mindfulness
FOR LIFE

Dr Stephen McKenzie has over twenty years of experience in researching and teaching a broad range of psychological areas, including depression, dementia, substance abuse, and most recently, mindfulness. Dr McKenzie has a unique ability as a lecturer, researcher and writer to present potentially complex information in a warm, engaging and entertaining way. He is currently a lecturer and research fellow at Deakin University's School of Psychology, where he is investigating mindfulness as a clinical treatment.

Dr Craig Hassed is an internationally recognised expert in mindfulness who has widely presented at national and international seminars and conferences and has published extensively in the areas of mind–body medicine and mindfulness. Dr Hassed devised and presents an innovative mindfulness training program for medical students at Monash University. His program has also been included in elective programs at other universities in Australia and overseas. He has worked with many other experts in the area of mind–body medicine and mindfulness, and has been instrumental in promoting mindfulness as a simple, natural and accessible technique for enhancing wellness, preventing and managing illness, and improving performance within health, educational and corporate settings. Dr Hassed is the founding president of the Australian Teachers of Meditation Association.

mindfulness
FOR LIFE

Dr Stephen McKenzie and Dr Craig Hassed

EXISLE
PUBLISHING

First published 2012

Exisle Publishing Pty Ltd
'Moonrising', Narone Creek Road, Wollombi, NSW 2325, Australia
P.O. Box 60–490, Titirangi, Auckland 0642, New Zealand
www.exislepublishing.com

National Library of Australia Cataloguing-in-Publication Data:

McKenzie, Stephen Paul.

Mindfulness for life / Stephen McKenzie, Craig Hassed.

ISBN 9781921966033 (pbk.)

Includes bibliographical references and index.

Mindfulness-based cognitive therapy.

Hassed, Craig.

616.891425

Designed by Christabella Designs
Typeset in Bembo 11/16.5
Printed in Australia by McPherson's Printing Group

This book uses paper sourced under ISO 14001 guidelines from well-managed forests and other controlled sources.

10 9 8 7

Disclaimer
While this book is intended as a general information resource and all care has been taken in compiling the contents, this book does not take account of individual circumstances and is not in any way a substitute for medical advice. Always consult a qualified practitioner or therapist. Neither the author nor the publisher and their distributors can be held responsible for any loss, claim or action that may arise from reliance on the information contained in this book.

To Melanie, Miranda and Deirdre
With love and gratitude

CONTENTS

FOREWORD

Why is it that mindfulness has become so popular? Why has mindfulness gained such widespread acceptance amongst the medical and scientific communities? And why are so many people attracted to learning and applying it in their daily lives? The answer is really quite simple. Mindfulness works!

As this excellent and timely book explains, 'mindfulness is the practice of paying attention — knowing where our attention is and being able to choose where to direct it'. This way of training our mind leads to increased awareness, the capacity to give our full attention to everything we do, and it helps us to learn how to let go of judgment, along with stress and anxiety. Mindfulness provides a reliable means for establishing peace and clarity amongst a complex and busy world.

The wonderful reality of mindfulness as a state of mind is that not only does it work but it is also easy. It is easy to teach, easy to research, easy to learn, and easy to apply in daily life.

Mindfulness for Life has many strengths. Firstly, it has been written by two leaders in this field who are teachers, researchers and practitioners. Craig and Stephen both speak from their personal experience of this practice, but then they add the combined benefit of their many years of teaching and researching the subject.

In the book they clearly set out the benefits of practising mindfulness in a formal sense by sitting down and paying attention to the present moment, free of judgment or distraction. What they then describe is how readily this formal practice translates into a way to live our lives, moment by moment, being mindful.

Another great strength of the book, and why so many people will benefit from reading it, is that the authors examine the real-life experiences and the associated research that accompanies applying mindfulness in three major areas of life: medical and pre-medical conditions, personal development and spiritual development. This combination of personal accounts from people who have transformed their lives through the simple practice of mindfulness, along with highly accessible summaries of the relevant research, makes for compelling reading.

Do read this book. Do give it to someone you care about. The evidence is clear. Mindfulness has the real potential to generate inner peace, foster physical and psychological healing and lead to a heightened sense of wellbeing and connectedness. This book tells you how to do it and will support you becoming more mindful.

Ian Gawler OAM
Author of *Meditation — An In-depth Guide*
and *The Mind that Changes Everything*

PART 1

MINDFULNESS
What is it and can it help?

CHAPTER 1

Introduction to mindfulness

Where are you now?

Which of the following makes you happiest: being distracted by pleasant imaginings, being distracted by neutral imaginings, being distracted by unpleasant imaginings or paying attention to what you are doing? Well, according to a recent study from Harvard University, simply paying attention to what we are doing makes us happiest.[1] This might seem strange because mostly we think that our daydreams, especially the happy ones, are interesting and the source of much of our contentment. Perhaps by the end of this chapter the relationship between our attention and our happiness will make a lot more sense. This book is simply about paying attention — in other words, mindfulness — and the profound happiness and health benefits that this can give us.

Have you ever walked into a room and forgotten why you went there? Have you ever waited for the weather report and when the forecast is given not even hear what the weatherperson says? Have you ever driven your car somewhere and not remembered the journey? Do you ever find yourself in a conversation with somebody and then suddenly wake up to the fact that you are not taking in a word of what they are saying? Do you ever find yourself reading a book (not this one, we hope!) and realising halfway through the chapter that you haven't taken in a word? Well, if you answered yes to any of these questions, then you know something about what it means to be unmindful.

Our tendency to not be fully present in our life as it happens has vast implications and can result in our missing out on our full life potential. Being unmindful means wasting our lifetime, missing important information, increasing our risk of physical and social accidents and communicating more superficially with other people. Importantly, it makes us unhappier than we realise and more vulnerable to stress and poor mental health and all of the harmful physical consequences that can follow. We will discuss this in more detail later.

Whether unmindfulness is more common today than it once was is hard to say, but mostly these days we find ourselves rushing, rushing, rushing from cradle to grave without ever really appreciating the bit in the middle. If we are not distracted by speeding through life then we might find ourselves distracted by boredom and inertia. Whether it is too fast or too slow, modern life just doesn't seem balanced. Looking at the pace of our modern life and its constant bombardment of information and disinformation, it would be reasonable to conclude that we have created a world that almost encourages the problem.

Although it often seems that our unmindful and unhelpful mental state is our only choice, it isn't. Being mindful rather than mindless is literally so simple that a child could do it, and they frequently do practise mindfulness, often better and more easily than adults do. When was the last time that a young child told you, with a frown, that he or she was far too busy worrying about what interest rates will be like when they grow up to go outside in the sun and play ball with you? Mindfulness is our natural state. The rewards of improving our mindfulness are great, but this requires effort and patience — even though the process is so natural that it could accurately be described as effortless effort.

What is mindfulness?

What *is* mindfulness? Perhaps the simplest way to describe it is to say that mindfulness is the practice of paying attention: knowing where our attention is and being able to choose where to direct it. A slightly more technical definition would be 'attention training' or 'attention regulation'. After all, we accept that physical training is vital for a healthy body, so why not accept that mental training is just as important for a healthy mind and life? We could even say that mindfulness is a practice that teaches us how to simply be ourselves, without having to be in some other place or time — or to be something else or somebody else other than what and who we are. The great American psychotherapist Carl Rogers, after many years of patiently listening to his clients tell him their problems, said that actually there is only one problem: to not know who you are. Mindfulness can give us back what we might think we have lost — ourselves.

Mindfulness is a form of meditation that has been widely practised for millennia, although interest in it and research on it and its clinical and daily life applications has increased enormously in recent years. This is an overnight lifestyle and clinical sensation that is thousands of years old. What do different meditation practices have in common, and what can they offer us? Formal meditation practices involve mental training that improves our ability to regulate our attention, so we don't get distracted by what makes us unhappy. The multitude of meditation practices available to us vary in the focus of attention they use and in what appears to be their aim, but actually they all aim to develop our capacity to focus attention on something specific.

Our body can be a very useful focus of our attention because, conveniently, it is handily available and is always in the present moment, never in the past or the future. Our body communicates with its outside world through its senses, and so in mindfulness practice our attention is naturally grounded in the present moment if we simply tune in to our senses — if we simply come to our senses. This will free our mind from its distracted preoccupation with a past that is already gone and a future that has never happened. This will allow us to richly experience what is going on in our life right now because we are actually paying attention to it. For example, in this state of full awareness of what is happening to us, right now, right here, we taste our food more, we connect more with our children, we work more efficiently and enjoyably, and we drive more safely. The cost of not paying attention may not be obvious unless we start to look closely at what is going on in our mind, and in our life.

We can use any of our senses to help us focus on the present moment. We recognise the importance of being connected in this way in our everyday language when we say we will 'be in touch' or we have 'come to our senses' or even we will 'wake up to ourselves'. If we are acting in such a way that shows that we are out of touch with present-moment reality we often describe this as being 'out of touch' or 'senseless'.

There are other forms of meditation that use a focus of attention other than our body, such as a mental image (imagery), a short mental statement of belief or aspiration (affirmation), a sense of stillness (stillness meditation) or a mantra, and these can all help us achieve peace, relaxation, a sense of connectedness, inner stillness or silence, insight, self-knowledge, better health, improved performance and, in a religious context, oneness with God or Self. Many people would also describe repetitive prayer as a form of affirmation or mantra meditation. What all forms of meditation have in common is that they can make us calmer and happier by helping us focus on what *is* rather than be distracted by what *isn't*.

The state of deep mindfulness could be described as a state of utter simplicity and naturalness. As in the old adage, 'When a wise man walks he just walks; when he sits he just sits; and there's nothing else going on.' Does this sound appealing? Does it sound good to just do what you are doing — whether it's working or playing — and not worry about anything else? Even focusing on a problem or a question in a mindful way is very different to worrying about it. One option is a grounded present-moment activity and the other involves aimlessly projecting into a future that has not happened but we imagine as real.

We will look at why being able to pay attention is so vital to our happiness and health in more detail in the remainder of this introduction and then in later chapters, where we will apply mindfulness to particular situations such as mental health problems, improving work and life performance, and managing symptoms and improving physical health. Mindfulness is like a multifaceted diamond that looks different depending on which facet you reflect.

When and where did mindfulness start?

We don't need a particular connection to a particular religion or wisdom tradition — by wisdom tradition we mean any knowledge system that can help us live our lives more peacefully and happily — to benefit from mindfulness, but knowing something about how it emerged from these traditions can deepen our understanding of it. Looking briefly at the historical context of mindfulness's modern popularity helps us understand what it is and how it can help.

We might think that mindfulness emerged from Eastern traditions, but actually the West also has a rich contemplative or mind-stilling history, even though for many centuries it has lost touch with these roots. Ancient Greeks including Pythagoras, Plato and Socrates wrote about it; and the Jewish, Christian and Sufi traditions also had their own contemplative practices. Maybe the West lost its contemplative roots when it started exploring and conquering our outer world, rather than exploring and making peace with our inner world. Maybe we have been so preoccupied with activity and busyness in the West, and increasingly in the East as well, that we are now mostly 'human doings' rather than 'human beings'.

The pursuit of material–external things as if they can provide deep and lasting happiness is contributing to a dwindling of real meaning and is a factor contributing to an increase in mental health problems. It just isn't possible to fill the hole inside us by piling up the things outside us. Until recent times there was possibly less disconnection between the inner and outer life in the East than in the West. Indigenous cultures too had their practices that deeply connected themselves to their world, not just through activity but through stillness.

The modern renaissance of interest in meditation and how it can help us — right here, right now — started with some cultural cross-pollination between East and West in the nineteenth century. While the West gave the East new technologies and vast potential for economic development, the East gave the West important philosophies such as those contained in ancient Indian Vedic philosophical texts like the Upanishads and *Bhagavad Gita*, and in practices like yoga and meditation that were based upon them. Thousands of years ago Buddhism grew out of the Vedic tradition and gave us philosophies that helped us to accept reality with greater equanimity, and meditation practices that are now commonly used by 'modern' Western psychotherapies such as Acceptance and Commitment Therapy (ACT). For something to be almost universally explored and practised by so many cultures suggests that there is something very universal and important about it.

Eastern philosophy influenced many great writers and philosophers in the West including Ralph Waldo Emerson, Hermann Hesse and the Transcendentalists. William James, generally considered to be the father of modern psychology, was profoundly interested in spiritual experiences, clearly seeing that being able to train and direct our attention is vital to our optimal functioning and happiness:

> *The faculty of voluntarily bringing back a wandering attention over and over again, is the very root of judgment, character, and will. No one is* compos sui *[competent] if he have it not. An education which should improve this faculty would be the education par excellence. But it is easier to define this ideal than to give practical directions for bringing it about.'*[2]

Although the West recognised the great importance of training our attention, the mind-stilling practices that help this happen weren't widely known until the late twentieth century. In the early twentieth century, however, Carl Jung was also interested in the connections between psychology and spirituality. In science, too, the great physicists of the early and mid twentieth century including Einstein, Schopenhauer, Schrodinger and Pauli were as interested in the powerfully practical Eastern philosophical texts and principles as they were in physics.

Meditation was and is the key to bridging the philosophy of peace and happiness and the experience of peace and happiness. This practice was first popularised in the West in the late 1950s when the Maharishi Mahesh Yogi introduced Transcendental Meditation, a form of mantra meditation, to California. Pictures of the Beatles sitting at the feet of their teacher deeply etched the notion in the 1960s that mediation was 'cool' into a younger generation that craved deep life meaning and was keen to challenge accepted dogma. In the following decade the first scientific research on the new and cool ancient meditation phenomenon was performed by Dr Herbert Benson at Harvard University. Our stress response had previously been described by Dr Hans Selye, who started his stress research in 1936, published *The Stress of Life* in 1956, and coined the term 'stress'. Benson realised that meditation produced the opposite of the stress response and coined his famous term 'The Relaxation Response' in his popular book on the topic.[3]

Despite promising early findings, meditation wasn't widely taken up as a foundation for psychotherapy until the 1990s, although a wider field of science called mind–body medicine and its main offspring, Psychoneuroimmunology (PNI), has grown steadily in popularity over the past 40 years. Our increasing understanding of the mind–body relationship has certainly provided a useful way of explaining mindfulness. The increasing interest in mind–body medicine shown by those working in traditional Western medicine has paved the way for the past 10–20 years of explosive growth in interest in meditation more generally, and mindfulness in particular. It could even be said that you can't truly understand the relationship between mind and body without also understanding the role of consciousness — attention. The increasingly impressive scientific research into practices like mindfulness has moved them into mainstream modern culture and healthcare and out of their association with 1960s hippy culture, and before that with the Buddhist-influenced 'beat' generation of the 1950s. What Western medicine really needs now is to develop its explanation of the mind–body relationship into an explanation of the *consciousness–mind–body* relationship.

The vital ingredients of mindfulness are found in all the world's great wisdom traditions and cultures. There's nothing particularly Eastern, or Western, about being aware of the present moment, or the simple act of breathing, or paying attention, or being able to objectively stand back from your thoughts and experiences; these experiences are universal. Each culture and indeed each individual eventually discovers this and describes it in their own way. Mindfulness practitioners who came from the Buddhist tradition such as the Dalai Lama and Matthieu Ricard, and the mindfulness repopularising pioneer Jon Kabat-Zinn, have made an enormous contribution to the modern application of and research into mindfulness, but even they wouldn't say that you need to be Buddhist in order to live mindfully. Mindfulness is becoming increasingly widely known in popular culture through modern–ancient classics such as Eckhart Tolle's *The Power of Now*.[4] The principles of mindfulness are in the public domain and readily available to you right now, right here.

Where next?

The barriers between philosophy, religion, science and popular knowledge are now being broken down as more and more researchers and psychologists are inspired to explore mindfulness at a whole new level. This research can increasingly help ordinary people greatly improve their lives by understanding what it is to be mindful and how this can help reduce unhappiness and even a range of life-threatening conditions. We will discuss this later in this book.

John Teasdale, Mark Williams and Zindal Segal, for example, took Jon Kabat-Zinn's Mindfulness-Based Stress Reduction (MBSR) and developed what they call Mindfulness-Based Cognitive Therapy (MBCT) for managing depression — with outstanding results. Davidson, Lasar and others have been inspired and encouraged by the Dalai Lama to scientifically investigate the neuroscience of the contemplative — mind-stilling arts — to study the brain. The fruits of their work are showcased in the Mind and Life Institute, which now hosts dialogues in many of the world's most respected educational and research institutions.[5] Norman Doidge's book *The Brain that Changes Itself* is a fascinating introduction for anyone who would like to understand neuroplasticity, that is, how the brain works and adapts itself depending on our environment and how we think and act.[6]

The mindfulness genie is now well and truly out of its bottle.

CHAPTER 2
Foundations of mindfulness

Are you there yet?

The first two sections of this chapter may be of great interest to you, but they may also get uncomfortably philosophical in places if you want to cut to the mindfulness chase, as it were, and get to the more obviously practical bits. The philosophical bits will make a lot more sense after you have actually practised mindfulness. If you suspect that you're not especially interested in the philosophical roots and wider implications of mindfulness at this stage, then just simply and mindfully skip these sections and move on.

The active ingredient of mindfulness is the ability to be present and aware of what is actually happening to you, by not allowing your attention to drift off to your daydream world — of what happened to you yesterday, or might happen to you tomorrow. This is what is meant by the popular practical philosophical advice to 'wake up to yourself'. Instruction in just how to pay attention to what is, and therefore wake up to the reality of who you really are, can be found throughout recorded history in many, if not all, the world's great cultures and wisdom traditions. This makes sense if mindfulness relates to something essential to realising our potential, understanding ourselves and overcoming suffering.

Mindfulness isn't a new concept. You have almost certainly practised mindfulness intuitively and spontaneously already at some stage of your life, even if you only stumbled across it by accident and didn't know what it was called, or even that it had a name. It is a wonderful paradox that when you are truly mindful, mindfulness doesn't have a name, or need one. You might have been mindful when you really looked at a sunset or at a child smiling and you didn't want to be anywhere else, or with anything else, or maybe you were momentarily forced into mindfulness by some great disaster such as when you woke up from your sleepiness to realise you were about to drive your car off the road and the only thing you had time to do was to mindfully save yourself by really attending to the road, rather than thinking about what you ought to do, or could do, or had once done.

Unfortunately we often don't acknowledge what our mindful moments can teach us. In the words of Winston Churchill, 'Once in a while you will stumble upon the truth but most of us manage to pick ourselves up and hurry along as if nothing had happened.' Churchill's interpretation of history as 'just one damned thing after another' could also be applied to our own histories, if we are not mindful.

Don't panic!

Mindfulness is simply a name given to something that you already know so well that it doesn't need a name. There are a vast number of quotes from the world's great wisdom traditions that can help us remember what we already know, at a deeper level than what we might be familiar with experiencing, and that are essential to our human condition. Before you mindlessly recoil from our lurking quotation marks, contemplate the words from the great modern wisdom tradition of Douglas Adams' *Hitchhiker's Guide to the Galaxy*: 'Don't panic!' The world's great wisdom and literary traditions often use allegory and metaphor to explain the unexplainable, and knowing this can help you remember what they are trying to remind you of. For example, arguably the most famous speech from all of English literature begins: 'To be or not to be, that is the question,' from *Hamlet* by William Shakespeare.

That really is the question, then and now: how to be yourself. So much of our life is spent wanting to be somewhere else or trying to be somebody else, or wishing for some other time; this is the unmindful craving for what we don't have that advertisers and politicians skilfully appeal to in order to manipulate consumers and voters. This is an ancient tactic: to delude us into believing that we want what we don't have and can never have — something else.

Rather than viewing mindfulness as an esoteric concept unrelated to our everyday life, it can more accurately be seen as a self-defence course in sanity. With the increasing complexities of our modern age it has become even easier to forget

rather than to remember how to simply be, and to simply be where we are —
here — and who we are — *ourselves* — and to live our life when it's actually
happening — *now*. Poor Hamlet, like the rest of us, wasn't in a very clear state
of mind when he haunted himself with his family ghosts, and so he never worked
out how to mindfully respond to his life stage. Hamlet described his mind as
being somewhat foggy, or in Shakespeare's more poetic language, 'sicklied o'er
with the pale cast of thought'. Does that sound familiar?

Controlling or clarifying our mind is actually infinitely simple, as well as
notoriously difficult:

> *The mind is fickle and flighty, it flies after fancies wherever it likes: it*
> *is indeed difficult to restrain. But it is a great good to control the mind;*
> *a mind self-controlled is a source of great joy ... Hidden in the*
> *mystery of consciousness, the mind ... flies alone far away. Those who*
> *set their mind in harmony become free from the bonds of death.*

Dhammapada *from the Buddhist tradition*

If we could spend just a few minutes practising mindfulness it could teach us
the ultimate truth of what this quote says about the fickleness of our mind
and how it wants to run off to join the circus of its own dream world, which
it takes to be real, if we don't wake up to it. This is the 'parallel universe' or
'twilight zone' in our own heads — brimful of hopes, anxieties and fears —
that distracts us from the actual life we are living. As the Harvard study referred
to in Chapter 1 concluded: '... a human mind is a wandering mind, and a
wandering mind is an unhappy mind. The ability to think about what is not
happening is a cognitive achievement that comes at an emotional cost.'[1]

As we will further explain later, the trick to mastering our mind with all
of its thoughts and emotions isn't so much a matter of trying to control it, but
rather of learning not be controlled by it. The key to self-control is to not
struggle with what we are experiencing but, paradoxically, to achieve control
by not trying to control. Struggle is exhausting and dispiriting and just makes
us sink faster into the quicksand of our anxious and preoccupied thoughts,
whereas mindful non-attachment gives us peace and freedom by helping us
out of the quicksand altogether.

As we mentioned in Chapter 1, an essential element of mindfulness is the importance of the 'now' moment. In fact you can't actually live in a moment that isn't now. It's only by taking our imaginings about the past and future to be real that we create the illusion that the past and future actually exist, but even thoughts about the past and future only ever take place in the now. The present moment is a bigger issue than we might think. In it is not only freedom from the burden of our past or future — vital to understanding the nature of depression or anxiety — but the present moment is also where we find wisdom. For example: 'Acquire a good name, and you acquire fame, but acquire wisdom, and you acquire eternity; awaken to Reality in the timeless moment of the eternal now.' (*Pirkei Avot* from the Jewish tradition.)

Plato also described time as an illusion, in his book *Timaeus*: 'Time is a moving image of eternity.' Indeed, in those moments when we are most present, perhaps when we see something so beautiful that it stops our mind in its tracks, or when we are truly 'in the zone', time almost seems to stand still. Maybe you've had such an experience, or watched such an experience, or heard a description of how somebody could suddenly do what they ordinarily couldn't do. There are many examples of this, from elite sportspeople such as Roger Federer who described a state in which his tennis game seemed to play itself, or Shane Gould who described how she sometimes went into her swimming races in a timeless, spaceless zone of infinite opportunity. There are also many examples of this state being experienced by ordinary people such as the frail and elderly lady who somehow found the strength to move a car off a trapped relative.

Life is fleeting. The ever-changing parade of our life experiences, both internal and external, is an observable fact, and the sooner we get used to this essential feature of our life state the better off we will be. We don't have any choice about our and our world's basic impermanence, and no end of wishful thinking will change this one jot. In the words of the Sufi poet Omar Khayyam:

> *The Moving Finger writes; and, having writ,*
> *Moves on: nor all thy Piety nor Wit*
> *Shall lure it back to cancel half a Line,*
> *Nor all thy Tears wash out a Word of it.*

We can decide how we will relate to the ever-changing passing parade of the days of our lives: we can choose whether they become a soap opera or a great work of life art. Attachment, getting stuck with objects, thoughts, emotions and events is described by many wisdom traditions as the source of all of our problems:

> *Dwelling on sense-objects gives birth to attachment, attachment gives birth to desire. Desire (unfulfilled) brings into existence the life of anger. From anger delusion springs up, from delusion the confusion of memory. In the confusion of memory the reasoning wisdom is lost. When wisdom is nowhere, destruction.*

> Bhagavad Gita *from the Indian Vedic tradition*

We try to cling to the bits of life that we like and push away those we don't like, which although this is understandable and well intentioned, is what causes our troubles. When the parts we try to cling to or push away are the reality of our present-moment experience, this clinging and avoidance can be a recipe for an anxiety disaster. To be peaceful and happy we have to accept things that we don't like when they come, and we have to let go of things that we do like when they go. Unfortunately, common experience also shows us that we often push away things that are good for us, such as physical activity or broccoli, and cling to things that aren't good, such as too much TV and chocolate. Non-attachment, on the other hand, allows us to make wiser choices about what to pursue and how hard to pursue it, and also how to finally free ourselves and experience contentment.

It is obvious that our life and experience changes from moment to moment. This is the whole nature of the transience that so many wisdom traditions keep reminding us of — 'this too will pass' — even a traffic jam, even a toothache, although Shakespeare did say that 'there was never yet philosopher that could endure the toothache patiently'. Nevertheless, it's obvious that there is something in us all that is always watching our passing parade. In the midst of all of what seems to change, this inner observer is stable and permanent. Every moment there is an aspect of ourselves watching those events — our consciousness. The importance of distinguishing between what is transient and what is permanent is at the core of all wisdom traditions; it could even be seen as the essence of wisdom itself. Being grounded in that aspect of ourselves that is both enduring and peaceful even in the midst of apparent calamity has long been associated with better mental health as well as happiness, and this could even be seen as the 'I' of the storm.

> *Even a happy life cannot be without a measure of darkness, and the word happy would lose its meaning if it were not balanced by sadness. It is far better to take things as they come along with patience and equanimity.*

> *Carl Jung*

All this might merely remain a philosophical abstraction unless we actually use the above wisdom in practical experience and application. We will now mindfully turn our attention to this.

Who can mindfulness help?

As we mentioned earlier, mindfulness is like a multifaceted diamond. A much fuller discussion about how you can use mindfulness for particular life situations will be explored in coming chapters, but it is worth giving you a sneak preview here of some of these uses. People often think of mindfulness as a relaxation exercise because relaxation is a common consequence of it. Mindfulness, however, is primarily a practice in training attention, and relaxation is more of a (welcome) side effect. People often get interested in mindfulness because they like the idea of being able to relax more easily or cope better with stress and anxiety. This is useful on one level but it is potentially a problem on another. If we get too preoccupied with our goal of relaxing then we might find ourselves becoming extremely tense and frustrated if the practice doesn't turn out the way we expect it to, as quickly as we expect it to.

Bart Simpson's famous unmindful question, 'Are we there yet are we there yet are we there yet?!' generally results in stress for him and for us too if we try too hard to do anything, even relax. Aiming at any goal, understandable and attractive as it may be, is paradoxically the opposite of mindfulness practice. Having a goal is a future-focused event, whereas mindfulness is all about the present moment. All of your pleasant and unpleasant experiences will inevitably come and go, it's only how you relate to them that really matters. If we learn to be at peace with, or less reactive to, our anxiety or tension then it greatly helps us to not amplify their impact when they do arise. Then they can come and go more readily, without us worrying about them. If we remain mindful no matter what goes on around us, then our mind-created 'disasters' can actually be our greatest friend and teacher.

> *If you can keep your head when all about you*
> *Are losing theirs and blaming it on you …*
> *If you can meet with Triumph and Disaster*
> *And treat those two impostors just the same …*
> *Or watch the things you gave your life to, broken,*
> *And stoop and build 'em up with worn-out tools …*

> If *by Rudyard Kipling*

If we can welcome the very things that we usually try to avoid as opportunities to cultivate a different way of being with them, then we will really make progress towards happiness and peace, easily, quickly and naturally.

Mindfulness has been successfully used to help people with a variety of conditions, including chronic pain and depression. Anxiety, along with the many associated states that this contributes to, is automatically reduced through a mindful rather than a mindless response to life. This acceptance of all experience will greatly benefit those who suffer from any of many conditions that can — but don't have to — make life a misery, even if that condition is life itself, or rather our reaction to it. Mindfulness, therefore, has many powerfully practical applications, including:

- mental health: depression-relapse prevention, anxiety, panic disorder, stress, emotional regulation and enhancing emotional intelligence, improvements in sleep, personality disorders, addiction.
- neurological: structural and functional changes in the brain,

neurogenesis (enhancing the capacity of the brain to generate new brain cells), better executive functioning, increased blood flow, and possibly the prevention of dementia.

- clinical: pain management, symptom control, coping with illnesses such as cancer, metabolic benefits, hormonal changes and changes in genetic function and repair.
- performance: sport, academic, leadership.
- spiritual: deep peace, insight, oneness.

If we view mindfulness merely as an exercise in managing stress, then many of us who may greatly benefit from it may not use it or think it is relevant to us if we are not experiencing stress at the time. Mindfulness, therefore, is a simple skill but one with many different potential uses and beneficial side effects. Mindfulness isn't just about helping us manage our illnesses and symptoms; it's also about helping us to understand ourselves better — to positively enhance our wellbeing and to help us make better use of our full attributes and potential. Mindfulness is a life skill that we can all benefit from.

What other treatments or healing traditions does mindfulness relate to?

Mindfulness is an active ingredient of many other approaches and therapies. Yoga and Tai Chi, for example, are as much about training the mind to be non-reactively aware as they are about learning physical postures. Other forms of physical therapy use attention including Feldenkrais and the Alexander Technique. Although the term mindfulness wasn't in wide use at the time, 'sensate-focusing exercises' were introduced decades ago as a part of sex therapy to help unhook the attention from anxiety about performance and help people engage more fully with the intimacy and connectedness of the experience. This may even have ancient origins in the *Kama Sutra*, an ancient Sanskrit sex manual.

Contemplative practices and wisdom traditions are now making a significant contribution to modern psychology and psychotherapy, such as the MBSR and MBCT previously mentioned. To train ourselves to 'go behind the thinking mind' helps us to understand it better and cultivate the mind and its potential more consciously. For example, there are many dialogues and interest groups examining the potential of Buddhism to inform modern psychotherapy, and pain clinics used mindfulness practices of awareness combined with acceptance well before this ancient spiritual-based practice achieved its 'overnight' success.

Mindfulness is also a prominent part of Acceptance and Commitment Therapy (ACT) and Dialectical Behaviour Therapy (DBT), which have been used to help many mental health problems, including some that have been considered hardest to manage, such as addiction and borderline personality disorder. The fact that mindfulness is a single skill that has such a profound range of applications suggests that it is an essential part of our human make-up, which can be remembered and adapted and applied in many and various ways.

Where to from here?

In the next chapter we will explore the practical benefits of mindfulness in your daily life. This will include mindfulness meditation and the principles of mindfulness-based cognitive strategies. We will cover these practices and principles in more detail in later chapters, when we will explore the applications of mindfulness to particular situations and health problems.

CHAPTER 3

The practical application of mindfulness

It's one thing to say that mindfulness is great and that it will help us with so many things, but it's another thing to be able to practise it or apply it to our daily life. That's exactly what this chapter is about. Applying mindfulness is incredibly simple, and if you're confused about how to practise it by the end of reading this chapter then we haven't done our job of explaining it very well at all. Actually, the more we learn about mindfulness the simpler it gets — perhaps it would be better to say that learning about mindfulness really just means dropping our unnecessarily complicated ways of thinking and living. There's an old saying that is appropriate here: 'When a wise man walks he just walks, when he sits he just sits, and there's nothing else going on.'

What could be simpler than that? Just because practising mindfulness is simple, however, that doesn't mean it's easy. Riding a bike is simple but it's not easy — well, not until we get the knack, maybe after falling off a few times!

As we've mentioned, mindfulness is simply about being aware of what's going on in our body and our mind, and paying attention to our life — to the external world as well as the internal world. Mindfulness is both a form of meditation (the formal practice) and a way of living with awareness (the informal practice). It is also the basis for us learning to think in a different way, and can help free us from our destructive thought processes, rather than try to change them. We will now explore the formal and informal applications of mindfulness.

The formal practice of mindfulness meditation

Formally practising mindfulness meditation doesn't actually require formality or rigidness, nor do we need to get esoteric about it. This really just refers to those times of day that we set aside from other activities to consciously practise being mindful. (The informal practice of mindfulness simply means practising being mindful within the flow of our daily activities, but we will discuss this later in the chapter.)

Mindfulness meditation is the cornerstone of our being able to apply mindfulness in all the other ways we will discuss throughout this book. It's a practice that basically involves sitting upright and still in a chair with eyes closed and focusing on something.

The aim of mindfulness meditation isn't necessarily to have a peak experience in the chair — to feel eternal bliss or universal empathy — although there's nothing wrong with that! There's also nothing wrong with experiencing deep peace or contentment while practising meditation, but the aim is to cultivate a greater sense of awareness when we get out of the chair and re-engage with our life after our formal practice. That practice might only take up 10–60 minutes of our day, but the rest of our day occupies something over 23 hours. What's the point of trying to have a few peak experiences for a few minutes if it's not also helping us to live the whole of our life in a way that helps us live better and longer?

The aim of mindfulness meditation isn't to relax; although again, there's nothing wrong with relaxing! In fact this is very good for us and it's a common and useful side effect of mindfulness meditation. But as soon as we fixate on an expectation that we have to relax we can get very tense trying to make it happen.

We can return to the example from a famous modern philosopher here, and use this example as it's probably meant to be used: to show us how not to live. Bart Simpson's 'Are we there yet are we there yet are we there yet?!' mind madness will drive us all mindless if we let it, whether we're travelling, mediating or otherwise engaged in living our life. Furthermore, we can miss the point that some of the most useful practice we will ever do will involve learning to respond differently to uncomfortable sensations, thoughts and emotions than we normally do — mindfully rather than mindlessly. Our habitual reactivity and non-acceptance of the things we find uncomfortable only makes our experiences of them worse.

So, to use an analogy, formal mindfulness practice is a bit like doing the work in the gym that helps us build up the stamina and strength that's going to help us for 24 hours a day. Consider, however, that the mind will come up with almost every excuse under the sun to not practise mindfulness. We remember, 'Oh, it's time to practise my meditation!' then the mind chips in with, 'But I'll just do this first.' We probably won't remember for another three days, then the mind comes in with, 'I'm too tired to practise now!' Too tired to do nothing? Does that make sense? Or how about, 'It won't work anyway, I'm too tense!' But isn't that the perfect time to learn to respond to tension differently? And then there's, 'I'm cruising! I don't need it now, so what's the point?' Don't we practise it so that the ability is there when we aren't cruising but are taking on mental water faster than the *Titanic*? Let's say we've developed a regular practice pattern, then the mind whispers quietly into our ear, 'Not tonight!' Pretty soon one night off becomes two and then three until we have to think hard to remember the last time we practised.

Then there's probably the most popular reason of all that the mind comes up with for us to not practise: 'I'm too busy!' Now that's a goodie because it's the type of excuse the mind can use any time — it can always find something else more important to do. But what's more important than finding peace? The mind is all about do, do, do. Doing is fine, but when we forget how to be then the doing has come at a grave cost. Being busy is a great reason to practise mindfulness because there is no efficiency without attention. Sharpening attention is like a woodcutter sharpening their axe — those few moments will save a lot of time in the long run.

The bottom line here is that there is no reasonable reason to not practise mindfulness meditation, but it takes some clarity of purpose, insight and determination to establish and maintain our practice. The mind is a creature of habit, even if those habits don't serve us very well, so we shouldn't be surprised that our mind resists moving from habitual to conscious mode, and tries to stop the merest suggestion of the light of awareness breaking through.

Commas and full stops

The formal practices of mindfulness meditation of 5 minutes or more can be compared to 'full stops' punctuating our day. How smooth would the flow of words in a conversation be without at least the occasional pause? Supplementing these full stops with regular short mindful pauses of anywhere between 15 seconds to 2 minutes might be compared to 'commas'. Like a book, a day that is not punctuated makes no sense.

If you are new to mindfulness, a good 'starting dose' is to practise for 5 minutes twice daily. Before breakfast and dinner are good times because after food is a low point for the metabolism and sleep can occur more easily then — that's a good power nap but it's not mindfulness meditation. The duration of practice can be built up to 10, then 15, 20 and even up to 30 minutes or longer if required depending on your time availability, motivation, needs and commitment.

In many programs that use mindfulness meditation in the management of conditions such as recurrent major depression or severe chronic pain, the amount of practice is around 40 minutes a day. We can't really say that the evidence confirms that 40 minutes daily will help us to recover sooner than 10 or 20 minutes a day will in such situations, but if tradition, clinical experience and the opinion of experts is anything to go by, we can expect that 40 minutes a day will help us better and faster than 10 minutes will. For lesser problems we may not need as much practice, but a good general rule to remember is that results don't come without effort — even effortless effort.

Although we have said that meditation is best practised before our morning and evening meals, that's a rule of thumb and not an absolute. If we forget then, we practise when we remember and have the opportunity. If our day is full of unavoidable emergencies, then we practise when we have finished dealing with them.

Commas during the day can help us be mindful for the whole of our day, including when we're not meditating. Even pausing for long enough to take a couple of deep breaths can help us break our mindless build-up of unconscious mental ability and tension. A good time to practise our life-punctuating commas is when we are in between activities. For example, we might have just finished work and be in the car ready to drive home — take a few moments to be mindful. We have just completed one job and are about to pick up another — take a few moments to put some space between the jobs. We are about to go into an interview — take a few moments to be present. We are just about to have lunch — we could take a few moments to prepare to taste our food, and not just bolt it down without enjoying it or even noticing what we are eating.

For our longer practices of mindfulness meditation — our full stops — it can be helpful, wherever possible, to have a quiet place in which to practise without interruption. This doesn't mean that mindfulness can't be practised anywhere, anytime; indeed, it's important for the practice to be as 'portable' as possible. If interruptions do occur then it helps to not be concerned, but rather just deal with them mindfully and then, if possible, go back to the practice. When sitting down to practise it helps to have a clock within easy view to help reduce anxiety about time. Just open your eyes when you think the meditation time might be up, and if the time is not up yet move back into the practice. An alarm can be useful but make sure it's one that won't jolt you out of meditation.

We can move into the formal practice of mindfulness by using the sense of touch, focused on the body and/or breath. We can also use another sense such as hearing, or a combination of senses. The important thing about the body and the senses is that they are always in the present moment, so they help to bring our mind into the present moment. Contact with any of the senses will automatically unhook our attention from the mental distractions that otherwise hijack our attention.

Position

We recommend the sitting position for meditation because you are less likely to go to sleep in an upright position. In sitting for meditation, it is best if your back and neck are straight and balanced, which requires a minimum of effort or tension to maintain the position. If you have a meditation stool you can sit with your back away from the back of the chair, which helps your spine find its natural position. Lying down can also be useful, particularly if deep physical relaxation is the main aim of the practice, or if your body is extremely tired or you are in pain or ill. The ease of going to sleep while lying down, however, is not usually desirable, unless you are practising mindfulness meditation late at night or you need a power nap.

Having firstly read the rest of this section, removed any restrictive clothing and spectacles, and settled into your preferred meditation position, let your eyes gently close. You can practise with your eyes open, as the Dalai Lama does, but closing your eyes can help bring your other senses, which we tend to under-utilise, into play.

The body scan

The body scan is the most widely used and generally the best mindfulness practice to start with. Begin by being conscious of the whole body and let it settle. Now, progressively become aware of each individual part of the body, starting with the feet. Let the attention rest there a while, feeling whatever is there to be felt. Then let the attention move to the legs, stomach, back, hands, arms, shoulders, neck and face, pausing for a while at each point. Take your time with each body part — how much time you intend to dedicate to the total practice will determine how long you spend with each individual part.

The object of this practice is to let your attention rest with each body part, simply noticing what's happening there, what sensations are taking place, moment by moment. In the process we naturally practise cultivating an attitude of impartial awareness; that is, not having to judge experiences as good or bad, right or wrong, nor do we need to cling to the bits we like and push away the bits we don't like. Even if there is not much sensation in one or other part of the body we simply notice that lack of sensation. It's helpful to practise being at ease with our moment-by-moment experience just as it is, even if it's uncomfortable. As we said at the outset, mindfulness is simple but not necessarily easy. We may soon discover that it is our reactivity to emotional and physical discomfort that amplifies our experience of it and the suffering it produces. There's no need to change our experience from one state to another or to 'make something happen'. Our state will change from moment to moment without us having to do anything — we just flow with it.

Observing our mind judge, criticise, worry or become distracted, for example, are simply mental experiences, like the physical sensations, to observe non-judgmentally as they come and go. As often as the attention wanders from an awareness of the body, simply notice where the attention has gone and gently bring it back to the part of the body you were up to. It's not a problem that thoughts come in or that your mind gets distracted; they become a problem only if you make them a problem.

A sense of clarity or insight often arises during meditation, which might lead to a temptation to race off and start planning things or sorting out problems. As tempting as that might be, delay such activities until after the practice is over and then use the mindful state for useful work. Let the transition from formal mindfulness meditation in stillness to mindful activity be seamless.

Although it might not be obvious throughout formal mindfulness practice, we are not only practising attention. We are also practising qualities such as an attitude of acceptance, a spirit of inquiry, equanimity, patience and even courage. When we practise these qualities in the meditation chair we soon start to find that we take a bit of them with us when we get out of the chair.

Breathing

Attending to your breathing is another form of mindfulness meditation that can be learned and practised. Just as the attention can be rested on the sense of touch through the body, one particular aspect of what the body does is particularly useful for mindfulness practice: the attention can be rested with the breath as it passes in and out of the body. The point of focus could be right where the air enters and leaves through the nose, or it could be where the stomach rises and falls with the breath.

Just as in the body scan, no force is required to be mindfully aware of your breath, and in mindfulness meditation there's no need to try to regulate your breathing — let the body do that for you. It's pretty good at it if we refrain from interfering with it. Again, if distracting thoughts and feelings come into awareness, just be aware of them and let them come and go by themselves. There's no need to 'battle' with these thoughts or to 'get rid' of them. There's no need even to try to stop these thoughts coming to mind, or trying to force them out. Trying to force thoughts and feelings out of our mind just feeds them with what they feed on — attention — which makes them stronger, and increases their impact. We're simply practising being less preoccupied about them or reactive to them. They will settle by themselves and all the more quickly if we learn to not get involved in them. We don't have to fight with the thought trains, or get on them. Similarly, we don't have to breathe in a particular way to practise mindfulness, just to be aware of the breathing as it is.

Listening

We can also use listening to mindfully meditate — the practice of restful attentiveness is similar to the body scan and mindful breathing. Here we're simply practising being conscious of the sounds in our environment, whether they are close or far away. As you listen, let the sounds come and go and in the process also let any thoughts about the sounds — or anything else for that matter — come and go. Keep gently bringing your attention back to the present when it wanders.

Sooner or later it tends to dawn on us that most of the time we're listening to mental chatter, so the value of listening mindfully is that our attention isn't being used to feed the usual mental commentary. It's this commentary that is so full of habitual and unconscious rumination, worries and negative self-talk.

Other senses

Any of our senses can be used for mindfulness meditation — even taste or smell. Wine enthusiasts may not think of themselves as practitioners of mindfulness meditation, but the focus and attention they bring to looking at, smelling and tasting a good bottle of wine is like a meditation in itself; similarly, the smell of coffee that the coffee enthusiast treasures so much is a moment of mindfulness. Sight can be rested with an object if we are practising meditation with our eyes open. Any of these senses can help us to come into the present or, as the saying goes, come to our senses.

Jon Kabat-Zinn popularised what's called 'the raisin exercise'. He used it to help introduce people to the concept of mindfulness meditation. In this practice he invites people to use each of their senses over a few minutes to investigate a raisin, as if they have never experienced one before. The practice ends with feeling the raisin in the mouth and then biting into it. It can be very revealing how much of a difference there can be between a common experience we generally take for granted and the same experience done with attention. You might like to experiment in this way yourself. If you don't have any raisins you can adapt this practice for use with chocolates or vintage wine! Other mindfulness trainers we know, working in corporate environments, have replaced the 'raisin exercise' with the 'Belgian chocolate exercise'. Needless to say, the main problem with the Belgian chocolate exercise is the temptation to put in too much practice!

Moving meditation practices

There are moving mindfulness meditation practices such as walking meditation. These can be helpful if we feel quite unsettled or if we are finding it hard to pay attention during a sitting meditation. In this we pause before setting off on a slow and deliberate walk back and forth along a line (or in a circle or labyrinth) during which we aim to feel the whole experience of our body as it moves, from the tip of the toes up. We can practise returning to the activity as our mind wanders off. This can be a confronting practice because walking is a lot harder sometimes when we're not doing it in our habitual way. We can also be confronted by our constant desire to 'get somewhere' ('Are we there yet?'), so this process can be a great remedy for impatience. Then there's the challenge of getting over feeling silly for walking so slowly. Maybe we can draw inspiration for our mindful walking practice by watching some of the walks developed by Monty Python's Ministry of Silly Walks — but then again, maybe not.

Other body-based activities such as yoga or Tai Chi also emphasise the importance of attending to our body as it moves, and not to other bodies, no matter how heavenly! In that sense these are really mindfulness practices as much as they are methods of training the body to be more flexible or balanced. Hence they provide benefits well beyond physical ones.

Finishing

After practising mindfulness meditation for the allotted time, gently allow your eyes to open. After remaining settled for a few moments, mindfully move into the activities of the day that need your attention. The mindfulness practice isn't finished when you get out of your chair — it has just begun! Move back into your day-to-day life with the intention of doing it mindfully, with the same quality of attention you brought to the formal practice.

The informal practice of mindfulness

Any activity done mindfully is a form of mindfulness. If we're paying attention while brushing our teeth then we're *being* mindful. If we really taste our food, listen to what our conversation partner is saying, or pay attention to what we are reading, then we're *being* mindful. If, on the other hand, we notice that our mind has wandered off into its own little world while we're walking down the street (and are about to step into a rut), and we drop our mental activity and come back to paying attention to the walking — feeling the steps on the ground, the breeze on our face, the sounds going on around us, the sights and colours — then we are *practising* mindfulness.

Practising mindfulness away from the meditation chair (or stool, cushion, mat, bed of nails, or whatever) as we go about our daily life is the informal practice of mindfulness. The active ingredient of being mindful is that we are conscious of what is going on but not in a self-conscious kind of way — so, paying attention rather than thinking about ourselves.

Let's illustrate this with an example. A young mother told a story during a mindfulness class about being at the beach and wanting to be fully mindful, to be fully in the moment. She was trying so hard to pay attention to the experience and savour it that it was quite hard work and she didn't actually feel overly connected. Her head was full of thoughts like, 'Is this mindfulness? Am I paying attention? What should I be experiencing?' Then her four-year-old daughter came up to her and wanted to play. Without thinking about it the mother 'dropped' her mindfulness practice and they started to play — building castles, being pirates and all the kind of stuff that kids like to do at the beach. This woman wasn't deliberately practising being mindful but she said that on reflection she felt so much more connected than she had when she was thinking about being mindful.

When we're really connected through our senses our mind isn't thinking, or at least not in its usual noisy, distracted way. When we're thinking, even about paying attention, then we're not fully connected to our senses. Even when we're practising mindfulness meditation and we notice that our attention is right with the breathing or whatever we're paying attention to, and then our mind chips in with: 'Oh, look at me, how mindful I am. I'm so connected, so present!' We can back it in that that's exactly the moment we stopped being mindful. That's fine, we just need to drop the mental chatter and come back to the breath or whatever we were paying attention to.

Lesson number one: thinking about mindfulness is different to being mindful. Thinking about mindfulness or why we aren't mindful can be as big a distraction from the present moment as worrying about what might or might not happen at work next week.

Mental chatter, whether about daydreaming, reminiscing, worrying or being mindful, anxious or depressed, is just a different form of what is sometimes called default mental activity. Default mode is when our mind slips into automatic pilot. Interestingly, or perhaps worryingly — depending on what attitude we take — the areas of our brain that are activated in default mode are the same as the ones affected by Alzheimer's Disease later in life.[1] It may be that the long-term effects of all this distracted mental activity aren't good for our brains. Equally interesting, and perhaps more comforting, is the research indicating that the practice of mindfulness helps our brain conserve its brain cells, particularly in the learning, memory and higher functioning centres.[2]

So, the informal practice of mindfulness is very simple. Just as we practise during the formal practice, when the attention goes off during day-to-day life we just notice in a non-judgmental kind of way and gently bring the attention back to the here and now — again by getting back in touch with our senses. No more thought is required.

Mindfulness as a foundation for cognitive therapies

Is mindfulness just about paying attention in a present-moment, non-judgmental way? Well, yes and no. Yes, it's that simple, but further than that, mindfulness helps us to pay attention to our own mind and that means that over time we come to understand a little more about how it works. Our mind isn't as different from other people's minds as we like to think, so coming to understand our own mind better helps us to understand other people better as well.

Psychotherapy means therapy for the mind; cognitive means the way the mind thinks (that is, cognitions are thoughts). As we practise mindfulness formally and informally over time we come to understand a little more clearly what thoughts are driving us and what effects these have, such as driving us to mindlessness. It's like when the lights go on we start to see things that were going on in the dark before.

One woman, for example, at about four weeks into a mindfulness course, started to notice how repetitive, angry and judgmental her internal conversations tended to be, whether directed at herself or others. She had never really seen it before, how repetitive it was, how unfair the judgments tended to be, nor how divisive an influence it was between herself and others. Because she noticed it in a mindful kind of way — as an interested observer and not by judging it — her thoughts from this stage on started to have a less significant influence on her.

One man working in a demanding professional position noticed how tense he tended to get over the things that were going on in his imagination. When something happened his mind would jump to a conclusion, his imagination would swing into overdrive and he would get worried, angry or apprehensive, depending on just what his imagination was doing. When he started to notice this, he created the opportunity to get back in touch with present-moment reality and respond to the situation, moment by moment, on its merits.

Another woman noticed, almost like a blinding flash one day, the thought going on in the background that had been the source of nearly all her stress and negativity: 'I'm not good enough.' She had never noticed it before but once she did she saw it popping up all over the place, causing tension and fear where none was due. She didn't need to think, 'I am good enough'; trying to replace the positive for the negative can be a bit of an exhausting tug of war in itself. Although the thought was deeply rooted in her past and upbringing, all she needed to do was notice the thought when it arose and not keep reinforcing it by getting taken in by it now. The past was being healed automatically and naturally by her choice to give her attention to the present moment and not have to relive and re-suffer the past.

Jon Kabat-Zinn's MBSR (Mindfulness-Based Stress Reduction) was used as a foundation for MBCT (Mindfulness-Based Cognitive Therapy) developed by the psychologists and researchers Mark Williams, John Teasdale and Zindal Segal under the guidance of Jon Kabat-Zinn. These two models for applying mindfulness are the two most widely taught and researched around the world. Other increasingly popular forms of psychotherapy such as Acceptance and Commitment Therapy (ACT) and Dialectical Behaviour Therapy (DBT) are very much based on mindfulness principles.

Basically, mindfulness teaches us to think differently. In the following sections we will summarise some of the key principles in the change of thought and perspective that mindfulness offers us. This is abridged from the complete *Stress Release Program* written by one of the authors back in 1991, when developing meditation as a basis for stress management for GPs, through Monash University and the Royal Australian College of General Practitioners.[3]

Perception — seeing what's really there

Our 'stressors' are the people, situations, events or circumstances that trigger our stress — our fight-or-flight response. If a venomous snake is just about to strike us and we get ready to run away then that seems like a pretty useful activation of our fight-or-flight response, but even an imaginary stressor will activate this response if we take our imagination to be real. Consider, for example, that the peak period for heart attacks is early Monday morning, around wake-up time. The day hasn't even begun and the biggest demand so far is to throw off the blankets. Generally no stressors in the form of venomous snakes have slid out of the wardrobe, and yet we start reacting to all the stuff our mind starts projecting, about what might or might not happen in our imagined day at work. If there's a heart attack waiting to happen then this is a pretty good trigger for it.

Reducing stress mindfully isn't so much a matter of replacing a stress-laden perception with a falsely positive one, such as looking at life through rose-coloured glasses or trying to pretend that that venomous snake isn't really there, or that it really loves us (at least enough to not bite us). If we're looking at a snake then hopefully we'll see it as a snake and respond accordingly before we get bitten. But if we see that the snake only exists in our imagination then there's no need to run or hide, or even to worry.

So, taking imagination to be real is the first distortion of perception that comes with unmindfulness. Reality is a piece of cake to deal with compared to our imagination taken to be real. We can always respond appropriately to reality, but responding to our imagination is like fighting a phantom that never gives up.

Sometimes what we're reacting to really is there, but we may perceive it to be bigger or more threatening than it is. A mouse, for example, is just a mouse, despite the fact that we may perceive it as a man-eating monster and scream and panic. The physical discomfort that we actually experience in the dentist's chair is generally minor compared to the level of intense suffering we produce for ourselves. In fact, we have probably had that root-canal mentally a thousand times before we ever get to the chair. If pain isn't amplified through the lens of fear and anticipation, or if it's experienced as a part of something we willingly participated in like a sporting or other voluntary recreational activity, then it would barely raise an eyebrow, let alone our pulse. The remedy to all this unnecessary suffering is to simply pay attention to what's actually being experienced, rather than blindly react to what we project on to situations.

When we are unmindful our thoughts unconsciously colour the way we see the world and its events. A simple comment from someone can be turned into a major criticism if it's distorted and exaggerated by our insecurities and self-criticisms. Vanity can be equally unmindful and blinding and can stop us from seeing the fairness of someone's criticism or the deceptiveness of someone's flattery. The most unfortunate thing is that, being on automatic pilot as we often are, we may be totally unaware of this whole process. From the perspective of mindfulness, pleasant misperceptions, expectations and mental projections are just as distracting and problematic as unpleasant ones are. In mindfulness, all we ask is to see things as they are — no more and no less.

Letting go — freedom through non-attachment

There's an old story about how monkeys are caught. Pots with narrow necks are buried in the ground and inside them hunters place something tasty to eat. Then they wait. The monkeys soon discover the tasty treats and slip their hand into the pot, grasp the contents, and then try to extract their fist laden with goodies. Unfortunately for them the fist is now too wide to fit through the mouth of the pot so they scream, believing themselves to be trapped. Voila — a trapped monkey! Trapped by its mind. From our human position it seems obvious that if the monkey would just let go it would be free. Silly monkeys! But perhaps, for most of our life, we are like the monkeys, with the way we hold on to things and won't let go.

To relax, mentally or physically, we don't have to 'do' anything. We merely have to stop doing something — holding on. In this way mindfulness is about 'non-doing'. Not holding on could be called detachment or non-attachment. Non-attachment is often misunderstood: it's not about getting rid of, cutting-off from, or denying what's going on, it's about not being bound to it.

It is an understandable mistake to think that sensations, thoughts and feelings, particularly the ones we don't like, have a hold of us. Mindfulness may well show us that it's the other way around — *we* have a hold of *them* — because we identify ourselves so closely with them. The tension we experience, like the sense of being trapped and out of control experienced by the monkeys — is because we latch on to and pull against what is taking place. But all these experiences come and go if we let them. If we hold on then we feel imprisoned, influenced and even dominated by them. Control, on the other hand, naturally restores itself when we let go of attachment.

Experiences in the form of situations, sensations, thoughts and feelings come and go all the time, whether we want them to or not. This is the natural and inevitable flow of life. If we forget that simple truth then we will soon be in for some problems. Some experiences we engage with, and others we don't, but being bound by our experiences is an unconscious habit, not a necessity. It feels like a great relief to let go, not because it's foreign to us but because it's natural. We become so habituated to tension that we have come to believe that tension is our natural state. We were not born anxious, preoccupied and distracted — we have managed to think our way into those states over a long period of time.

Some practical examples will help illustrate what's meant by 'holding on' and 'letting go'. Consider, for example, that, consciously or unconsciously, we have a self-image. It could be that we think of ourselves as being smart, kind or resilient. When that image is challenged — say we do something we see as stupid — we soon realise how attached to our ideas about ourselves we are. This will be experienced as tension and accompanied by emotional pain, mental agitation, embarrassment, fear and all the rest. If we're a little less attached we may acknowledge the stupidity and be thankful for the useful if uncomfortable lesson we've learned. To preserve our smart self-image in the face of evidence to the contrary, we may desire to cover up the blunder, or justify it, or try to win the argument whether we're right or wrong, rather than be thankful for being corrected.

The language we use is instructive. We don't tend to say that we *consider* an opinion, rather we *hold* an opinion. If we hold on to it tightly then we're much more likely to feel attacked if it is challenged, or deflated if it is proved wrong. This is fertile ground for conflict and loss of objectivity. Although this habit is common and happens to us all, if we are a little more mindful, we have the opportunity to choose whether or not we want to keep repeating it. If we really notice the effect we will likely choose a different way of relating to our thoughts.

We often hold on to desires whether they're useful or not. For example, we might find ourselves wanting to eat more than we should and then experience the pain that comes with over-indulgence. We might try to maintain a larger mortgage than we can comfortably afford and then find that our life gets dominated by it. We can cling to relationships even when they are toxic, possessions that just clutter the house and memories — to the extent that we can't be content in the present moment. We might determinedly stick to a fixed plan about how an event should go, even when circumstances unfold in such a way that makes it impossible. Clinging to the pleasant stuff can be just as problematic as clinging to the unpleasant stuff.

There are some common misconceptions about letting go. First, that letting go is about not responding to life, even when a response is called for. Mindfulness helps us engage and respond when we need to, but by first having let go of the tension and resistance that often gets in the way of that response. Second, that letting go is about giving everything away. We don't have to literally give everything away, only our attachment to it. Mind you, if we give up the attachment then we might find that we do literally give a few things away as a result. Third, that letting go means getting rid of what we don't like; for example, 'If I let go of a depressive feeling then it will go away.' It might, but it might not, or at least it might not for a little while. If this assumption is working away in the background then we can get very frustrated when the thing we don't like is still there. Fourth, that letting go means becoming inert. On the contrary, in letting go we tend to become more able to respond freely and without the limiting effects of anxiety, worry or preconceived ideas. Like the monkey who learns to let go, we're free again.

Acceptance

There is nothing either good or bad, but thinking makes it so.
William Shakespeare, Hamlet

An important principle related to letting go is acceptance. Whatever is happening is happening. There's no denying that. If at one moment there is comfort, peace, success or happiness then so be it. Enjoy it but remember that it will change. Equally, if there is an experience of pain, anxiety, failure or depression then so be it. Be patient in the presence of it and remember that it will change.

Life is constantly trying to teach us that experiences — pleasurable and painful — come and go whether we like them or not. As it says in 'the serenity prayer' — 'God grant me the serenity to accept the things I cannot change, courage to change the things I can, and wisdom to know the difference' (Reinhold Niebuhr) — we should try to change for the better what we can change, but wisdom lies in being able to recognise the things we can't change and therefore accept them. A crucial factor in how much impact an experience has on us is the attitude we bring to it. If we're mindful while drying the dishes then it might help us not to break them, but if through inattention we break a plate then non-acceptance will only make us feel worse — it won't change what's happened and it won't bring back the plate. It's wiser to use our time and energy repairing mistakes and then, because we're learning to be more mindful, resolve to pay more attention. Inattention costs.

Dealing with pain — or emotional discomfort for that matter — is another example. If our body has chronic pain then being at peace with it isn't easy but it will greatly reduce the suffering associated with it. In fact, our emotional reactivity to the pain merely makes us ever more vigilant for it and sensitises the brain's pain pathways to register more pain. Likewise with emotions: if a depressing thought or feeling comes to our awareness we may find that the non-acceptance of it leads to a cycle of rumination that merely imprisons our attention on it all the more.

Conversely, with acceptance and non-reactivity comes a growing ability for us to let the unpleasant physical or emotional experiences flow in and out while being less moved by them. This also allows our attention to gently come back to the present moment. One university student with a long background of depression found this to be the case after a few weeks of patient practice. The less reactive she was to these thoughts the easier it was to let them come and go. In one of those breakthrough moments it clicked that her thoughts had no grip on her. She said, 'I believed that because I had a depressing thought I had to think it. Now I realise I don't. I don't have to do anything about it, in fact the less I do the better. It's been very liberating for me.'

Presence of mind

The present moment is the only moment that's real — the past and future aren't. The past and future never actually exist. We may habitually think they do, but they are actually always outside the reality of our actual experience, although in the present we may notice that the mind imagines and projects into what it imagines the future to be, or what it thinks the past was. Yes, the residual effects from past thoughts, feelings, actions and decisions may be with us now, but those effects are also only ever observable and experienced in the present moment, which is timeless, and therefore eternal.

One of the authors (the mindful one?) had an experience of being apprehensive about a significant public speaking engagement the following day. 'Will it go well or will it go badly?' While standing at the sink washing the dishes he thought to himself, 'I hope I'm in the present moment tomorrow.' All of a sudden, as if waking from a dream, it seemed ridiculous that practising absent-mindedness in the form of worrying about the future was going to be a good preparation for being present. 'If I want to have a chance of being present tomorrow I ought to practise being present now, which means paying attention to the dishes!' Life became simple again and a state of mind was being cultivated that might actually be useful if the speaking engagement actually eventuated the following day.

When we say that someone has 'presence of mind' we are describing a state of being focused, responsible, brave and capable. When we deal with a challenging situation with presence of mind we notice that a feeling of calm is a conspicuous part of that state. On the other hand, if we take time to investigate what's going on in our mind when we experience anxiety, fear, depression or worry we will notice that this involves the mind unconsciously slipping unseen into a future that hasn't happened, or a past that has already come and gone. In the meantime, our focus goes from what's happening here and now, so we don't enjoy the present moment and our experience of it is clouded by our mental projections. We take our imaginary world to be the real world, and the real world doesn't get a look in. When our attention is on the here and now, our thoughts of the past or future aren't in the picture and therefore can't cause the emotional upset that they often do. Absent-mindedness is the opposite of presence of mind. If we are absent with or without leave then we are not here, now.

In our re-created past we tend to replay old events like replaying old movies: often embellishing them, ruminating on regrets, re-experiencing old hurts and criticising ourselves for old mistakes. Have you ever had an argument with a family member in your mind while you were driving home? There we are, outraged at all the things the person is saying to us (in our imagination, of course) and then in we go with all guns blazing. Then we wonder: 'Where did all that come from?' Maybe we've been on the receiving end of someone's fertile imagination? When we mistake imagination for reality we're merely arguing with ourselves and projecting our unreality on to others. If they have been unconsciously doing the same thing to us then we may find that when we arrive home we walk into a barrage of criticism and blame over which we feel unfairly accused. That's not a good recipe for successful communication!

In our imaginary future we tend to imagine problems that never happen. This is sometimes called 'catastrophising'. As Mark Twain said, 'I've had a lot of catastrophes in my life, and some of them actually happened.' We concoct anxiety and fear, dwell on rigid ideas about how things must turn out, and pre-judge situations and conversations long before they happen, if they ever happen. Then we often become anxious about how to get things to go the way we assume they must, and feel frustration or grief because they don't go according to those preconceived ideas. We prejudice events, which simply means that we judge them before they happen.

Mindfulness quickly teaches us how often the mind is distracted with thoughts about the past and future. In fact, if we have even a few moments in the present we should be very proud of ourselves — after a few weeks of practice we may realise that it's the exception rather than the rule. Realising more fully how much of the time we are not present is not a matter for concern — it's a sign of progress!

'What about planning and preparation?' you might ask. Planning and preparation can be as much present-moment activities as anything else can. If we plan or prepare then it's useful to do it with attention, and not with worry or rumination. Planning and preparation are present-moment activities, but when we notice ourselves worrying, and all of the physical effects that come with it, we can be confident that the mind has slipped out of the present moment into what it assumes the future will be, and it will be off-task to boot.

Being in the present is something we tend to avoid. Living in the 'here and now' doesn't mean becoming a hedonist who doesn't care about the results of actions, nor does it mean not caring about the future, or having no plans or goals. It does mean that we let the future come to us moment-by-moment as we practise dealing with each moment on its merits, patiently directing our attention to what the moment requires.

A student of one of the authors had the experience of being so preoccupied about a future exam that he couldn't focus on the study required to prepare for it. Does that make sense? We can be so anxious about the outcome of an interview that we go into it tense and unfocused. Who knows, even if we get the job we want so much, time may reveal that we were better off without it. A sportsperson can be so concerned with the outcome of a match that they lose concentration on the game or behave in an unsportsmanlike way that they will later regret. We can be so preoccupied about all the work we have to do that we feel exhausted before we have struck the first blow. We can keep replaying a past unpleasant argument to the extent that we distort current interactions and relationships to the point where we can't move on.

When we're not present we're unable to clearly see and understand the thoughts and feelings that actually motivate our actions, and their consequences. The question is — are we going to keep living under the tyranny of our past or our imagination about our future, or are we going to live the life we are meant to be living, now?

Listening

Here we go; Shakespeare again. Do you know how Hamlet's father, the king, was murdered? He had poison poured into his ear while he slept. What's that got to do with anything, you say! Well, have you ever wondered what sort of poison is pouring into our ears every day without us noticing? Maybe we're more like King Hamlet than we realise.

During day-to-day life, what do we spend most of our time listening to? It might be the birds singing in the trees, or the drops of rain falling on an iron roof, or the sound of children playing. It might be that we listen enthusiastically and intently to the conversations we are having, or the ambient traffic noises on the way home from work. Chances are, however, that it's not! Mindfulness quickly shows us that we spend most of our time listening to our endless internal dialogue. When we're stressed, worried, afraid, angry or depressed this internal dialogue has a particular tone to it and constantly reinforces and justifies itself. One of our favourite forms of internal chatter is to endlessly criticise, particularly ourselves. But if this were broadcast on a cable channel would we tune into it? Would we pay good money to listen to it? What would we call it: channel M for misery?

When we're unmindful we have little choice or awareness of what we're listening to. If we examine it we notice that the internal chatter is repetitive, and has a personal sound, as if it were 'me' talking to myself. But who is 'me', who is talking, and who is listening? In a more mindful and objective state, of course, we can start to view this mental chatter impersonally and we realise that our mind is just yabbering away to itself, trying to convince itself of something or other while we're simply noticing, quite unaffected. That's interesting. Mental chatter is just mental chatter. We don't have to believe it, react to it, dissect it or even be interested in it. That's a relief.

The internal chatter only allows us to give partial attention to what's going on around us, including our conversations with others. Miscommunication is the source of much stress and it causes misunderstanding, conflict and loneliness. We may have noticed that when we argue with someone we usually don't actually hear what they are saying. While the other person is speaking we generally listen to what we are going to say next, based on what we assume they are saying. This could, of course, be very different to what they are actually saying. We may not feel heard because the person we are miscommunicating with is probably doing the same thing. If we observe an argument objectively we may get the impression that neither person is hearing what the other is saying, and the simple reason for this is that they are probably not! We could be forgiven for assuming that in order to be heard we need to raise the volume which, of course, won't work. Listening will work.

It doesn't have to be as dramatic as that. Unmindfulness can include not hearing a person's name when they're introduced because we're chatting to ourselves about 'What impression am I making?' A teacher tries hard to explain how to solve a vital statistics problem and the student, with glazed eyes, doesn't get it because their attention is stuck on their internal dialogue of, 'I hate statistics, vital or otherwise, and I can't understand any of it! Why have I got to do it anyway?'

True listening means listening with attention and a quiet mind. It's more than just hearing words; it includes seeing under the surface to what the other person is really experiencing. For example, if we fully pay attention we might notice the fear that generally hides beneath anger; the anger is just a cover. Even though a person may not say much verbally, if we are attentive we often understand an enormous amount about what their needs, feelings and grievances are under the surface and can be more helpful, compassionate or conciliatory, as needed.

To be less oppressed by negative emotions we need to recognise when we are listening to internal chatter and then redirect our attention back to what's taking place in front of us. Effective communication begins with mindful listening.

Emotions

There is an aspect of letting go, which we have already considered, that requires a special mention, and that has to do with our not getting so attached to emotions. Emotions are the powerhouse or energy store behind our thoughts, actions and physiology. Learning how to relate to and express them is what psychologists sometimes call 'emotional regulation'.

We often get caught up with certain emotions no matter how much harm they cause to ourselves or others. Even when we do notice the effect of negative emotions we often replace one with another, like replacing anger with self-criticism. Something our experience may have taught us is that the more we fight with or dwell on these emotions the more they become like a black hole for our attention and the more they impact us.

Emotions, of course, don't have a hold on us; we have a hold on them. Some we grip very tightly. The more reactive we are to them the more they wire themselves into the circuitry of our brain, making it more and more likely that the same patterns will keep repeating themselves. Rather than feeling trapped by this fact we should feel empowered by it because the reverse is also true: the less reactive we are to emotions, through acceptance and non-attachment, the less binding they are and the more they become unwired in our brain. As paradoxical as it may seem, the less we try to get rid of them or criticise them the more they will recede of their own accord. We may not be able to stop the trains coming, but we can decide which ones to get on, and the less we get on those unhelpful thought trains the less likely they will be to keep coming.

Negative emotions tend to get in the way of our natural disposition for positive ones. The negative ones can become so habitual that we can think they are more real than the positive ones. When we are less preoccupied by negative emotions we make space for the deeper, stronger and more useful emotions to surface. For example, the contentment that can come with mindfulness meditation will come by itself if we let it.

Sometimes negative emotions can be strong and persistent, like depression or panic. You might have noticed this. It's often useful to seek professional help and support to deal with them, but where there is objectivity and motivation, our emotions, even strong negative or positive ones, can be impartially observed — just like our thoughts can. We can develop acceptance and the choice of whether to go with them or not, remembering that those we latch on to will be the ones that will habitually control us. The mindful approach to emotion doesn't mean suppression or trying not to have these feelings, it just means adopting a different relationship to them.

Negative emotions are reinforced, justified and perpetuated by unreasonable and ruminative thinking. When we see their unreasonableness and destructiveness clearly we start to lose our appetite to keep feeding them.

Any emotion, of course, can have its time or place. A positive emotional state doesn't necessarily mean agreeing with everyone all the time or being at the whim of others. There may be times when we need to confront an issue or stand up for a principle with clarity and conviction. Here fear may need to be let go so that courage or resolution can surface. Even anger can have its place and as such it's not always negative. It may be appropriate in a given situation and to suppress it would be harmful. Appropriate or 'mindful' anger, however, is born of a clear perception of a situation, isn't excessive, lasts only as long as it is needed, isn't venomous and never has any harmful intent in it towards ourselves or others. It is supported by reason, includes an emotional strength to deal with a situation, and doesn't leave a residue after the event is over. We feel in control of it, not controlled by it.

Inappropriate or unmindful anger, on the other hand, is the opposite of all these things.

It's interesting that the person we punish most with our negative emotions is ourselves, although we aim them at others. This is a destructive way of reducing the unrest we feel. Other people, being in the same predicament, also take their negative emotions out on us, so the cycle keeps repeating. We don't have to watch world politics for long to see unmindfulness on a global scale.

Forgiveness, from a mindfulness perspective, isn't something that we have to employ. We don't have to forgive if we don't want to, but mindfulness encourages us to look at the impact of non-forgiveness. If we look at the cost of being unforgiving, we may realise how much it costs us and so we might like to then experiment with forgiveness. Opening our heart can be something we first experiment with in small situations and then in bigger ones. Nobody can do it for us. Over time, mindfulness breeds the self-awareness that leads to compassion and tolerance for others. Self-criticism isn't a part of the mindfulness process, because it tends to be destructive. We can practise self-criticism if we want to but it doesn't help much. Useful and objective self-evaluation is constructive, but criticism is disabling and energy-sapping, and it slows and sabotages learning.

Negative feelings tend to have their origins in, and are fuelled by, the past. We replay unpleasant memories and continually re-experience and reinforce the deeply entrenched hostility, negativity and stress that inevitably goes with it. The mindful way out of this predicament is to just observe emotional states impartially, be present, and exercise a moment-by-moment choice of which emotions to embrace, and which to let go. This is central to the management of anxiety and depression and other common but actually unnatural and potentially remediable psychological states, which we will explore in coming chapters.

Expanding self-interest

It is surprising that with so many people around us we often feel isolated, lonely and at cross purposes with others. As obvious as it may sound, it's easy to miss the fact that our own wellbeing is inseparable from the wellbeing of those around us, although we may be separated by things such as distance, culture or social status. Our interests are inextricably linked. In the words of the poet John Donne, 'No man is an island'. African Ubuntu philosophy answers the question, 'How are you?' with 'I am well if you are well!'

As we work ourselves into a negative stress spiral we become more and more self-centred — ego-centred — so our view of the world gets smaller and smaller until it has shrunk to just 'me' in my own private world. When we are mindful, often after a significant breakthrough in our stress insight, we tend to become more connected and attentive to the needs of others. Indeed, it's hard to care for others when we don't feel good about ourselves.

If we feel like we are constantly battling everyone else — and everyone is battling against us because they are thinking the same way that we are — then how can we feel anything but stressed and tired? If we asked ourselves, 'Would we survive more happily and effectively on a life raft where people looked after each other or on one where people looked after themselves only?' the answer would be obvious. Which sporting team is more successful and enjoyable to play in: the one with team spirit or the one where the players play for themselves only? Unfortunately, the 'me attitude' sacrifices our prosperity as well as our emotional and physical wellbeing. This is of immense practical importance if we are to understand how intimately our individual and collective wellbeing are entwined.

What are the barriers that stop us from being on the same side as others, even in our own team? How can these unnecessary barriers and conflicts between people be broken down? The natural life remedy is to pay attention, let go, listen and tune into our emotions. Mindfulness can help us focus and grow our perspective from the small claustrophobic 'ego boundary' to increasingly include the family as a whole, workplace as a whole, community as a whole, and eventually the universe as a whole. To find out if this way of living will help our happiness and others' happiness we have to experiment with it and test it.

An essential aspect of expanding our broader self-interest and happiness needs to be mentioned — in the process of caring for others it is important that we still allow time for self-care. Mindful self-care isn't selfish but is actually a vital aspect of being able to care for others in a sustainable and enjoyable way.

Let's finish this chapter with a quote from the great scientist and philosopher Albert Einstein:

A human being is a part of the whole, called by us, 'Universe,' a part limited in time and space. He experiences himself, his thoughts and feelings as something separated from the rest — a kind of optical delusion of his consciousness. This delusion is a kind of prison for us, restricting us to our personal desires and to affection for a few persons nearest to us. Our task must be to free ourselves from this prison by widening our circle of compassion to embrace all living creatures and the whole of nature in its beauty. Nobody is able to achieve this completely, but the striving for such achievement is in itself a part of the liberation and a foundation for inner security. [4]

CHAPTER 4

The science of mindfulness

This chapter provides a summary and focuses on some of the science and evidence on mindfulness and its clinical effectiveness. We'll try to make sure that it's not too dry, but if science is really not your thing then please avert your eyes now and go on to the next chapter. Later chapters will look at how mindfulness is applied to various physical and mental health issues, but we hope this one will help you feel motivated that mindfulness is a useful thing to do — and realise that it's much more than just sitting down doing a lot of nothing.

Preventing and managing chronic illnesses and the symptoms associated with them isn't something that our conventional healthcare system does really well, with examples including asthma and chronic pain. It's one of the main reasons why people in the West are increasingly turning to complementary and alternative medicine. Take depression as an example. Depression is predicted to be far and away the greatest single burden of disease — that is, it will create greater disability than any other condition — in developed countries by the year 2030.[1] This trend has been gathering momentum over the past 60 years. The causes of mental health problems involve many factors including our coping style, upbringing, lifestyle (for example, poor diet and lack of exercise) and environment, but inattention may be a much more important factor than previously thought. Unfortunately the biomedical approach to managing depression has placed far too much emphasis on medications and far too little emphasis on all the other factors. The pharmaceutical treatments for depression aren't as effective as many doctors and patients assume they are. Some recent reviews of the evidence suggest that antidepressant drugs are only as good as placebos (sugar pills) for mild to moderate depression.[2,3] For severe depression, patients start to get an effect that can be attributed to the chemical action of the drug; up to that point, the effect is based on a person's belief in what the drug will do, not the chemical itself.

That doesn't mean that there's nothing a person can do to manage their depression — far from it. It's just that the best approaches in the long term need to include training people to use their mind better. This is where mindfulness comes in. It's probably the research on the use of mindfulness for depression that has created more interest in mindfulness than any other single area, and this has stimulated a lot of other research.

Does paying attention matter?

Although we may think that we're happiest when we're thinking about all the wonderful things we did last summer or what we have planned this coming weekend, according to a study from Harvard University we're happiest while our minds aren't wandering from what we are currently doing.[4] This was tested by giving people an iPhone and phoning them at random times during the day and asking them three questions. One: At this moment rate your happiness from 1 to 100. Two: What are you physically doing? Three: What is your attention on (unpleasant, neutral or pleasant daydreams, or were you paying attention to what you were doing?)? It seems we're happiest when we're paying attention to what we're doing. The authors concluded that the 'human mind is a wandering mind, and a wandering mind is an unhappy mind. The ability to think about what's not happening is a cognitive "achievement" that comes at an emotional cost.' Why? When we're inattentive our mind is most vulnerable to slipping into its habitual low gear — rumination and worry — which are central to depression and anxiety.

Clinical applications of mindfulness

The list of applications of mindfulness in healthcare and education keeps growing year upon year (Table 1).[5] The research into preventing relapse in depression has probably caused more interest than any other single application.

Table 1: Some clinical benefits of mindfulness-based meditation

Mental health

- Depression–relapse prevention
- Reduced anxiety, panic disorder and stress
- Better emotional regulation
- Greater emotional intelligence
- Management of addiction
- Better sleep
- Helping manage psychosis
- Borderline personality disorder
- Better control and less avoidance

Neuroscience

- Structural and functional changes in the brain
- Preservation of brain cells and generation of new brain cells (neurogenesis) particularly in the memory and executive functioning centres, which is important for preventing dementia
- Reduced activity in the amygdala, which is associated with aggression
- Enhanced attention and self-regulation

Clinical

- Pain management
- Symptom control
- Coping with major illnesses such as cancer
- Reduced allostatic load (long-term stress response)
- Metabolic benefits
- Hormonal changes
- Improved genetic function and repair and possibly slower ageing
- Reduced incidence of illnesses associated with ageing and poor mental health
- Facilitation of healthy lifestyle change

Improved performance
- Sport
- Academic
- Leadership

Spiritual
- Deep peace
- Insight
- Oneness
- Transcendence

Mindfulness and the fight-or-flight response

When we aren't paying attention to the present moment we often perceive stressors in our imagination that don't actually exist. Our body doesn't distinguish between imaginary stressors and real ones: if it gets the message from our mind that we're under threat it turns on our stress-response alarm system. This amplified level of stress takes a toll on our mental and physical health, especially over the long term. The fight-or-flight response is a natural, necessary and appropriate response to a threatening situation — if it's based on a clearly perceived actual, real-time, threat: say, confronting a hungry tiger or an angry employer. The resulting turbo-charge of energy happens in order to preserve life (Table 2).

Table 2: The fight-or-flight response

This response is associated with the following reactions in our body and mind.

Increased blood flow
- Dynamic circulation: elevation of blood pressure and heart rate, and the strength of the heartbeat

- Blood flow is diverted away from gut and skin (meaning that the gut shuts down and we go pale) and is diverted to the muscles ready for action
- Sweating in order to regulate temperature while we exert ourselves

Increased metabolism
- Increased metabolic rate
- Increased respiration and opening up of airways to get lots of oxygen onboard and to breathe off carbon dioxide
- Mobilisation of energy (glucose and fat) stores

Arming defences
- Blood gets thicker (platelet adhesiveness) ready to stop bleeding faster
- Mobilisation of immune cells ready to fight infections

Preparing for tissue repair
- Mobilising inflammatory hormones (for example, cortisol, cytokines, interleukins) to help repair tissues damaged while dealing with the threat

Alertness (mindfulness)
- Attention centres in the brain activate
- We pick up a lot more information about what is going on in the environment

When we appropriately switch on our fight-or-flight response we don't experience it as anxiety but rather as a surge of energy that is associated with an increase of mindfulness. On the other hand, when we inappropriately switch it on we experience it as anxiety and we do it because we're unmindful. All the switched-on chemicals and processes are all dressed up with nowhere to go and nothing to do, except create trouble in the form of symptoms and disease. The name given to the long-term over-activation of the stress response is 'allostatic load'.[6] This is like physiological wear-and-tear on our body and is seen in chronic depression and anxiety (Table 3). If we want to accelerate our ageing process then this is the best way to do it. The positive message is that these effects can all be reversed over time with the regular practice of mindfulness. What goes up comes back down again and what goes down comes back up. Focusing our attention on the here and now helps us to see which stressors are actually real and which ones are in our imagination.

Table 3: High allostatic load can, among other things, lead to the following reactions

- Immune dysregulation (lowered defences against infections and increased inflammation)
- Hardening of the arteries (atherosclerosis), which leads to cardiovascular disease
- Metabolic syndrome (high blood pressure, high blood lipids, high blood glucose and increased weight around the trunk)
- Thinning of the bones (osteoporosis)
- Loss of brain cells (accelerated ageing or atrophy), particularly in the hippocampus and prefrontal cortex (learning, memory and executive functioning areas of the brain), which predisposes to Alzheimer's Disease in later life[7, 8]
- Growth and increased reactivity of the amygdala (the fear and stress centre of the brain)

Stress, attention and performance

Stress is often valued as a way of improving performance. To an extent, stress is good or at least better than apathy as far as being productive is concerned. The relaxation associated with apathy and lack of focus should, however, not be mistaken for the relaxation associated with the inner calm and focus of mindfulness. Furthermore, too much stress is associated with a lack of focus, poor performance and an increased number of mistakes. Depressed hospital doctors, for example, make more than six times as many medication errors compared to non-depressed doctors doing the same job.[9] The chapters on performance (Chapters 18, 19 and 20) will explore this in more detail.

Mindfulness also enhances executive functioning associated with an area of the brain called the prefrontal cortex. Executive functions include short-term (working) memory, processing information, attention regulation, making decisions, emotional regulation and prioritising. Mindfulness training stabilises this area of the brain and helps it to function well whereas an overactive stress centre (amygdala) hijacks this area of the brain, making effective functioning difficult, if not impossible.[10]

Sports people notice that they function best when they are focused. As an article about sports psychology put it:

> Mindfulness is vastly different than the way many athletes conceive it, and it offers many benefits to focusing and athletic performance. Mindfulness teaches athletes to focus on the present rather than dwelling on past mistakes or future results. This present focus enables athletes to be more alert to relevant performance cues and allows them to more easily disregard distracting cues.[11]

Another challenge in truly focusing is the prevalence in our modern world of 'multitasking'. Although we can do many things at once, contrary to popular belief we just can't do them all well, nor do we have in-depth or rewarding experiences while our attention skims across the surface of life. To illustrate, the chance of having a motor vehicle accident within 5 minutes of using a mobile phone is over 400 per cent higher than what it is normally.[12] Many work environments are so fast these days (some people call it 'hyperkinetic') that we become conditioned into very short attention spans. This is called 'Attention Deficit Trait' — the tendency to be inattentive — and it's a big reason why smart, capable people underperform.[13]

The modern myth of efficiency and fullness of living being the result of multitasking is one that we should question. Let's not confuse busyness with productiveness. You may have noticed that you are increasingly likely to be asked, 'How are you, keeping busy?' as if busyness is now all that matters.

Furthermore, the lack of enjoyment (anhedonia) that is a central part of poor mental health is a direct result of a lack of engagement with life as it unfolds. One of the greatest benefits of mindfulness is an increase in the richness of life as well as in our capacity to tell the difference between real and imagined stressors.[14]

Learning to pay attention is therefore central in improving our performance and efficiency, deepening our enjoyment of life and protecting our mind from the destructive cognitive processes behind poor mental health. Mindfulness training isn't about avoidance; it's about engagement. Avoidance and distraction are the *problem* — mindfulness is the *remedy*.

Mindfulness and mental health

Mindfulness has been seen for millennia as a means for reliving suffering. In our modern day we give 'suffering' different names, such as depression, stress and anxiety. As we mentioned in previous chapters, mindfulness is more than meditation, it's also a foundation for various forms of psychotherapy.

Jon Kabat-Zinn developed Mindfulness-Based Stress Reduction (MBSR) for the management of stress and chronic pain at the UMass Medical Center in Worcester, Massachusetts. Mindfulness-Based Cognitive Therapy (MBCT) was developed by some prominent psychologists by the names of Teasdale, Williams and Segal from the work of Jon Kabat-Zinn for application in managing depression. MBCT was initially found to better than halve the relapse rate for people who have had recurrent depression in the past, compared to treatment as usual.[15] It also improves mood, anxiety and coping in people dealing with major and life-threatening illnesses such as cancer.[16]

Conventional cognitive therapy aims to change people's thoughts, whereas MBCT aims to change people's relationship to negative thoughts and emotions (non-attachment).[17] It has been found through various forms of brain imaging (brain scans) that changes in brain function during mindfulness include increased signals in brain regions related to mood regulation and attention control, with an increased release of dopamine — a brain chemical associated with feeling good.[18, 19] It has also been found that mindfulness reduces levels of some of the inflammatory chemicals we release when we are stressed, such as cytokines, which cause a range of symptoms associated with depression.[20]

Mindfulness not only reduces depressive symptoms but also reduces the reactivity of the amygdala, which is overactive in people with depression.[21] In adolescents, mindfulness reduces symptoms of anxiety, depression and somatic distress, and increases self-esteem and sleep quality.[22] Improving sleep is likely to be one of the most important reasons why mindfulness is therapeutic for depression. (We discuss this further in Chapter 16.)

Depression and anxiety often co-exist so it is important to find approaches that are therapeutic for both. Mindfulness seems to do that. It helps with generalised anxiety and related symptoms such as social anxiety disorder.[23]

Mindfulness programs have also been found to reduce stress, anxiety and depression among high-performing students, such as medical students. At Monash University a six-week mindfulness program has been part of the core curriculum since 2002, and our research indicates that the students who have participated are more resilient and have better mental health as a result.[24] A program developed by a former Monash tutor for the University of Tasmania medical course has shown similar findings.[25] Research undertaken by the authors indicates that medical students who have been taught about mindfulness and its clinical applications are far more likely to be disposed to recommend it to their patients.[26]

Mindfulness is just as important for health professionals as it is for the people they look after. For example, it has been found to enhance doctor wellbeing, reduce burnout (burnout is measured by its effects on emotional exhaustion, depersonalisation, lack of personal accomplishment) and mood disturbance, and increase empathy, responsiveness to patients and conscientiousness.[27]

A range of mental health benefits have also been found for teachers who learn mindfulness,[28] and mindfulness programs are increasingly being adapted to schools. One of the authors has been involved with running mindfulness programs for staff and senior students. For example, a program for year 12 students found that those who learned mindfulness performed significantly better on the General Health Questionnaire (GHQ) than did year 12 students who didn't.[29] The wider interest in mindfulness has led to it being a topic at a range of education-related conferences.

One study on primary school children had them complete the Strengths and Difficulties Questionnaire (SDQ) and a modified version of the Children's

Depression Inventory (CDI) — pre and post mindfulness program. There was a significant decrease in both scales on overall average scores and the number of children diagnosed with mental health problems. For example, we found that 25.6 per cent of children scored in the borderline or diagnostic category for the SDQ pre mindfulness program, but only 16.3 per cent post. This suggests that mindfulness training warrants consideration as an element of a whole school mental-health promotion program.[30] A range of mental health benefits are also found for teachers who learn mindfulness — which is comforting because they probably need it more than their students do!

Mindfulness-based strategies have also been applied to patients with schizophrenia who are in remission, with some promising results,[31,32] although the current evidence suggests that mindfulness may not be appropriate for people with psychosis. Mindfulness improves function and reduces anxiety in many patients, including those with schizophrenia, therefore helping avoid a relapse of schizophrenia. It may also be helpful in reducing the intrusiveness of hallucinations by helping patients to be less distracted by and reactive to them. Mindfulness for schizophrenia shouldn't be seen as an alternative to medications, and it should be used by experienced mental health practitioners. Intensive practice or retreats should probably be avoided in managing psychosis.

Neuroplasticity

Contrary to what has been taught in medical schools for decades, we now understand that the brain is constantly rewiring itself, throughout our life. Neuroplasticity simply means that the brain (neuro-) can change or adapt (-plasticity) depending on what we experience and how we train it. From a therapeutic point of view it means that we can 'unwire' unhelpful patterns of thought and behaviour and wire in helpful ones.[33] Mindfulness research is changing the way we understand the brain, and the Mind and Life Institute is a collection of leading scientists exploring this field.[34] If you would like to read further on this topic, Norman Doidge's book *The Brain that Changes Itself* gives a great overview of this subject.

To summarise some of the key findings about mindfulness and

neuroplasticity: brain scans measuring the thickness of the 'grey matter' in long-term mindfulness meditators indicate that this is thicker, particularly in the areas associated with the senses, memory, emotional regulation, paying attention and executive functioning.[35] Blood flow to such areas of the brain is also increased.[36] This confirms what people report about functioning better, and also indicates a slowing of ageing of the brain by reversing the negative effects of the high allostatic load discussed earlier.[37, 38, 39]

Leisure activities during which we don't pay attention (such as watching TV) are associated with higher rates of attention deficit problems in children and roughly a fourfold increased life-long risk of developing Alzheimer's Disease[40, 41] — compared to those whose leisure activity requires attention, such as reading, playing board games, playing musical instruments and dancing.[42] The amount of screen time that a lot of young people now engage in — the average is about four hours a day — may have as important implications for the health of their brains as it does for levels of obesity and physical inactivity. It seems clear that the brain thrives on attention and engagement and it wastes away with inattention and disengagement. Essentially, if we're engaged with life then we're more likely to be enjoying it — so enjoyment and a healthy brain go hand in hand.

There are particular areas of the brain associated with the experience of empathy and compassion, and it seems that over the long term these areas of the brain become more responsive — wake up, if you like — when people learn to meditate on compassion.[43] There should be nothing surprising in the finding that if we pay more attention, including to the person in front of us, we will relate to them a whole lot better. Compassion may be a natural side effect of attention and a lack of compassion a side effect of inattention.

It is because of mindfulness's capacity to foster compassion that it also helps to prevent 'carer fatigue' or 'carer burnout' because it can teach us to be compassionate to ourselves as well as others. This is illustrated by a study of an eight-week mindfulness program for doctors that was associated with improvements on all measures of wellbeing. The more mindful the doctors became the less burnout (emotional exhaustion, depersonalisation, personal accomplishment) they experienced, the greater their empathy and responsiveness to the psychosocial aspects of their patients' situations, the less mood disturbance they experienced, and the more conscientious and emotionally stable they became.[44]

Default mental activity

There are two main types of brain activity that depend on how focused or connected we are: active engagement (tasks associated with paying attention) and default states (when our mind is inattentive, idle, recalling the past, daydreaming, ruminating).

Brain regions active in default states in adolescents and young adults are not only associated with depression, but also show the early changes found in the elderly with Alzheimer's Disease.[45] This may have to do with wear and tear on the brain through all the aimless mental activity associated with constantly going over the past and the stress this causes.[46] Default mental activity is largely to do with thinking about our ideas about ourselves — our imaginary selves. This is why it is so much a part of depression and anxiety. Mindfulness is the direct remedy for default mental activity because when we are paying attention it doesn't find a way in.

Mindfulness and ageing

Work led by Australia's Nobel Prize-winning researcher Elizabeth Blackburn has found that mindfulness may slow genetic ageing and enhance genetic repair.[47] We will explore this topic more deeply in Chapter 6.

Mindfulness, addiction and lifestyle change

Stopping smoking or any other addiction isn't easy and to do it we have to learn to deal with cravings. The common way to deal with cravings is to suppress them, but this comes at a mental health cost. A study on the effectiveness of suppression versus mindfulness for coping with cigarette cravings reported that the mindfulness group reduced smoking and also achieved a far more stable affect (mood) and reduced depressive symptoms, whereas the suppression group found that their mood significantly declined.[48]

Acceptance therapy, a core element of mindfulness training, has been found to be effective for alcohol and other forms of substance abuse because it helps to reduce the negative mood, distress and craving that are such common triggers for relapse.[49, 50, 51] Vipassana meditation has also been studied as a therapy for addiction among prison inmates: it led to a decrease in alcohol-related problems and psychiatric symptoms and to increases in positive psychosocial outcomes.[52] We will explore the topic of addiction in more depth in Chapter 9.

Mindfulness-based skills have been central elements in most successful lifestyle programs for chronic illnesses such as heart disease and cancer. The Ornish program is probably the best-known example. We will explore these programs more deeply in future chapters on heart disease and cancer (Chapters 13 and 14).

Meditation and emotional intelligence

Research has found that people who rate highly on mindfulness scales also rate highly on emotional intelligence (EI)[53] and empathy.[54] EI has a number of elements, including self-awareness, self-regulation, empathy, motivation and social skills. This is one of the main reasons that educators and leadership trainers are becoming more interested in mindfulness — because it is associated with the qualities that make up good social beings and responsive leaders. We will explore this more deeply in Chapter 21.

Mindfulness and eating disorders

Mindfulness is a promising approach to the management of eating disorders. It possibly works for this by increasing our awareness of our eating behaviour and physical cues, helps us deal with self-criticism and negative self-image, and assists us in managing impulsivity and negative emotions.[55] Mindfulness programs for eating disorders such as binge-eating are designed to help people control their responses to their varying emotional states, make conscious food choices, develop an awareness of hunger and satiety cues and cultivate self-acceptance.[56]

Interviews with women going through such programs report that they experience a transformation from their emotional and behavioral extremes, disembodiment and self-loathing to an inner connection with themselves resulting in greater self-awareness, acceptance and compassion.[57] We will explore this more deeply in Chapter 12.

Mindfulness and cancer

A study on cancer patients who learned mindfulness in their cancer management had significantly lower scores for negative mood, depression, anxiety, anger and confusion, and they also had more vigour. They also had fewer overall physical and stress symptoms.[58] Mindfulness has also been shown to reduce cortisol levels and inflammation in cancer patients — signs of a poor prognosis — and improve immunity and quality of life.[59, 60] We will explore this more deeply in Chapter 14.

Mindfulness and pain

Mindfulness meditation is associated with a significant reduction in pain, fatigue and sleeplessness, and with improved function, mood and general health for people with chronic pain syndromes.[61, 62, 63] One of the main reasons for this is likely to be the reduced emotional reactivity to pain that reduces the suffering associated with it.[64] We will explore this topic more deeply in Chapter 11.

Mindfulness and immunity

Mindfulness training improves immune function because it has the opposite effect to the stress response and allostatic load that disrupt immunity. For example, people within the workplace show better immune response to vaccinations and increases in antibodies after an eight-week mindfulness program.[65] Mindfulness and compassion meditation practices are also associated with reduced inflammation,[66] and may therefore be important in the management of a wide range of inflammatory and autoimmune illnesses such as asthma, arthritis, dermatitis, Multiple Sclerosis and Inflammatory Bowel Disease.

Mindfulness and sleep

Mindfulness helps to significantly improve sleep quality by helping people go to sleep more easily, have a longer sleep duration and require less use of sleep medications.[67] Enhanced sleep may be part of the explanation for mindfulness reducing depression in those with chronic insomnia.[68] We will explore this topic more deeply in Chapter 16.

Meditation and control

We can't always control the things that happen to us, which might be what makes life the adventure that it is, but we can have more control over our responses to life events and our attitudes to them. Mindfulness helps us to develop more adaptive and less avoidant coping styles, which helps us to learn faster and to get on with dealing with situations — rather than putting them off.[69, 70] This is important for mental health, which will be explored in depth particularly in Chapters 6–8.

What does it all add up to?

In summary, what mindfulness can teach us may be tremendously useful for our physical and psychological wellbeing because it: improves how effectively we function; positively changes our bodies physiologically and metabolically; has indirect benefits by improving our lifestyle; enhances our relationships and compassion to others and to ourselves; improves the way we cope with life challenges; and enriches our enjoyment of life.

PART 2

MEDICAL AND PRE-MEDICAL CONDITIONS THAT MINDFULNESS CAN HELP WITH, AND HOW

CHAPTER 5

Mindfulness as a clinical treatment and prevention

It has taken mindfulness thousands of years to be an overnight modern clinical success. There is a growing realisation that this is a technique that can restore the foundations of mental and physical wellness — even to people who think they have lost it forever — as well as help people maintain mental and physical wellness. The recent upsurge in interest in mindfulness as a therapy as well as a lifestyle-enhancing option derives partly from a growing objective evidence base of its scientifically measurable benefits. It also derives from a growing desperation.

An increasing number of the world's population are now realising that the only way 'out' is 'in' — that we are running out of other options. The rapid increase in the complexity of our modern problems means that our last as well as our best option for a solution is to finally wake up to ourselves, to become fully aware and fully accepting. This realisation might not seem like a blessing but maybe it's the most powerful kind of blessing — a blessing in disguise.

There's a fairly obscure idea tucked away in a fairly obscure ancient Indian wisdom tradition known as the 'yoga of desperation'. This arises when our situation looks so completely bleak that all we have left is a truly magnificent last opportunity for peace and wisdom and happiness, just when it looks like our existential goose is cooked. This can happen when things are just so bad that our minds have to stop making them worse by trying to make them better, and we can be blessed by a state of simultaneous awareness and acceptance — a state of enforced mindfulness. There's a quote by former Israeli diplomat and politician Abba Eban that goes along the same lines: 'History teaches us that men and nations behave wisely once they have exhausted all other alternatives.'

The growing body of objective evidence that supports the clinical as well as the practical uses of mindfulness is difficult to ignore, even by the scientists and clinicians who sometimes display an unscientific tendency to ignore or oppose anything that's new, or at least new to them. The progress of medical and psychological science can seem painfully slow to watch, partly because it's vital in these areas to not make avoidable mistakes — new theories and treatments are rightly not accepted until there's a substantial body of evidence that supports their usefulness and safety. This progress can be even slower than it needs to be, however, when vested interests protect the current way of doing things, even if this means unfairly and unscientifically ignoring or criticising potential improvements.

The advantages of mindfulness therapies over other therapies, particularly drug therapies, include their ability to:

- prevent mild conditions or propensities from developing into full-blown clinical conditions such as depression and addiction,
- be practised by oneself with or without a therapist,
- provide a non-invasive, non-stigma-producing ('healthy' people also practise it) alternative,
- offer a wellness-based rather than a sickness-based remedy for a range of conditions,
- result in significant clinical improvements relatively quickly and inexpensively, compared with other therapies, and
- meet Hippocrates' first principle of medicine: to do no harm; mindfulness practised appropriately causes no side effects, except for an increase in wellbeing.

As we mentioned in the beginning of this chapter, mindfulness can restore as well as enhance health. In the following chapters we will give practical explanations of how and why mindfulness can help anyone with any of a range of mental and physical conditions. The special benefits of mindfulness as a clinical technique include its unique ability to explain illnesses at a deep causal level by illuminating why things go wrong, which makes it an especially powerful prevention as well as cure. If you are suffering ill health, the road to recovery might seem like it's a thousand miles long, and dark. To combine metaphors from two ancient wisdom traditions, one Chinese and one Indian, a journey of even a thousand miles begins with a single step, and your lantern only needs to cast enough light to cover the single step that's in front of you. Mindfulness may well be both the first step on our journey to wellness and also the lantern that lights your way.

CHAPTER 6

Stress and ageing

Sandra looked older than her years. She was in her late thirties and came in regularly for ongoing counselling as part of her drug rehabilitation program. She'd had a difficult upbringing with a mother who drank too much and a father who disappeared from her life when she was three. Sandra's mother had a number of de-facto relationships and two of her partners had sexually and physically abused Sandra throughout much of her teen years. Since leaving home at sixteen, Sandra had spent much of her time living on the streets until her early twenties. She had been on and off hard drugs — she has been off them for the past six months — and had three children whom she greatly loved, to two different fathers. Sandra still smoked and took prescribed medications from her GP. Because of the drug issues, her children had spent much of their lives in foster care but were back with Sandra.

Sandra was living on welfare because of difficulties holding down a regular job but was doing her best to make ends meet. Sandra was the kind of person, however, who always managed to get up no matter how many times she was knocked down and she had been very courageous and determined to get her life back on track. As a part of her therapy she was making sincere efforts to learn to be more mindful and to live more consciously without being such a prisoner of her unhappy past.

The problem of stress and ageing

In this chapter we will expand a little on what we mentioned in Chapter 4 relating to stress — a term we will broadly take to be unhealthy states of mind and emotion — and how it affects our ageing. This will help us understand how mindfulness not only helps with stress, but also how it seems to slow the ageing process. Although it's still early days as far as the research is concerned, and although we haven't arrived at the end of the journey yet — as far as completely proving the effects of mindfulness meditation on slowing ageing — we will say that the signpost is pointing in a very interesting direction.

In Chapter 4 we looked at the short-term activation of our stress response and the long-term overactivation of it, the latter of which leads to high 'allostatic load'.[1] We described this as a physiological wear and tear on the body and learned that it is seen in chronic depression, stress and anxiety. Your car mechanic would probably tell you that if you flog your car it will cope pretty well for a time, but it won't last you as long as it would if you looked after it, and its parts will wear out a lot faster. Well, it's no different with our body. If we wanted to accelerate our ageing process, then mindlessly flogging our body is the best way to do it. Ageing is unavoidable but how we age is largely up to us.

Epigenetics, telomeres and telomerase

We thought that some fancy words might impress you, perhaps even make you think that we know something that you don't! Although we hope you're impressed, we suspect that the principles these words relate to will probably be quite intuitive to you, although you may not be familiar with the details. So let's spend a little time exploring genes, epigenetics and telomeres.

There are a lot of things taught in our universities and medical schools for generations that 'ain't necessarily so'. One of them is that the way our genes (our DNA) express themselves is pretty much predetermined. 'If it's in your genes then that's the end of the story. It will come to pass.' That belief potentially leads to a kind of scientific fatalism or learned helplessness. If we get genetically tested for one condition or another and find that we 'have the gene' then we might feel like we're perched precariously on a genetic time bomb, just waiting to go off.

We now know, however, that what we used to think about genes and how they work simply isn't true. Why, for example, do some people get an illness like bowel cancer when others with the same family history and diet don't? Why do some people get the chronic illnesses associated with ageing at an earlier age than others do? Why do some people look as though they are ageing faster than others?

Epigenetics is an emerging field of science that tells us that our genes and the way they express themselves are anything but set in concrete. Our environment, lifestyle and state of mind have profound effects on how our genes express themselves, for better or worse. We can increase our likelihood of getting an illness we're genetically disposed to — whether it's heart disease, cancer, MS, addictions or depression — depending on the things we do (lifestyle), the things we think (state of mind), and the things we're exposed to (environment).

What we also know now is that we can age faster or slower depending on the things we do, the things we think and the things we're exposed to. We won't go into diet and exercise too much here, as important as they are, but will focus on the mind because that will help us understand the potential importance of mindfulness for improving genetic repair and slowing the genetic ageing process.

Australia's Nobel Prize-winning researcher Elizabeth Blackburn discovered telomeres and telomerase and demonstrated their importance in the ageing process. What are telomeres? They are located on the ends of the long strands of interwoven DNA, which are the molecules at the centre of our cells that contain all the information they need to function and produce whatever they need to produce. Telomeres function something like the little plastic bit on the end of our shoelaces — to stop the DNA from unravelling. As we age the telomeres get whittled away and an enzyme by the name of telomerase works away trying to repair the telomeres. The shorter the telomeres get the older we are genetically and the more chronic illnesses associated with ageing we are prone to, from heart disease to cancer to arthritis. When the telomeres get worn short enough the DNA unravels and the cell dies. Like the ends of our shoelaces, when they get shorter and shorter in response to what we're doing to them, eventually they don't do their job very effectively anymore.

We know that a good diet and regular physical exercise help slow the ageing process and keep our telomeres intact. That's just another reason why eating a healthy diet and exercising regularly is good for us. We also know that our state of mind has a profound effect on the rate at which our telomeres age. Ageing, however, isn't just about our telomeres, but let's look at them closely because they illustrate the relationship between the state of our mind and the state of our body so well.

Work by Elizabeth Blackburn and her team has found some interesting relationships between our state of mind and our rate of ageing. For example, a study on healthy post-menopausal women found that the combination of lower optimism and higher pessimism was associated with shorter telomeres, greater inflammation and increases in the risk for disease, and early mortality.[2] In other words, by middle age the women with a tendency to pessimism were approximately ten years older genetically than optimistic women. One could save on a lot of anti-wrinkle cream at that rate!

That women exposed to domestic violence experience chronic stress and report worse health than women who aren't is well known, but we now also know that a big part of the explanation for this is the resulting wear and tear on the telomeres.[3] Another study on healthy pre-menopausal women showed that psychological stress associated with higher oxidative stress (oxidation is a part of ageing, like when an apple is going brown), lower telomerase activity and shorter telomere length added the equivalent to between nine and seventeen years of accelerated ageing. The effect of ageing wasn't due to the events going on in the woman's life but how well she coped with them.[4] This raises the question, of course, of whether learning to cope better with our life events will slow our ageing process. It seems that the answer is yes.

Post-traumatic stress disorder (PTSD) associated with childhood trauma has also been associated with increased risk for age-related diseases, rapid loss of telomere length and early mortality.[5] Children with greater exposure to institutional care have significantly shorter relative telomere length in middle childhood — the longer the institutionalisation, the shorter the telomeres.[6] Early adversity and how we learn to cope with it has potentially profound effects on a molecular level for the rest of our life. Although most of the studies in this field have been done on women, there's no reason to believe that it's any different for men.

The more positive side of what might look like a very gloomy ageing coin is that we can do a lot to turn this process around. So, for example, physical exercise has been found to protect our bodies and telomeres from the damaging effects of stress. Sedentary women were fifteen times more likely to have short telomeres in relation to significant life stress compared to women who exercised regularly.[7]

What we find even more interesting is that when we change our state of mind we change what's happening to us on a molecular level, right down to the very core of our cells. As we said previously, we can't always control the things that happen to us, but we *can* have more control over our responses to life events and our attitude to them — mindfulness helps us to do that. It has been found that mindfulness may slow genetic ageing and enhance genetic repair by increasing the effectiveness of our telomerase.[8] It's fascinating to consider that we can help our bodies do their own genetic engineering by sitting on a cushion and paying attention. There's still a long way to go as far as this research is concerned, but although we may not have arrived yet at the end of that journey we are passing some very promising signposts.

The brain

We discussed this in Chapter 4 to some extent, but it's worth expanding on a few points here. The bad news is that we know that increased inattention, stress and poor mental health accelerates the ageing of our brain cells (neurons) — but can the process be reversed? Well, the good news is that yes, it can.

Brain scans measuring the thickness of the 'grey matter' in long-term mindfulness meditators indicates that it is thicker, particularly in the areas associated with sensory input (we connect better with the world around us), memory (we remember more in both the long and short term because we are paying attention), emotional regulation, the attention centres (we attend better) and the executive functioning region (we think, plan and choose better).[9] This indicates that mindfulness meditation slows down the ageing of the brain by reversing the negative effects of the high allostatic load that we discussed in Chapter 4. Leisure activities that engage our attention literally help keep us young — it's natural to be creative and to explore our environments. It's not so natural to spend our life 'veging out', which isn't to say that the occasional veg-out can't be very useful and enjoyable.

Mindfulness can help us make all of the other healthy lifestyle changes that may help slow our ageing process and reduce our chances of developing the illnesses associated with it. All of the above points also have important implications for preventing or slowing the progression of dementia.

Over the last six months Sandra has made great progress in moving on from her troubled past. Although her mind habitually wanted to dive back into the past she found that the mindfulness practice helped her to come back to what she was doing now. Sandra had gone around those loops in her thinking many times and she was sick of always arriving at the same place — it was time to move on. She had also made a number of changes to her diet and exercise levels and had found the mindfulness practices very helpful in getting off the cigarettes. She enjoyed nothing more than the early morning walks with her children along the waterfront. This was when she felt most present and alive — the healthy benefits were a nice side effect but were a secondary concern. Some part-time work had come her way, which helped to make ends meet. Who knows what was happening in the core of Sandra's cells? All she knew was that she was feeling a whole lot better physically and emotionally, and people were telling her that she was looking younger all the time.

Take-home tips for a mindful response
to stress and ageing

- Recognise that what we think affects what we do and that what we think and do affects our body.
- Recognise that stress comes from our *reaction* to what happens, not from what happens.
- Take an active interest in health by developing interests and activities that will stimulate our brain and body.
- Be aware of, accept and enjoy life as it really wonderfully is — at any age.

CHAPTER 7

Anxiety

Georgia was a young, intelligent and capable woman aged in her late twenties who worked in marketing. Although she had a long history of low-level anxiety, part of which she had inherited from her parents, it had never been enough to interfere significantly with her life — until six months ago. Recently life had become more demanding at work, as well as socially and at home. Her sleep had become affected in part due to an irregular lifestyle and the various energy drinks she used to boost her flagging energy levels, but also in part to an increasing tendency to worry. Then six months ago Georgia had her first panic attack, out of the blue, while driving her car. This shook her up and she started to anticipate the possibility of another attack in an even more public place. Sure enough, such an attack did come on while she was at work. Although everyone was very understanding and sympathetic, Georgia wasn't so gentle on herself. She became hyper-vigilant for signs of anxiety and when she experienced them she tried desperately to make them go away. Unfortunately this didn't make them go away; in fact, it made them all the worse.

Over the next couple of months Georgia's panic attacks came more frequently and stronger, to the point where she was experiencing them on and off for hours in the day. She couldn't leave the house, couldn't work, couldn't socialise and her life became isolated and bleak. After another couple of months it was apparent that wishful thinking wasn't helping, nor was a growing sense of helplessness. Georgia saw her GP, who did some tests to be sure there was no major physical illness to explain the problem, which there wasn't. Georgia said that she wanted to learn to manage the problem herself and didn't want to go on sedatives or other medications because she felt, with her personality, she would be addicted in no time. Her moment of facing up to her demons had come ...

What is anxiety?

Have you ever been anxious? Have you ever wondered what really causes your anxiety? Let's consider what anxiety is — from a mindfulness perspective — and whether there's something we can do about it. It might seem radical, but we can even consider the possibility that it's possible to make anxiety, and the deep human suffering that underlies it, disappear into irrelevance.

According to the ancient Indian wisdom tradition of Ayurveda ('ayur' — life; 'veda' — wisdom) anxiety is the cause of all of our health problems, mental and physical. That the mind profoundly influences our health is not a new concept, although the increasingly popular field of research called mind–body medicine can make it sound like it is. The research by Elizabeth Blackburn and her colleagues that we described in the previous chapter, and the research of Herbert Benson and his team at the Harvard Mind–Body Institute, show that our stress genes can be accentuated by poor living and quietened down by mind–body techniques such as meditation.[1] This demonstrates the profound practicality of science meeting life, in this case the science of epigenetics. How's that: tweaking our genes with our mind and attention. What next?

One of us once did a fifteen-day Ayurvedic treatment in a small, humid and dusty Ayurvedic hospital, in a small, humid and dusty southern Indian city called Quilon. During his initial week as an Ayurvedic outpatient he spent several hours every morning waiting for his four-handed medicinal oiling and oral herbal treatment, in a very appropriately named waiting room. On the waiting-room wall facing him was a painting of a serene blue god holding what looked like a pitch fork. This was the great Hindu deity Shiva.

'What's he doing here?' he eventually asked one of his impending oilers.

'Shiva is god of destruction and medicine.'

'Um, isn't that an odd combination?'

'No! To be healed you must first destroy what is not true!'

Shiva is symbolic for consciousness so perhaps that has something to do with healing. According to Ayurveda, anxiety comes from feeling separated. We can see ourselves as separate from our community, or from our family, or from the human species, or from our idea of what we would like to be, or from anything. It doesn't much matter what we think we're separate from, if we think we're separate, instead of being 'at one with everything', then our idea can fill our world with lots of potential competitors and threats. Of course, our anxiety may also be related to being asleep, metaphorically speaking.

Curing anxiety may be quite simple, conceptually at least. But just because it's conceptually simple doesn't mean that it's practically easy. It will take a fair bit of effort and a fair amount of courage, but if we're up for it then mindfulness may be just the thing we need — to see the cause and to apply the remedy. Popping a pill (prescribed or unprescribed) seems easy but it will at best only cover up the symptoms, leaving the cause unexamined and, sometimes, make the problem worse.

On one level all we need to do to be free of our anxiety is to restore our natural connectedness — unity. To do this we just need to be mindful, rather than mindlessly feeding the kind of ruminative patterns that makes us feel separate. Anxiety can be seen as modern mass mindlessness, which isn't just a personal affliction. Anxiety is a condition that can affect whole societies and entire ages, and this current age is pretty good at generating and perpetuating anxiety. A society is just like any person in it, who can get mentally and physically sick when they get so distracted by their desires that they forget what makes life truly valuable — living consciously, which simply means being present and awake.

Let's look at the separation issue first. Western psychiatry actually has a similar slant to ancient wisdom traditions on why people develop anxiety and anxiety-related illnesses: we get anxious when we lose sight of our centre or sense of true self. Developmental psychology also adds something to the growing non-denominational wisdom database. At the age of about eighteen months we develop a sense of being a separate ego, which leads us to what the philosopher Neale Donald Walsh called our actual original sin — self-obsession or thinking about our (separate) selves. Connection is very important at any age, but particularly in our early developmental stages. Dan Siegel, a child psychiatrist, writes at length about this in his book *The Mindful Brain*.[2] We can see the potentially self-destructive loss of our wisdom of knowing who we really are as the delusion of thinking, rather than being. We literally start to think our way out of our connection, out of our present moment and out of happiness. It might not be a coincidence that we develop our sense of a separate self and language and possibly also time at about the same age.

The idea that we create a false and separate sense of self, and that we get anxious when we lose contact with our true self, might even be a missing link between psychiatry, psychology and philosophy — and between ignorance and knowledge.

So what then can we do about our anxiety? Nothing. That might sound a bit defeatist but it isn't. Our experience with anxiety will have taught us, again and again, that the more we fight it the more entangled in it we get. In a paradoxical kind of way, learning to notice the physical and emotional experiences associated with anxiety in a more mindful way teaches us a few basic truths. First, these experiences are transient — they come and go. Second, they come and go more easily when we don't get so reactive to them or fixate on them.

Mindfulness practice could be seen as an effortless action that links our experience and knowledge, and our surface and deeper selves. The result of this reunion with reality is that we don't have to do anything to heal ourselves or to be ourselves. We can learn just to be content with what is. If we can simply become fully aware of what actually is, of who we actually are, then we can lose our preoccupation with what isn't, and what we aren't. We can therefore experience reality without thought or mood, and reunite with the deep peace that our natural state consists of. The trick to finding peace is all about learning to be at peace with our moment-by-moment experience.

Anxiety and being awake

Now for the being-awake issue. As we discussed in Part 1, when we are daydreaming and distracted — whether about what we imagine the future to be or the replays we have packaged from the past — we create a world of imaginary stressors, and our body activates itself in response. The loss of capacity to distinguish between our imaginations and reality leaves us tremendously vulnerable to anxiety and depressive rumination. This world in our head tends to lack perspective, rationality or stability. The more we elaborate on it the more complex and convoluted it gets. Mindfulness is the gateway out of this dark and threatening internal world and into the fresh air and daylight of reality. It's a form of metaphorical and literal waking up out of our internal dream and into the clear space of the present moment. Life is no more complicated or threatening than the thing that's happening right now. If we pay attention in the present we will find that 99 per cent of the time we are getting anxious when there's nothing much happening — just making a cup of tea, sitting on a train, lying in bed, waiting for an appointment. Our senses are the gateway into the present moment — see, hear, touch, taste, smell. We have to come to our senses if we want to transcend anxiety.

The problem of anxiety

A possible fringe benefit as well as a possible cure of anxiety is the realisation that no matter how anxious we think we are, we're not alone. There are a lot of anxious people out there, thinking that they are alone. The United States has approximately half of the world's psychiatrists, as well as approximately half of the world's lawyers. A central principle of statistics is that association doesn't mean causation, because there might be something happening at a deeper level that's actually causing both associated phenomena — in this case psychiatrists and lawyers. It might be interesting then to consider what could be simultaneously causing the proliferation of both psychiatrists and lawyers, and maybe anxiety is the common denominator.

There are over 40 million adults in America diagnosed with an anxiety disorder, often by psychiatrists. This means one in five American adults is clinically anxious, and the figures aren't a lot different in other developed countries. What sort of a world are we creating for ourselves? There are many more people who *haven't* been officially diagnosed with anxiety, so 20 per cent is just the tip of the iceberg. Psychopathology isn't a binary condition that you either have or you don't — there are levels of affliction. We can all have the same problem to a greater or lesser extent. The question is, whether we're an individual or a country, which direction are we heading in — are we moving towards more anxiety or less?

Rates of anxiety differ greatly in different societies, which might say something about its cause. Perhaps surprisingly, anxiety rates in traditional communities or less developed countries are extremely low. Anxiety rates in large cities worldwide are, however, far higher, which suggests a grass-is-greener attitude that leads people in many countries to leave their small societies and travel to big cities. Perhaps this attitude of always looking for something better or bigger explains the 'progress' of societies, into psychopathology. People are usually happy in traditional societies because they mainly know what's expected of them and they naturally feel connected to their communities. This is simple when you and your family have been in the same place for 3000 or so years. It's easy, however, to feel cut off and alienated and anxious when you've just arrived in a city of mega millions. Being connected actually means a lot more than just having lots of people around us.

Anxiety treatments

There are numerous treatments available for anxiety and, as with most things, some of them work better than others do. As usual, treatments tend to be based on underlying theories. Some important theories that underlie common treatments for anxiety include the behavioural and learning model, the cognitive model, the psychodynamic model and the physiological model.

A common psychotherapy for treating specific phobias is systematic desensitisation. This isn't as painful as it sounds, usually, and involves pairing scary stimuli such as spiders, snakes and dentists with nice stimuli, such as feelings of relaxation and self-mastery. This is done bit by bit, for example starting off with showing a snake-phobic client a rubber snake and then encouraging them to feel relaxed with it. Eventually the phobic client may be presented with a gradation of increasingly challenging situations, all the while pairing the relaxation response with it, for example ending up cheek to cheek (or whatever) with a real live python. This treatment arose from the association and conditioning learning models that see anxiety as a learned or conditioned response. Whatever has been learned — and wired into the brain — can be unlearned and unwired again.

Another common psychotherapy for treating anxiety is Cognitive Behavioural Therapy (CBT). This involves encouraging people with clinical anxiety to examine and eventually improve their destructive thinking habits that cause and perpetuate their anxiety. For example, 'If Jane/John doesn't agree to go out with me when I ask her/him tomorrow then I will probably end up alone — forever! Contemplating life without Jane/John, whom I met two days ago, is so utterly devastating that I can feel myself freezing with anxiety — which Jane/John will surely notice and then reject me! I'm a nobody if she/he won't go out with me!' CBT derives from a cognitive behavioural model that emphasises the relationship of our thoughts to our behaviours and emotions, including anxiety. In CBT one would examine, question and challenge these kinds of thought patterns.

Psychodynamic therapies for anxiety consist of working with clients to identify the underlying reasons for anxiety, such as past events or relationships, that haven't been adequately resolved. These therapies originated in the psychoanalytic theories of Freud, who saw all behaviour, and especially maladaptive behaviour, as strongly influenced by unconscious conflicts.

Drug treatments for anxiety consist of a direct and immediate response to a highly aroused physiology, involving the administration of drugs such as sedatives or tranquilisers. This approach has been accused of conceptualising anxiety as being treated only at the level of its symptoms, as if it doesn't have a deeper cause that can be understood and treated. Drug therapy for anxiety can cause more problems than it cures because taking anti-anxiety medications can make people feel tranquilised, they can be habit-forming, and if the underlying causes aren't addressed they can make people's lives feel like emotional rollercoasters of uncontrollable ups and downs. This contrasts with non-drug options such as mindfulness that can make people's lives steadier.

Mindfulness and anxiety — the evidence

Mindfulness could be seen as a response to anxiety that involves changing our behaviour at its causal level. There's vast and longstanding experimental evidence that demonstrates that meditation-based practices such as mindfulness reduce anxiety.[3] Indeed, this was one of the first conditions that meditation and mindfulness techniques were scientifically shown to be effective for. Scientific research was undertaken in the late 1960s and early 1970s into the benefits of meditation techniques such as Transcendental Meditation (TM), which clearly demonstrated their substantial anxiety-reducing benefits. Objectively measurable benefits of TM such as stabilisation of irregular heart rates, changes in blood pressure and reductions in adrenaline were found although experience had demonstrated these benefits thousands of years ago.

A key pioneer of modern mindfulness as clinical therapy, Jon Kabat-Zinn, published the results of an important early study of the effectiveness of mindfulness that he undertook with colleagues in 1992.[4] The results of this study showed that the group administration of an eight-week mindfulness training program significantly improved the symptoms of 90 per cent of participants, who were all diagnosed as suffering from either generalised anxiety disorder or panic disorder. The participants' improved anxiety levels were maintained at three-month follow-up testing, and also after another three years, when the researchers found in a follow-up study that most of the participants were still practising mindfulness.[5] Indeed the depth of the benefits offered by the practice of mindfulness extends to improvements in brain activation pattern and antibody levels.[6] More recent research shows that mindfulness not only helps people's mood to improve but it also quietens the stress/anxiety centre of the brain, called the amygdala.[7]

A recent study used a meta-analysis to pool the results of 39 separate scientific studies of the effectiveness of mindfulness-based treatments for a total of 1140 people with anxiety and mood disorders.[8] A meta-analysis is basically a statistical melting pot into which meta-chefs throw the results of many individual studies so they can boil them all down into one large result. The results of this statistical feast clearly showed that mindfulness improves anxiety and mood in cases that most obviously need improvement. The results of 39 studies into the relationship of mindfulness to anxiety can be succinctly summarised as: mindfulness reduces anxiety.

Mindfulness and anxiety — the benefits

So what can mindfulness offer you if you are experiencing a level of anxiety that's making your life feel worse than it needs to be? What can it offer you if you are free of anxiety and would like to stay that way? Being mindful simply means being with what's actually happening right now in your life, and not ignoring it by trying to replace it with something in your imagination whether it's better or worse.

There is a story about a man who goes on a long journey. He comes to a huge chasm and the only way to cross it is via a swing bridge. Just as the man approaches the bridge, out from behind some bushes jumps an ugly, fierce-looking ogre. The man reels backwards and the ogre steps forwards, and as it does it gets even bigger. The man steps back further and the ogre steps forward and gets bigger again. The man keeps going further and further back and the same thing keeps happening. By this time the ogre is huge and about to grab hold of the man and devour him. At this point the man has a (most welcome) mindful moment and notices what's happening. He says to himself, 'Well, I keep stepping back and the ogre keeps stepping forward and getting bigger. I'm just about done for, so I've got nothing to lose. I wonder what would happen if I stepped forward?' The man stepped forward and to his surprise and relief, the ogre stepped back and got a little smaller. Encouraged, he kept stepping forward, and the ogre kept stepping back — until eventually the man was on the verge of the bridge. By this stage the ogre was small enough to fit on the end of the man's finger, so he picked it up. He was curious about what this creature was so he asked the ogre for its name. The ogre replied in a small, squeaky voice, 'My name is Fear!' The man blew fear off the end of his finger and continued on his journey.

There are a few lessons in this story. The first is that avoidance is like stepping back — the fear steps forward and gets a bit bigger every time. We don't escape from it but we actually confirm the fear and reinforce the thoughts, feelings and behaviour that are reinforcing it. The second lesson here is that we have to accept where we are and pay attention to our experience and not turn away from it. What is our experience trying to teach us? We should be interested and welcome what's happening so that we can look at it and therefore understand it. Mindfulness will help us to do this — not just while we're sitting in the chair doing the formal practice, but more importantly when we get out of the chair and go about our daily life.

Anxiety is based on some habits concerning the way we think and how these habits affect our body. The greatest challenge to living life mindfully is the habits that we can mistake for our life. Sometimes our habits mainly consist of us getting into difficult situations and then responding to them difficultly, such as with anxiety rather than with acceptance, or with learning enough about life's accidents to not mindlessly repeat them. Our habits can get so deeply entrenched in us that they affect our body and mind at a cellular or structural level. Anxiety, therefore, is a habit that can be even more destructive and unconscious than smoking or taking drugs. How then do we use mindfulness to break our anxiety habit?

To begin with, it's unhelpful to get anxious about anxiety. Paradoxically, often the best way to improve something — to restore naturalness to what's become unnatural — is to accept it. To get less anxious we need to accept that there's something going on in our life that we're not comfortable with, that we're not mindful of, and this can help us develop insight into what's causing our anxiety. The ancient Greek philosopher Epicurus said that this is a key to our being happy: knowing what it really is that's making us anxious. Maybe this isn't our new job or spouse or prison sentence. Maybe it's actually something far deeper — a fear of being found out, of being exiled, of being alone. All fear is really just the fear of us losing our individual idea of ourselves, which is what we think death is, so to break our fear cycle we need to realise who we really are and what we really want.

Every time our mind wanders off into its own world of rumination or worry, or we notice our body switching on the stress response, we need to see what's going on and come back to our existential 'terra firma' — that's another way of saying coming back and getting in contact with what's in front of us, now. To fight with our anxious thoughts and feelings and to try to suppress them is to reinforce them. So let's be matter-of-fact about them. Let's be nonchalant about anxiety.

Our biggest fear is of losing the things we're attached to, whether it's an idea we hold about ourselves or a possession, or anything else. If we didn't have all of these attachments then there would literally be nothing to fear. This is sometimes called non-attachment. We can hold on to all of this stuff if we want to but at least we should notice the cost that this brings. At least our holding on to it will be a conscious decision rather than an unconscious habit. Of course, if we do examine what's going on we will more than likely notice that letting go is the better choice.

Mindfulness can help us to see ourselves in the world of mirrors. The mindful state of simple awareness and acceptance is our truly connected state, and this is a state of love. Love isn't clinging, because clinging breeds fear. Love is all we have left when we finally let go of our fear. The Canadian poet/singer/songwriter/monk Leonard Cohen once described love as our engine of survival. Being mindful means accepting what's happening right now in our life, including the sensations that we are experiencing right now; sensations we don't have to label as anxiety or anything else.

There's a psychological model of emotion known as the 'two-factor theory'.[9] This states that our emotions have two components: a physiological state, such as of high arousal, and also a pattern of thinking that appraises that state. We might therefore think of our physiological state as being one of 'excitement' or 'anxiety' depending on our thinking habits. The relevant point here is that a physiological state is just a physiological state — sensations are just sensations and aren't a problem unless the mind gets involved and thinks they are. Mindfulness trains us at both a psychological and, eventually, a physiological level to not overreact to what happens in our life and to simply live.

Georgia was very diligent, courageous and faithful in her formal meditation practice. For over an hour a day she practised not fighting with the feelings and thoughts of panic, which wasn't easy considering how long she had practised fighting against them. She also practised being more present and taking a more accepting attitude towards her day-to-day experiences. Over the first week her major insight was that the anxious feelings that she thought would come and never go did come, and also went — they were transient. By the second week she was getting the knack of not fighting with or resisting them and was curious to notice that this led to them not escalating so much. By the third week she wasn't feeling the need to try and get rid of them and was gaining confidence that she could ride these waves of panic rather than be swamped by them. She was welcoming the very thing she had been resisting because it gave her the opportunity to learn how to relate to it in a different way. By the fourth week Georgia was disappointed. The panic attacks weren't coming anymore. There she was waiting in the water with her mindfulness board ready to surf and there were no waves. Georgia was one courageous and determined young woman.

Take-home tips for a mindful response to anxiety

Not so helpful

- Get anxious about anxiety.

Helpful

- Trace the cause of anxiety to its source and develop insight into what's actually making us anxious.
- Stay aware and accepting of what's really happening — right here, right now — inside our body, no matter what's happening outside of it.
- Stay in close contact with our deeper self as the witness of what is happening, rather than identifying with the happenings.
- Be patient with ourselves and let the mindful process work.
- Consider doing a mindfulness course or some mindfulness-based therapy.
- Tune in, not out.

CHAPTER 8

Depression

Kat was a twenty-year-old university student. Outwardly she had everything going for her but inwardly it was the opposite story. Although she didn't let on to her friends, Kat was almost constantly critical of herself, going over the clumsy things she said, and what people thought about her, and whether she would ever get anywhere, and whether her boyfriend really did want to be with her. On and on and on ran this incessant and judgmental commentary on her life. Endlessly she would try to work herself out, beat herself up about past mistakes and plan so hard that she would be sure nothing would go wrong, but it always did.

Kat did get anxious about many things but it was more her mood that was the major concern for her. It had been low and getting lower for months. Her sleep was often disturbed but she had managed to continue to get to uni although she was not doing as well in her studies as her abilities would have allowed. Although Kat sometimes wished she wasn't alive, she had never actually thought of taking her own life. Then it came to crunch time. Kat knew she wasn't getting anywhere trying to work all this out for herself; in fact, she was making things worse. She needed to talk to someone and try to get some perspective on what was going on. Kat went to her GP, who said that he wasn't an experienced counsellor but he could prescribe antidepressants, or he could suggest seeing a psychologist or psychiatrist. She wanted to learn to deal with it herself and thought perhaps there were some strategies she could learn, so she went to the university counselling service.

The counsellor was experienced in a range of approaches, including mindfulness. When the principles of mindfulness were explained to Kat it seemed to resonate with her, so they set out on a six-week program, at the end of which they would take their bearings. Kat learned a mindfulness meditation practice as a way of being more mindful in daily life and then explored a range of cognitive strategies based upon mindfulness. The counsellor said that for mindfulness to be effective it would take effort on Kat's behalf, a commitment she was prepared to make.

The problem of depression

Depression has been described as the common cold of psychopathology, but being common doesn't make it natural or inevitable. So what really is depression and can it be successfully treated or even prevented? There are many different ideas about what depression is and isn't, but most of them centre around the notion that if you're depressed there's something wrong with you, and you need to find somebody to fix you — fast. So what's actually wrong with you if you have an unwelcome visitor such as the one that Winston Churchill called his 'black dog'? Not as much as you might think there is. Depression didn't stop Churchill from winning a world war, or stop Buzz Aldrin from landing on the moon, or stop JK Rowling from making a billion or two with *Harry Potter*, or stop Agatha Christie from writing a classic play called *The Mousetrap* that premiered in London's West End in 1952 and is still running, or stop William James from being the great pioneer psychologist that he was, or stop Mozart from being Mozart, or even stop Mark Twain from being a great humorist and writer. Maybe one solution to depression is to stop trying to figure out what's wrong with us, and to just experience more fully and mindfully what's going on in our life and what's right with us.

If you're depressed, or if you're close to somebody who is, or if you have some other deep personal connection with depression, you don't need us to tell you what a huge and global problem depression is. It's enough of a problem if it's a problem for you. The point of throwing a few depression statistics at you, though, is to show you that nobody with depression is alone in their suffering, even if they think they are. Chances are high that just about every human being living on this planet today, especially in the more 'developed' bits of it, will personally experience at least a mild form of depression at some stage in their life, or know somebody who will. We're all constantly moving along a scale of mood between really happy and really sad. Somewhere along that scale an arbitrary line is drawn and we say below that line a person is depressed, above it they're not.

More than one in five people will have an episode that would be diagnosed as depression and almost one person in six will experience depressive symptoms intensely enough to require treatment at some stage in their life — one in five females, and one in eight males.[1] Depression accounts for approximately 75 per cent of psychiatric hospitalisations, and approximately 75 per cent of the inmates of nursing homes and psychiatric institutions are depressed.[2] There is evidence that long-term depression leads to dementia and to other serious consequences of people switching off their own mental life-support systems.

As previously mentioned, depression is overtaking heart disease as the developed world's most destructive disease. It is predicted that by the year 2030, if trends over the past 60 years continue, depression will be way out in the lead.[3] This rise in depression isn't just a matter of us being more aware of it — it's a real rise. What's going on? All this has been taking place in a time of unprecedented economic prosperity, technological advancement and the availability of antidepressant medications. If happiness were truly dependent on such things we should collectively be over the moon, as well as able to land on it. So what are some of the factors behind the rise of depression?

Having an unhappy or traumatic upbringing can predispose us to depression, as can a family history of the illness. Unsupportive relationships, marital break-up and a poor work environment can also predispose us to depression. Special risk factors include physical conditions such as thyroid problems, brain injuries including stroke, heart disease and chronic pain; and also personality characteristics such as shyness, unassertiveness, low self-esteem, perfectionism, social anxiety and sensitivity to criticism; and environmental characteristics such as isolation and being in a threatening environment. Lifestyle issues can also be major contributors. Alcohol, smoking and other drug abuse are all risk factors. Insomnia is a major risk factor. A lack of sunlight is an issue, particularly in winter months. Physical inactivity, particularly a lack of aerobic exercise, and a poor-quality diet are risk factors. And, importantly, unmindfulness or inattention leaves us vulnerable to depression.

The positive side of the coin is that with all these things that we know contribute to depression it gives us a whole lot of things we can do to prevent or manage it. The main prevention, and possibly the most important — which we are exploring in this book — is mindfulness.

Types of depression

Depression isn't just ordinary misery; it's something even more serious. *The Diagnostic and Statistical Manual of Mental Disorders*, regularly published by the American Psychiatric Association since 1952, has been seen as a scientific bible for the diagnosis of mental conditions including depression, and is broadly accepted as being accurate and clinically useful. The current version emphasises the great diversity of depressive symptoms, which can mainly manifest as agitation and irritability in some people, and as sleeping or eating too much or too little in others, or as feeling guilty and worthless in yet others. The bottom line of the depression experience, though, is, according to the *Manual* at least, a general loss of interest and pleasure in life and its activities.

Table 1 summarises the major types of depression described by *The Diagnostic and Statistical Manual of Mental Disorders, Fourth Edition.*[4]

Table 1: Types of depression

- Major depressive disorder — a depressed mood that lasts for at least two weeks. This may also be referred to as clinical depression or unipolar depression, which means there are no symptoms of bipolar disorder.
- Major depressive disorder with psychotic features — a depressed mood that includes symptoms of psychosis. Psychosis involves seeing or hearing things that are not there (hallucinations), feeling

---

everyone is against you (paranoia) and having delusions (beliefs that are not true but are still believed even in the face of evidence to the contrary).

- Major depressive disorder with melancholic features — a depressed mood that is characterised by a loss of pleasure in activities (anhedonia).
- Bipolar disorder (once known as manic-depressive illness) — this involves periods of feeling low (depressed) and high (manic).

Theories of depression

There are many scientific theories of depression, which tend to all arise from particular scientific evidence and be associated with particular treatments. There may be so many of these theories that it can be difficult to see that they actually aren't as different as they seem, and may just be emphasising different facets of the same complaint. This is often the case when there are so many brands on offer that you don't know what to buy or believe in. There's a story about an elephant and some blindfolded men that might help illustrate that sometimes our problems and disputes come from us only seeing a part of the whole truth.

A group of blind men were invited to feel an elephant and based on what they experienced to come up with a theory of what an elephant is. One blind man felt its tail and came up with: 'An elephant is like a brush!' One blind man felt its trunk and came up with: 'An elephant is like a hose!' One blind man felt one of the elephant's legs and came up with: 'An elephant is like a tree!' When they were asked to share their views each argued vehemently that they were each right and the others were wrong.

Well, they were all right, but if they took their limited experience as the whole truth then they were all wrong. Depression is an elephant the totality of which is difficult to see, and the underlying truth of which is impossible to understand, unless we uncover our eyes.

Aaron Beck and others developed an important theory of depression in the 1960s and 1970s that is known as cognitive theory.[5] They also developed an associated therapy known as cognitive therapy.[6] According to these practical theorists, depression isn't caused by negative life events, even though the people who suffer from it often think that it is. Although life events can trigger depressive episodes, depression is actually caused by distorted thinking processes. As the ancient Greek philosopher Epictetus said, 'Man is not disturbed by events, but by the view he takes of them.'

Maladaptive thoughts can lead to depressive feelings because, in scientific language, they introduce a B factor to the initial or A factor, the A being the environmental event — such as losing our job, or spouse, or even a football match. Next is the C factor, which is our emotional reaction to losing our job or spouse or the football match. This might be anger, depression, sadness, or even joy, depending on our perceived value of our job or spouse or which football team we support. The important point here is that most of us think that the environmental event (loss of job, spouse or even a football match) *caused* our emotional reaction. It actually didn't. If it did, we would have no choice of response to adversity and we would be the human equivalent of laboratory-conditioned rats. It's the B factor — our interpretation of events — that causes our emotional state. In slightly less scientific terms, the roller-coaster of our up and down mental and emotional states isn't driven by what happens to us; it's driven by the spin that our mind puts on what's happened to us.

According to cognitive therapists such as Beck there is a particular way of thinking that is very likely to make us depressed, and this is what they call global, negative and personal thinking. Let's say that our environmental event is getting a flat tyre on the way to an exam in a faraway place. Let's say that we habitually think in a way that's global, negative and personal. We might come up with a response to this actually neutral environmental event along the lines of, 'Bad things are always happening to me! I'm an idiot! I won't get to the exam in time now and what would be the point even if I did — I would fail! My life is as good as washed up.' A specific, positive and impersonal response might be: 'This road is particularly hard on tyres, so it's not surprising that I got a flat. It won't take me long to change the tyre, so there's every chance I can still get to the exam — for which I'm well prepared — on time.

If, however, I don't make it on time I will need to explain the situation to my examiners and find an alternate exam arrangement.'

Another important theory of depression is the learning-based theory developed by Martin Seligman and colleagues in the 1970s and 1980s.[7] Martin Seligman is, incidentally, even more famous now for helping to found the positive psychology movement. He has written very popular and helpful books about this such as *Learned Optimism* (the opposite of learned helplessness).[8] The basic theory here is that we can get depressed when we feel overwhelmed by life; out of control; out of our depth; helpless. Seligman's experiments showed scientifically what we already know unofficially: if you keep giving any life form more than it can deal with it's likely to give up, eventually, and get depressed.

One of the authors once performed a computer-simulation version of the learned-helplessness experiment that Seligman and his colleagues performed on animals and on (simulated) people. Even in the early 1980s ethics committees often successfully protected the general public from psychologists and psychology students and their sometimes inappropriately grand designs, so a computer simulation was a good way to learn something useful without damaging anyone more vulnerable than a computer. A highly challenging virtual simulated environment was created where participants' actions had no bearing on their outcomes, which led to a very strong simulated tendency to develop simulated depression.[9]

From a purely biomedical point of view, there is also the low-neurotransmitter-level theory that could be described as the medical model of depression. This sees depression as caused by low levels of neurotransmitter substances in the brain such as serotonin, epinephrine, norepinephrine, tryptamine and dopamine. A number of the inflammatory chemicals mentioned in other chapters regarding the high allostatic load are associated with depression, and can activate what is called the sickness response when they act on the brain. The symptoms of the sickness response include lack of energy, motivation and appetite — which is fine when we have the flu, but not so good when we are chronically ruminating about past events. To say, however, that low-neurotransmitter high-inflammatory substances *cause* depression is a little superficial and possibly ill-informed. Knowing that neurotransmitter substances are *associated* with depression doesn't tell us that they *cause* depression. It might well be the case that they are both caused by something else, like the way we think, live and relate to each other, and that low neurotransmitter substances are a result, rather than a cause of depression.

If the real cause of depression was just low neurotransmitter levels (for example, serotonin) then the real treatment for depression would be giving an antidepressant drug to increase neurotransmitter levels. The evidence shows, however, that the benefit of antidepressants for mild to moderate depression is a placebo effect — like taking a sugar pill you believe will improve your mood and so it does.[10] It's only in severe depression that there's some effect that can be attributed to the chemical action of the drug.

A recent large statistical meta-analysis incorporated the results of many individual scientific studies of the benefits or otherwise of antidepressants.[11, 12] Unlike most studies published in this area, this one actually invited science's poor relatives — the results of unpublished research — in from the statistical cold. This analysis showed that for mild and moderate depressions, antidepressants don't give people a clinically meaningful advantage over placebos. This result demonstrates some interesting medical and human principles. Firstly, if placebos can improve people's health, then the human mind must have an enormous capacity to *heal* the human body and mind that probably hasn't yet been fully explored. Secondly, the results of this study and others suggest that antidepressants tend to offer an initial reprieve from depression, until the people taking them revert back to their previous state unless they have learned to do something different. Thirdly, this study suggests that antidepressants are probably not the ultimate answer to healing depression. The mental health system invests too much energy and resources in these drugs to fully respond to the results of such non-supportive studies, often at the expense of other more beneficial therapies that address the deeper causes of depression.

There are also the theories of depression that we won't go into here but have been re-badged from 'psychoanalytic' to 'psychodynamic'. These basically see depression as being caused by repression and associated guilt.

According to various philosophical and spiritual traditions, a common form of depression could be seen as arising from mental, physical or spiritual exhaustion. We try to find fulfilment in pleasure and various superficial and material pursuits rather than in a deeper understanding of ourselves. Ultimately this depression is caused by anxiety — by the idea that I am separate and therefore I have to go all out to find or escape something *out there* to compensate. This is depression that comes from too much activity, or rather from too much mindless activity, aimed at getting and acquiring. According to these traditions depression can also come from mental, physical or spiritual lassitude — a deep jadedness that comes from seeing life as unfulfilling and uninteresting. The deep cause of this form of depression is also a feeling of disconnectedness from ourselves and the universe around us. Also associated with these traditions is the notion of natural laws and the importance of living a moderate, carefully paced and balanced life, rather than a life of haste and excess.

Another model of depression that may offer a broad insight is the idea of a pain body described by Eckhart Tolle in his popular philosophical/spiritual/healing book *The Power of Now*.[13] Tolle based this idea on his reading of works from various wisdom traditions and possibly also from modern psychology, and came up with an idea that perhaps links them. The 'pain body' is a monstrous sense of self as something deeply vulnerable, over-sensitive and keen to be upset by circumstances. The basic idea of this construct is that it's a mind-child creation of the individual sense of self — the ego — that wants nothing more than to create and protect a false identity of 'who I think I am' and will defend this idea even if it's to the death. Central to the idea of the pain body is an important characteristic of the person who identifies with being in pain or with being a victim. For some ambivalent, self-sabotaging reason we don't really want to be free of our pain bodies, maybe for the same reason that sometimes at least we don't really want to free of a destructive relationship or job. There's something comfortable and complacent about being what we usually are, even if it's painful.

The idea of the pain body is consistent with the observations of psychotherapists from a range of traditions who say that people who present to them with conditions such as depression usually tell them that they want to change and get better and be happier, but when it comes to actually challenging the ideas and behaviours that keep them miserable, they usually just let them go and grow. We all know what it's like to think one thing and yet do another — and then justify it. This idea is also consistent with learning theory: we usually don't keep repeating any behaviour unless we get rewarded for it in some way. This explains seemingly strange phenomena such as why the unruly behaviour of children in classrooms persists in spite of their being yelled at or otherwise 'punished' by their frazzled teachers. Being punished can be seen by at least some children as a form of attention, and can actually be a reinforcement rather than a punishment. In the case of depression we can get reinforced for being depressed if the reinforcer is a sense of identity, no matter how flawed — 'a poor thing but mine own', from Shakespeare's *As You Like it*.

Mindfulness-based approaches put an entirely new perspective on depression, emphasising that depression can be caused by inattention, attachment and not being present. Rumination about ideas of self, past and future, is the main cognitive style in depression. The more we identify ourselves with these depressive thoughts and elaborate on them the more we get bogged in this mental quicksand. Depression is associated with anhedonia (lack of pleasure) and poor functioning — both related to a lack of focus or engagement with what life is presenting, right here, right now.

Each of the theories of depression mentioned above has spawned associated therapies, which we will briefly talk about below and then we will explore the answers that mindfulness provides for depression.

Approaches to the management of depression

You might have noticed that there isn't really an impenetrable divide between each of the main scientific theories of depression, and that perhaps they are really just different descriptions of the same elephant. A psychopathology, by any other name, would be just as unpleasant to its experiencer — with apologies to Shakespeare. It's perfectly possible to believe in Seligman's depression theory without having to completely renounce Beck's, and to believe in Beck's theory without having to renounce Seligman's, and to believe in both and also to believe that repression and guilt can contribute towards depression, and at the same time to acknowledge that there are chemical changes in the brain associated with depression. There is a common element or elephant emerging here.

To believe that you are helpless or guilty is to have a negative belief. Learning and cognitive theories of depression are actually compatible and easy to combine to generate treatments that link behaviour and thought modification. This is the principle behind the most common psychotherapy used to treat depression — Cognitive Behavioural Therapy (CBT), which we will meet again soon. The mindful approach to treating and also preventing depression relates to all of the depression theories that we have described, and to their associated therapies. This might be a 'new' or 'deeper' or more 'all-embracing' approach to depression that combines other theories and yet transcends them. Mindfulness-based therapies also see thoughts and behaviour as being closely related and involve guiding people to a place above and beyond their addiction to thoughts — good or bad — rather than instructing them in how to improve their thoughts and behaviours. CBT, for example, focuses largely on examining the content of thoughts, whereas mindfulness examines our essential relationship to thoughts; that is, no particular relationship. No matter what the theory or treatment is that recognises it, the universal bottom line here is that thinking can cause vast human problems, including depression. An unquestioned belief that more thinking will eventually get us out of our mire may be the very thing that is driving us out of the thinking frying pan and into the thinking fire.

It may be that mindfulness is the missing link between all of the above theories of depression. This is a clinical and life behavioural remedy and prevention that all depression treatment roads may ultimately be leading to, no matter how rocky they may be.

Mindfulness and depression — the evidence

According to the official position of noted Harvard mindfulness researcher Ellen Langer, the opposite of mindfulness — mindlessness — causes *most* of the world's problems, including depression. According to the unofficial position of Ellen Langer, mindlessness causes *all* of the world's problems! This is actually what earlier great psychologists also said, such as Gautama the Buddha, or Plato about 2400 years ago — if somebody does something that you blindly react to, then the pain gets multiplied and eventually the whole world is in trouble. This process causes arguments, psychosomatic conditions, wars and misery. If anybody anywhere responds to their situation mindfully, not mindlessly, then the whole infectious misery buck can stop with them, and the individual's and the world's troubles will instantly start decreasing.

Ellen Langer is a prominent psychologist who gives us a refreshingly short list of psychological states that we can be in: either mindful or mindless. This contrasts with the psychological states described by *The Diagnostic and Statistical Manual of Mental Disorders*, which are many in number but don't include wellness. According to Ellen Langer most people, in most places, are mostly mindless. The good news is that we have considerable room for improvement.

Depression can be seen as an extreme form of mindlessness. What is the mind up to when we're not paying attention? It tiptoes off and starts to worry and ruminate. What are we listening to when we're not really listening to what is going on around us? An endless internal dialogue of self-criticism, self-doubt, negativity and all the rest. What are we trying to suck happiness from when we're not connected to what's happening in the present moment? We're trying to derive happiness in the imagination about some other place or other time, which is like trying to suck water out of a mirage. What are we fleeing from or wrestling with when we're not paying attention? All of the catastrophes our imagination can cook up.

Ellen Langer's view of depression is that it can be seen as what happens when our experience of life has gone stale. A lack of novelty can result in a filter between us and our experience of the beauty and wonder of life in general and also of our own life. This is why we experience anhedonia or a lack of pleasure with depression. Mindfulness directly treats depression whether we see it as coming from too much anxiety or too much lassitude, because in both cases what's gone wrong is our connection with what is, which is ever-changing, ever-novel. Taking a half-hour unmindful walk in the morning could be just another thing to fit into a packed and pressured day. If that walk is taken mindfully, however, it's a feast for the senses — an opportunity to clear the mind and a chance to connect with who and what passes us by.

There's a simple test of mindfulness, according to Langer, that can also give us a very rapid idea of how mindfulness might start to improve or prevent depression. Simply look at your finger for a minute or so. Is your finger interesting and engaging and new? Or is it the same old finger that is possibly even more completely and utterly uninteresting than it usually is? Now look at your finger again — and *really* look at it. There it is, pulsating with life. Look at its shape, colour, form and movement. Is there maybe a line on it or even a wart that you hadn't really noticed before? If you really look at or listen to or smell or taste or feel anything then you are being mindful, and it's easy to accept whatever you're experiencing, warts and all. Try doing the same with your life. Taste the foods you eat as if you have never tasted them before — because the truth is that you probably haven't really tasted them. Look at your spouse or partner as if you haven't really seen them before, as if for the first time.

According to Ellen Langer and other researchers who are interested in the potential of mindfulness to heal and prevent depression, the key to this approach is that mindfulness keeps us alive to the new. To avoid allowing life to get stale — just really attend to it. Mindfulness increases our natural ability to be creative, and can restore our natural creativity and also our natural humour. When we see the joke, when we see the solution, we are seeing something new, or something old in a new way; we are being mindful. Ellen Langer described a very simple experiment that shows the benefits of mindfulness for treating depression in people who haven't developed it yet.[14] One group of jaded orchestra musicians was instructed to add some novelty to their performance by creating some distinctions from past performances. Another group was instructed to re-create a past performance — to play as they always did. The results were measured according to objective criteria such as ratings by expert musicians, as well as by satisfaction of the performers. According to all criteria, the musicians who were doing something new, creative and mindful did much better than the musicians who did the same old thing. These musicians also played better together as a group, making for a richer and more satisfying experience.

Mindfulness and depression — the benefits

If we don't have an understanding of what depression is then it is hard to address the cause of it. Depression stems from something that causes even more harm than depression does, and that's human suffering itself, of which depression is perhaps the most obvious example. What most theories of depression hint at, without going so far as to offer a real understanding of, is that depression is a disconnection between the depressed person and their basic sense of being present in their life. Depression involves switching off, giving up, the development of hostility towards the individual self and others, a belief that what's bad is more real than what's good. All of this simply means that there's a lack of belief in, a lack of participation in, a lack of connection to, life.

Mindfulness therapies and practices may well offer depressed and potentially depressed people (that is, all of us) all of the benefits that other theories and treatments do, such as improving our thinking processes and even our neurotransmitter levels, but they also offer a lot more. The real potential benefit of mindfulness as a treatment and prevention of depression is that it doesn't directly aim at doing any of these things because it operates at a deeper level.

Depression is fundamentally an awareness problem that typically arises in response to an illusion of separation. This might have been caused by difficult life events, or by whatever other situation that's resulted in non-acceptance and therefore non-awareness. The active ingredient of the mindful response to depression is to simultaneously restore acceptance and awareness, and this is done automatically when we are mindful. This isn't accomplished by training us to think better thoughts, or even to change the contents of the thoughts, or by giving us drugs, but by guiding us in a natural process of regaining our lost life by simply encouraging us to connect non-judgmentally, vividly and completely with the unfolding of life as it takes place, moment by moment.

One common RSVP to the open invitation to be mindful is: 'Why would I want to pay attention to the people and events around me if I don't actually like them?' That's a fair question. Firstly, if the situation is a challenging one then it needs our attention if we are to have any chance of dealing with it. Secondly, if we look closely we may find that our attention may not be as engaged with the event as we think it is, and it is not so much the event itself but what we are thinking about it that makes it so onerous. For example, when we are with a person we may not like being with, we may not actually be listening to them but rather to our internal dialogue: 'When is this going to be over? I can't stand them ...' Or with a job: 'This is so hard. I'll never get through it. Why do I have to do it anyway ...?' Or when experiencing pain: 'This is so bad. I can't stand it. When is it going to be over ...?' Or stepping up to present in public: 'Oh no. I'm going to stuff it up. What will everyone think about me ...?' We could go on but we hope you get the idea. Paying attention helps to circumvent these well-worn thought patterns.

This emphasis on the new as a treatment for depression and as a general re-vitalising mental, physical and spiritual tonic links modern approaches to mindfulness such as Ellen Langer's with traditional approaches such as Vipassana meditation. The New York and Bodhgaya schools of applied mindfulness offer exactly the same antidote to depression, and also to less-clinical manifestations of being overwhelmed or jaded by life. Simply be aware of the ever-changing, ever-new quality of life — whether it's manifesting right here and now in the sensations of our body or in the traffic whizzing past us — and eventually the whole world will be new again and we won't be depressed. This is our natural state of wonder and beauty and we can all experience it when we are accepting and aware enough, when we are creative and free enough to realise that we are all playing essential parts of the orchestra of life.

Mindfulness-Based Cognitive Therapy

There is a wealth of scientific evidence that demonstrates that mindfulness-based treatments are very effective in improving people's depression levels. A great advantage of these treatments is that they offer these improvements in a wellness-based, life-improving context, and they don't cause negative side-effects or stigma.

Scientific studies have shown that mindfulness-based therapies compare well with Cognitive Behavioral Therapy (CBT) and are just as effective for less-serious forms of depression, unlike CBT, which isn't.[15] Recent studies have even shown that mindfulness can be an effective treatment for depression when given over the phone or via the internet.[16]

Jon Kabat-Zinn, along with a team of psychologists who took his work with Mindfulness-Based Stress Reduction (MBSR) and developed Mindfulness-Based Cognitive Therapy (MBCT) described much of this research in their book *The Mindful Way Through Depression*.[17] It has been found to more than halve the risk of recurrence of depression even for those who have had many episodes in the past.

In Chapter 3 we discussed the main elements of mindfulness in more detail, but here are a few key points. MBCT uses mindfulness meditation as its cornerstone, with up to 40 minutes' practice daily. This can be supplemented with some mindful yoga. We then use this as a platform to be more present in daily life, to engage more fully with events as they unfold, without getting ahead of ourselves with anxious anticipation and bias or behind ourselves with reliving the past and rumination. If our mind goes back into the past again, we just gently escort it back to the present moment using our senses.

Acceptance is a crucial element of mindfulness whether it's called MBSR, MBCT or anything else. We cannot stop depressive thoughts or feelings from ever arising nor need we. Our experience will have taught us that the harder we try not to have the thoughts and feelings we hate having, the more we focus on and amplify them. Try a simple exercise that can show us how useful it is to try to control your mind. Sit comfortably for a minute and *don't* think about pelicans. What you *can* do is accept your thoughts about pelicans or anything else as they arise, but change your relationship to them by learning that you can observe them not as facts but as just another passing momentary event. Psychologists like to call this meta-cognition. We can give attention to a thought if it's interesting enough or not give it attention, if we so choose. It helps to learn to be matter-of-fact about this process rather than judgmental about it. The less we engage with depressive thought patterns, the less disturbance they cause as they come and go. We think they have a hold on us, but it's the other way around. We have a hold on them and may not have realised that we won't let them go. We take them so personally because we latch on to them and have never learned to stand back from them with a little more objectivity. It gets easier, but it takes time and patience as we learn how to do this.

Kat made good progress with the counsellor. She made the effort to apply the mindfulness practices and reported her breakthroughs, challenges and insights each week so that she could learn from her experience. The most important insight she had, when the penny dropped after a few weeks, was that she had previously assumed she needed to work out her thinking, but she realised that most of what went through her mind was irrelevant or unhelpful. It suddenly occurred to her that she could stand back from her thoughts and watch them like a curious bystander. She said, 'I thought because I had a thought I had to think it. Now I realise I don't. That's the most liberating thing of all.'

Take-home tips for a mindful response to depression

Not so helpful
- Label what we're experiencing as either good or bad.
- Unquestionably believe in our diagnoses and prognoses. (We would be better off unquestionably believing in pixies!)

Helpful
- Practise being present and not living in a past that has already gone or a future that may never come.
- Do something new today or do something old in a different way, or even do something old in the same way but really attend to it.
- Enliven stale ideas by consciously examining them.
- Give more attention to life — the bits labelled as good and the bits labelled as bad. None of it stays the same, so we needn't cling nor resist but go with the flow of events as they unfold.
- See the funny side of something — of anything! The main difference between a sit-com and a drama is the perspective we take to the unfolding events. Stand back and look at how we are,

and how others are. If we can see the joke — a new way of looking at something — we're being mindful.

- Notice newness — be more and more aware of the subtle changes constantly taking place in our mind and body and life.
- Allow ourselves to unconditionally enjoy life.
- Give out, not up!

CHAPTER 9

Addiction

Joe was a star country footballer. Like most of the guys he played with and against he didn't see that he was an addict, and that his addictions were making his life worse than it needed to be, and his family's lives worse than they needed to be. During his occasional conscious and mindful moments Joe realised that maybe he was addicted, to the alcohol that he and his team-mates toasted their successes and consoled their losses with; but Joe didn't work out that what he was really addicted to was a dream.

Joe's dream was his idea that he was only worth anything when he was winning; this was when he could show a usually hostile and uncaring world that he was worth watching, worth something. Joe's dream idea of himself was a lot more fun than his usual idea of himself, as somebody who didn't really matter when he was not on the football field, or better still, in the pub with his team-mates after a win. Joe didn't really like his job of selling cars, even though he was sort of interested in them and he didn't mind talking to his customers about them. Most of the time, though, he didn't really tune in to what his customers were telling him, or even to what his family was telling him, unless it was about last weekend's game.

The only time Joe felt good about himself these days was when he saw himself as Joe the footballer, Joe the champion, Joe the guy people thought was cool. The only problem was that life's worthwhile bits only happened occasionally these days, and he still had to live with himself constantly. Joe's way out was to realise what he was really addicted to — a dream of champions. He would finally overcome his addictions and find real happiness, real peace, when he woke up to what he really was and had now.

What is addiction?

The *Macquarie Dictionary* defines addiction as: 'The state of being addicted to some habit, practice or substance, particularly narcotics.'[1] The great psychologist and philosopher Carl Jung said that: 'Every form of addiction is bad, no matter whether the narcotic be alcohol or morphine or idealism.' Incidentally, the syphilitic eighteenth-century French poet Charles Baudelaire came out in favour of addiction, with some practical advice that perhaps his poetic licence allowed him: 'Be always drunken, with wine, with poetry, or with virtue, as you will!' Maybe he wasn't quite ready to deal mindfully with his habits.

Maybe there's a common source of all addictions: the hellish craving for more than what we have. Like the donkey chasing the carrot, the lasting happiness we seek as addicts to anything is always just out of our reach. If we assume that happiness and pleasure are the same thing, then we might seek pleasure as a way to happiness. If they are not the same thing then that's a dangerous mistake. Shortcuts to happiness can turn into highways to hell.

We all have 'pleasure centres' conveniently located in our brain. This is sometimes called our 'reward system', or for those who like technical terms, the mesolimbic reward system. This is what makes what we need for survival pleasant, like food and sex. If they weren't pleasurable then we wouldn't do them and we wouldn't survive. Pleasure, then, isn't a bad thing in itself — it's a natural part of living. When our pleasure centre gets carried away by our pleasure-seeking behaviour, however, we get into a cycle of demanding more and more stimulation, for the same level of satisfaction. In the long run this actually ends up blunting our enjoyment centre and lowers our mood. Soon, if it's not being stimulated, it also starts to fire off anxiety messages when we think we're missing out on something, and then we're addicted.

Our search for happiness through pleasure can soon degenerate into a restless retreat from anxiety over which we have less and less control. This is a recipe for disaster, not happiness. Trying to suppress our desire to pursue the object of our addiction is fraught with tension and fear. This is quite aside from the fact that any particular substance, like alcohol, nicotine, heroin or even Big Macs can have its own chemical addictive properties. Some people, due to their genetic make-up, can have an inherited tendency to addictions. This means that it doesn't take much exposure to stress or substances to fire up their addictive cycle.

The flip side of chasing pleasure is running away from pain, whether physical or emotional. For example, if we experience emotional pain in the form of significant stress, anxiety or depression, then it's natural to want to be free of that pain. If we have constructive ways of getting to the cause of the emotional pain — such as improving how we think, live and relate to others — then all is well. If we just want to cover up our experience with a dangerous drug or activity, or ignore it, then it festers and becomes an even bigger problem.

Improving our mental health, learning to deal with anxiety and being able to 'surf' our addictive urges — to mindfully go with their flow — is an important life skill to learn. To do this we need to be mindful of our habits. When we do something again and again and again it very soon wires itself into our brain. This makes it more likely that we will do it yet again, especially if the behaviour is associated with a pleasurable experience. This is conditioning, which means that circuits in our brain get deeply reinforced, like a bush track etched with deep ruts — it gets hard to turn our wheels out of them and go in a different direction.

Maybe all of our addictions, physical and psychological, start with our lack of mindfulness. Maybe all addictions are simply cravings for something that we think is better than what we have — reality. This mindless craving is ultimately extremely harmful because it results in addicts trading in the reality of *now*, for the unreality of something better, *later*. This is always in another time, another place, another self. When we start craving, our imagination starts to fire up: 'How happy I'll be if ...' This is a long-running theme of advertising and popular movies, novels and stories including Jack's famous swapping of a perfectly good and real cow for the nursery-rhyme equivalent of a handful of ecstasy — magic beans to take him away from his real life and into a fantasy world of giant problems.

The problem of addiction

Addiction is a huge and rapidly growing global health problem. According to recent figures from the National Institute on Drug Abuse in the United States, which leads the world in drug addiction, more than 22 million Americans have a drug or other substance-abuse problem including alcohol. In Australia the estimated annual cost of alcohol and other drugs to the community is $15.3 billion, including crime, violence, treatment costs, loss of productivity and premature deaths.[2] The human cost is, of course, far higher. Around 10 per cent of adults have an official drug-abuse problem in 'developed' countries such as the United States, United Kingdom and Australia. Many more people, however, have an unofficial or potential problem.

More than 3.7 million Americans over the age of twelve have tried heroin at least once, over 10 million have tried methamphetamines such as ecstasy, and over 36 million have tried cocaine. These figures are similar in the United Kingdom, Australia and other developed countries. Developing countries such as India are starting to develop a similar problem. If we add prescription-drug addiction to the addiction epidemic figures, we need to add another 6.4 million abusers of mostly painkillers, tranquilisers, stimulants and sedatives, just in the United States. If we add non-prescription legal drug addiction, the mounting addiction toll gets even more alarming. Approximately one in five adults in developed countries smoke and approximately one in two adults regularly drink alcohol. Addiction is a modern plague.

What if we include addictions to potentially harmful behaviours as well as substances? These include gambling, food and even sex. The number of people who are addicted to at least some behaviour that isn't good for them is scary. According to the National Council on Problem Gaming in the United States, approximately 85 per cent of adult Americans have gambled at least once, and approximately 3 per cent are problem gamblers. These figures are again similar in other developed countries. According to the Centre for Gambling Research total annual expenditure on gambling in Australia rose from approximately $4 billion in 1978–9 to approximately $16 billion in 2003–4.

The Australian Bureau of Statistics estimates that in 2005 approximately 54 per cent of the Australian adult population was overweight, up from 45 per cent in 1995. If all of that doesn't tell you that you that might be more addicted than you think you are, the Society for the Advancement of Sexual Health estimates that 3–5 per cent of adults suffer from an addiction to sex! Any addiction, even to sex or chocolate, eventually causes suffering because any addiction involves a mindless compulsion to keep doing something even though it hurts ourselves and others.

Why then all this tendency for us to abuse drugs and other potentially toxic substances and activities in our modern world? Well, self-medicating with substances to make ourselves feel better, or cope better, or perform better is an understandable response to problems when we don't have better solutions. Using anything outside of us to make us feel better just covers up our problems, rather than gets to their cause, and only creates even worse problems than we began with.

When people abuse illegal or legal drugs, the obvious toxic effects of these addictions include loss of wellbeing because of their harmful effect on our mood and ability to function well. This substance abuse can cause acute and chronic ill health, from liver to brain disease. It can lead to disability, premature death including by suicide, lost productivity, and crime including property damage and assault. Addictions to food or social acceptance or power might not be as obvious as addictions to heroin or nicotine, but they can be as lethal. So why do we do this to ourselves and to others?

We are all potential addicts, although some of us are more vulnerable than others because of our environment and our genes. It seems like there's a huge range of addictions, and an even huger range of theories to explain them, but addictions all actually only have one basic active ingredient: the compulsion to do something that's ultimately harmful, even if we know it's harmful. Mindfulness can profoundly help people with a wide range of addictions because it offers the exact opposite of what the addictions take away — conscious living.

Addiction is a much bigger problem than most of us realise and it's a much bigger problem than most addicted people realise. The compulsion of a drinker to drink or of a gambler to gamble may not be so very different from the compulsion of a perfectly 'normal' person to run a red light or to say, 'Yes please!' when somebody with a frozen grin and a silly hat asks them, 'Do you want fries with that?' We don't just get addicted to drugs and alcohol, even though these are massive and high-profile problems. We don't just get addicted to the many other illegal and legal toxic substances that are now so common it is almost impossible to avoid them, whether they're cannabis, junk food or ecstasy. We even get addicted to invisible things, like the increasingly strange and scary chemicals infiltrating our food to make it seem to taste better, last longer or look better.

We can get addicted to harmful *experiences* that don't seem addictive, as well as to harmful *substances* that don't seem addictive. This includes getting addicted to stress, such as the stressful lives that can motivate and harm business executives, or the stressful adrenaline rushes that can motivate and harm elite sportspeople, criminals and sex junkies. There are more adrenaline addicts than heroin addicts. Perhaps obvious addictions are only the tip of the addiction iceberg.

Can addictions be cured?

So what can we do if we are addicted? Our addiction might be to a drug, or to alcohol or to smoking, gambling, driving too fast, using a mobile phone too much, or anything else. How can a manically unmindful business person or sportsperson see a connection between what they do and how they feel? How can *we* see a connection between what *we* do and how *we* feel?

Imagine that you are a smoker. If you are or were one then that shouldn't be hard. If you aren't a smoker then imagine something else you're drawn to so deeply that you can't seem to escape its gravity, even though it might be killing you, no matter how slowly. Maybe this is chocolate, or computer games, or gossip, or any of the million and one other things that 'do us' rather than 'us doing them'. The first step out of any addiction is to realise we are addicted.

Once we realise that we are addicted we can clearly see that our addiction is causing us more problems than we need, such as coughing in the night more than we need to if we smoke, or living with a higher chance of getting cancer than we need to, or paying a voluntary cigarette smoking tax that we don't need to. Imagine that we get so disturbed by our new insight that we decide to actually do something meaningful about ending our addiction. What?

Maybe we can instantly cure ourselves of our addiction to smoking or late-night chocolates or texting by working ourselves up into a steely resolve to just quit, right now, and never smoke a cigarette, or eat a chocolate, or text somebody who is in the same room with us again — cold turkey. Alcoholics Anonymous uses this strategy: 'Hello, I'm Joe and I'm an alcoholic!' The key idea here is that addictions are never really cured and we have to keep them permanently dormant by never exposing ourselves to what we're addicted to. That's one way.

Maybe we're keen to try gradually weaning ourselves off our addiction by substituting something less harmful for it. This strategy is used in methadone programs where people who are addicted to illegal substances like heroin are legally given something similar but less addictive. These programs haven't been hugely successful in weaning people off heroin, but some experts argue that they reduce overall heroin-related harm by reducing heroin-related crime.

Nicotine patches are another substitute-and-wean approach to treating addiction. The crucial idea here is that most people aren't just addicted to a substance, they're addicted to an experience. This includes the apparently profound pleasure of sucking in hot smoke and then blowing it out again. With the substitute-and-wean approach we try to pluck addictions out by their psychological roots. The nicotine patch eliminates the thrill of sucking, then reduces and finally eliminates the actual addictive substance — nicotine — by reducing and eventually ceasing the patches. These programs are effective for some people, but you could say that the real roots of addictions are even deeper than our craving for experiences.

Maybe we can distract ourselves from our addiction by getting really enthusiastic about something else. This is a similar strategy to that used by many parents. It's just too sad for everyone to snatch away the small plastic toy car that our precious child is playing with because they just might choke on it, without giving them something to replace it with, such as a toy truck that is too big to choke on. Maybe we can give up smoking by joining an indoor rugby team or taking up kayaking. Physical exercise is potentially very useful for addiction substitution because it creates wellbeing via the release of endorphins — happy chemicals in our brain. Physical activities can also improve our feeling of life mastery, as well as distract us from our addiction.

Distractions may not actually cure addictions, though. James Thurber wrote a story in *The New Yorker* about a bear who was addicted to alcohol and often came home late at night drunk, and terrorised his wife and cubs by falling all over the floor as a result of too much booze. One day the bear insightfully realised that he had a problem and took up gymnastics to channel his drinking energy into something more positive. After a while the newly disciplined bear developed such proficiency in his gymnastics that he often came home late at night, and terrorised his wife and cubs by falling all over the floor as a result of too much positive energy.

Addiction treatments

As with most conditions — physical, mental and spiritual — if you can't get enough relief from them by coming up with your own solutions, or by reading self-help books, or by mindfully changing your life, it might be a good idea to find a suitable therapist. There are plenty of therapies available for official addictions, although not so many for unofficial ones. There are therapies based on the above treatment principles of harm minimisation, and there are more serious treatments that force people to change their lives, at least temporarily, such as the detoxification units for people with serious alcohol and other addictions where they are forced to withdraw from them.

There are general therapies available to help people with addictions, especially easily recognisable ones, such as cognitive behavioural therapies (CBT), which attempt to treat addictions at the root level of the actual addictive thoughts and behaviours as well as by raising awareness about the life cost of addictions. These addictive thoughts and behaviours often end up creating a vicious circle. Addictive behaviour leads to low self-esteem, which leads to craving for the temporary escape from self-tormenting thoughts offered by the false friend of whatever addictive substance or experience we can get our hands on, fast. Therapies like CBT can be reasonably effective in reducing addictive symptoms but can be difficult for the people doing them to understand. People can also feel stigmatised by seeing themselves as being 'in therapy' and therefore lacking in some way. Also, not everybody is suited to changing their addictive behaviour by changing their addictive thinking patterns. This is especially true of people in potentially unreceptive mental states, such as those just out of a drug detoxification program.

Drug treatments for underlying causes of addictions such as depression and anxiety can be reasonably effective when there's a close link between a negative emotion and an addictive behaviour. These drugs include anti-anxiety medications and antidepressants, but they produce physical side effects such as drowsiness and agitation. They can also worsen the feelings of inadequacy that lead to addictions in the first place, when a treated person sees themselves as 'on medication' as well as 'in treatment'. Medications can even replace other addictions, rather than cure them.

Aversive therapy is sometimes used to help people with addictions, and it can be almost as painful as it sounds. One of the first R-rated movies — *A Clockwork Orange* — graphically showed the potential dehumanisation of this approach to mental health when Alex the juvenile delinquent was 'cured' through classical aversive conditioning. His violent and sexual tendencies were paired with electric shocks, which destroyed his aggression but also his ability to love music and life, as symbolised by the beauty of Beethoven's *Ode to Joy*, which was played while he was being shocked.

Mindfulness as a treatment and prevention of addiction

Mindfulness strategies and therapies are becoming increasingly popular ways of preventing and treating a wide range of psychological problems, including addictions. They are particularly effective at treating addicted people because they directly target an addiction's root cause. Also, they build on people's wellness, rather than merely responding to their problems.

There is a clear link between stress, negative emotions and addiction, so it's therefore likely that a technique that's highly successful at reducing stress can also greatly reduce addiction-related harm. Many substances and addictive behaviours are attempts to self-medicate the pain associated with stress.

Mindfulness has important advantages over CBT in that it is simple and natural. It has an important advantage over drug therapy in that over time it leads to positive side effects such as relaxation and deeper happiness, rather than negative side effects. A potential downside, if you can call it that, is that mindfulness takes patience, practice and sometimes a bit of courage. In time the apparent downside winds up being an upside because it can help us enjoy the benefits of patience and courage in our whole life.

We can learn mindfulness or undertake mindfulness therapy regardless of the state of our mind, or mindlessness, although it's difficult to engage properly with the process if we're acutely intoxicated — with anything. Mindfulness practice can profoundly improve our life if we have an official addiction, an unofficial addiction or a potential addiction. The first step in this process is to recognise that we might be addicted or heading in that direction. Mindfulness can give any addicted or pre-addicted person a life strategy or therapy that offers the combined benefits of CBT and drug treatment. It will eventually improve addicted people's thinking, behaviour and brain chemistry, without actually targeting any of them.

Once we become aware of an addiction, mindfulness can improve our life by encouraging us to be fully aware and accepting of it, warts and all — all by simply helping us develop more awareness of the sensations in our body without judging them or reacting to them. Fighting and suppressing our urges usually makes them worse, not better. Learning to notice these urges in a more detached way helps them come and go without our getting caught up in a mind war.

Mindfulness practices and therapies are a valuable self-development process (actually a self-re-development process) that offer us a gradual return from our stressed and addictive state to our more natural and happy state. We can all learn mindfulness and gain its benefits, whether or not we're suffering from an official or unofficial addiction. Mindfulness offers us a reunion with reality — now — and this can greatly help us recover from addiction or addictive tendencies by replacing our blind anger, anxiety and restlessness with patience, empathy and consciousness.

Mindfulness and addiction — the evidence

There is rapidly growing scientific evidence that demonstrates the usefulness of mindfulness for reducing addiction-related harm, including evidence that it can prevent relapse. Scientific studies such as that undertaken by Dr Katie Witkiewitz and others at the University of Washington in Seattle have clearly demonstrated the ability of mindfulness therapy to help prevent substance-abuse relapse.[3] Dr Witkiewitz described her results as showing that 'the meditative tortoise wins the race'.[4] These researchers suggested that because of the strong relationship between craving and negative emotions, mindfulness is particularly useful to people with addictions because it treats negative emotions and substance abuse simultaneously. If the underlying driver for resorting to a substance isn't dealt with then a potential vulnerability remains. Applying the principles and practices outlined in the anxiety and depression chapters are therefore also very relevant to managing addiction.

A small but encouraging study recently published in *Substance Abuse* showed that a mindfulness program improved the happiness, stress levels and mindfulness level of alcohol-addicted people, as well as reduced their craving.[5] This study specifically explored the relationship between mindfulness therapy and alcohol abuse, and the researchers concluded that addictive behaviour arises from a deeper psychological condition — unhappiness. Too many people who are 'cured' of their addiction soon revert back to their previous addiction-use levels. Mindfulness is a therapy that recognises and resolves the deep-rooted psychological or existential maladies that underlie addictions, and therefore it offers a more permanent cure than do other approaches.

A recent study provides important evidence that mindfulness therapy can effectively reduce the stress that may well be the real cause of addictive behaviour.[6] This was shown in a potentially highly difficult population: prison inmates with a long record of substance abuse. An intensive program of Vipassana mindfulness meditation practice over ten days was offered to prison inmates. The program resulted in 'significant reductions in alcohol, marijuana, and crack cocaine use and decrease in alcohol-related problems and psychiatric symptoms' after release from jail.[7]

Mindfulness and addiction — the benefits

Apart from the general principles of mindfulness outlined in previous chapters, there are some particular points worth making that can help an addicted person manage their addiction. A few of these are summarised below.

- Mental health: Improving mental health and managing stress is central to removing the hidden drivers to addictive behaviours.

- Imagination: The tendency to daydream about the substance or behaviour, imagining how happy we think we would be with it and how unhappy we are without it, leaves us vulnerable to relapse. This is almost like meditating on our object of desire, which only breeds attraction for it and keeps reactivating the circuits feeding addiction. Practising giving attention to our day-to-day life as well as learning formal mindfulness practices leave us far less vulnerable.

- Urge-surfing: Urges will arise. Our experience teaches us that fighting with them only draws more attention to them and creates tension, and sooner or later we give in. Urge-surfing means being able to observe the urge, and even the thoughts about the urge, but respond more gently than how we usually do. This means accepting our urges and letting go, not suppressing them — let the urge flow in and through you with less and less reaction or engagement with it. We don't even have to think that the urges shouldn't be there. In fact, we can welcome them every time they arise — as opportunities to be free of them.

- Engagement: Greater engagement with life and our enjoyment of it through giving more attention to it is vital to fill the vacuum left by the addiction when it's no longer there. Really tasting our food, really seeing the sunset, really noticing our child or dog playing in the park, smelling the roses or daffodils or gerberas — all the simple, wonderful moments can make our life much fuller and more sustaining.

Joe's wife Jane realised sooner than Joe did that they needed some help to improve their life together. Jane knew that Joe would resist going to a health professional such as a psychologist about his drinking problem, because that would mean admitting to himself and others that he had a drinking problem. So when a friend told Jane that she had done a course in mindfulness that helped her give up smoking because it helped her cope with her cravings, Jane began to hope that this might help Joe, if only she could convince him to try it. Jane didn't tell Joe that the mindfulness course would help him drink less, she told him that it would help him enjoy life more — the way that he used to. They did the course together. After a few weeks Joe woke up one morning feeling enthusiastic about the day ahead, rather than feeling like trying to go back to sleep again. He realised that this was the first morning in a long time that he had really woken up — to himself, to Jane and to his life.

Take-home tips for a mindful response to addiction

Not so helpful
- Lie to ourselves or others by thinking that what's hurting us is normal or okay or unavoidable.
- Wait until everything is going well before we are happy and comfortable enough with ourselves to not crave anything else.

Helpful
- Be aware that something we want badly might be an addiction or the start of one.
- Be aware that we can be addicted to things that aren't usually thought of as addictions. Anything that does us rather than us doing it is unmindful, unconscious and unnecessary.

- Be aware that if we keep living in a stressed or unfulfilled state we risk developing new addictions or re-inventing old ones.
- Follow the mindful living practices discussed in earlier chapters. These will make us less anxious, less depressed and more able to really concentrate on and enjoy what we're doing, right now.
- Understand that we can start on the road to recovery before we reach our front gate. We can peacefully accept what's happening inside our bodies, as well as outside them.
- Reach out and join something and somebody real rather than turn to alcohol or fast food or thrill-seeking as a substitute. Talk to somebody. Join a support group.
- Consider doing a mindfulness class or therapy.
- Accept now what's good in life, don't *except* it. What we give our attention to grows — whether that's flowers or weeds!

CHAPTER 10

Attention Deficit Disorders

Amanda took her seven-year-old son, Jack, to see her GP one day. She had been getting a lot of reports from his teachers that he had been very disruptive in class, was settling poorly in his work and had been falling behind the rest of the class. One of Jack's teachers suggested that he might have ADHD and that he should see a doctor to have the situation assessed.

Inattention and the modern world

Depending on what part of the world you live in, Attention Deficit and Hyperactivity Disorder (ADHD) is diagnosed in anywhere between 1 in 1000 and 1 in 10 children — boys more often than girls and in developed countries more than under-developed countries. In parts of the world where it is most common, like some states in the United States, it is probably the product of environment and upbringing, along with a tendency to over-diagnose the condition by attributing many behavioural or domestic problems to ADHD.

Research has shown that parents of children with ADHD have poorer quality family life, less parental warmth and higher depression and anxiety.[1] High parental stress and more inconsistent and hostile parenting are also associated with a greater chance of ADHD in the children. This doesn't mean that parents whose child has ADHD must be 'bad parents' but it may mean that the pressures, stresses and inattentiveness in parents are likely to manifest themselves one way or another in the children, and ADHD may be an increasingly common one. Time-pressured, frazzled and stressed parents may be a symptom of the society we have created for ourselves. It's all a part of an overheated and overly fast world.

ADHD isn't just about parenting, though. Research supports the view that a number of chemicals and food additives increase the risk of ADHD, and a healthy whole-food diet reduces the risk. The sometimes necessary but largely superficial response to the problem is to put an increasing number of children on amphetamine-like drugs, rather than address the underlying issues.

What we call ADHD may in fact be just the tip of a very large iceberg. Underneath the bit of the iceberg above the waterline where we see and name ADHD is a much larger bit pushing it up — that is, the whole community. It would seem that we have created for ourselves a world that is conditioning us to have shorter and shorter attention spans and leave many of our children vulnerable to attention-related problems. IT, media, upbringing, genes, lifestyle and environment all play a part, but more of that later.

Attention Deficit Trait

An article from the *Harvard Business Review* coined the term Attention Deficit Trait (ADT).[2] ADT — the tendency to have an attention that is constantly flitting — is a newly recognised neurological phenomenon and is a response to a hyperkinetic environment. Hyperkinetic is a way of saying highly paced, frenetic activity or, in more colloquial terms, everyone running around like chickens with their heads cut off. Put up your hand if your workplace is like this. Now put it down again because everyone around you is probably thinking you're a little strange for sitting there with your hand in the air.

The modern work and home environment is not only too fast-paced for too much of the time, but within it we are generally trying to deal with too much sensory and mental input. ADT can be controlled by engineering the environment and by taking greater consideration of our emotional and physical health. Suggestions by workplace experts include a range of strategies outlined in Chapter 19 on the workplace.

Working memory

Working memory is another term for short-term memory, which is our immediate memory of what's happening currently. It's like the information on the desktop of our computer that we're working with at any given time. A more technical description is the 'structures and processes used for temporarily storing and manipulating information'.[3]

The specific part of the brain responsible for working memory is largely the prefrontal cortex — the bit of the brain behind our forehead. It is, as has already been said, the area of the brain most involved in paying attention. It's well known that ADHD is associated with impairment of the areas of the brain involved in and activated by attention regulation, and this is why improving working memory helps to increase IQ and treat ADHD at the same time. It also explains why, even for people without ADHD, we perform more poorly — say, in exams — when under stress. A reduced working memory capacity leads to a pronounced increase in reaction time and errors.[4] If performance pressure harms our ability to succeed by harming our working memory capacity, one can only imagine what effect it has on a well-intentioned child trying to perform under the gaze of a well-intentioned adult putting pressure on the child to get the right results.

Media, attention and memory

Excess television has a negative effect on our capacity to pay attention, particularly for developing brains that need the direct engagement of the senses with the physical world to establish the connections they will need. Watching football on television, for example, is a totally different experience to playing it. Watching it requires no skill, creativity or engagement, whereas playing it demands attention. Children who watch higher levels of television by the age of three are significantly more likely to display attention problems at the age of 7,[5] let alone the higher risk of sleep problems and obesity. We were not evolved to live our life vicariously through a screen, even if it's a 52-inch LCD screen.

How much TV is too much? Most experts recommend no more than two hours a day of 'screen time' (television and computer time) for a child. With the average child in a developed country now having four hours of screen time a day, we have gone a little too far, but it's not an easy thing for time-poor and exhausted parents to find the time to spend with their children on other activities.

Other forms of media such as music can also have both positive and negative effects on a child's development and behaviour. Very fast-paced or aggressive music can produce more fast-paced and aggressive children — it's like we're winding up their little springs from an early age.

Whether or not we're aware of it, the kind of leisure activities we engage in have an effect on our state of attention and therefore our memory and performance. Passive leisure activities that lull us into a state of inattentiveness are not helpful. Number one among passive leisure activities is TV watching. Whether it causes dementia is a very hard question to answer definitively.[6] Just as not using our muscles leads to us not developing them in the first place, or their wasting away, not engaging attention means that capacity wastes away.

Alzheimer's Disease (AD) is also associated with problems with the prefrontal cortex and memory centre of the brain. According to research on the long-term effect of television viewing on the brain: 'For each additional daily hour of middle-adulthood television viewing the associated risk of AD development increased 1.3 times. Participation in intellectually stimulating activities and social activities reduced the associated risk of developing AD.'[7] Those who have less than average diversity in leisure activities, spend less time on them and practise more passive activities (principally watching television) were nearly four times as likely to develop dementia over a 40-year follow-up compared to those who rated higher than average on these factors.[8]

Multitasking

Then to all of the above we add Information Technology (IT). This is probably the main source of multitasking. Multitasking is probably something of an illusion or misnomer. What we're actually doing when we seem to be multitasking is task-switching. Computers can multitask; we can't. Switching attention happens so fast that it appears we are performing multiple tasks at the same time, when in reality we're switching back and forth between tasks.[9]

Dr Clifford Nass from Stanford University had this to say about the performance levels of extreme multitaskers:

> These are kids who are doing 5, 6, or more things at once all the time ... It turns out multitaskers are terrible at every aspect of multitasking! They get distracted constantly. Their memory is very disorganised. ... they're worse at analytic reasoning. We worry that it may be we're creating people who may not be able to think well, and clearly.[10]

It's not just kids who have problems with all this stuff. According to research, adult workers distracted by email and phone calls suffer a fall in IQ more than twice that found in someone smoking marijuana.[11] In other research, an increase in the amount of time university students spent instant messaging had the effect of increasing their level of distractibility in performing academic tasks, whereas the amount of time spent reading books reduced the levels of distractibility.[12] Russell Poldrack from UCLA concludes:

> The best thing you can do to improve your memory is to pay attention to the things you want to remember ... When distractions force you to pay less attention to what you're doing, you don't learn as well as if you had paid full attention. Tasks that require more attention, such as learning calculus or reading Shakespeare, will be particularly adversely affected by multitasking.[13]

The illusion is that we can do many things at once. Well, yes we can but we just can't do them as well as we think we can, although the reduction in our level of focus and performance isn't apparent to us. Simple multitasking, such as walking and talking at the same time, may be fine, but complex multitasking isn't such a good thing. Complex multitasking is where we are doing two things at once, both of which require a little more intellectual grunt, like driving a car and talking on a mobile phone at the same time. As has been previously mentioned, within 5 minutes of using a mobile phone while driving we are more than four times as likely to have a motor vehicle accident.[14] Although our aim in multitasking is to not miss anything, to have a fuller life and to be more productive, the reality behind the illusion is that all we get as a result of this habit is continuous over-stimulation, distractibility and a lack of fulfilment.[15] We actually become less efficient in task-switching, not better at it.[16]

What can be done about it?

Much of the above is the negative side of the coin. The positive side of the coin is not to believe that there's nothing we can do about ADHD. Apart from having an expert assessment from a suitably trained health practitioner and considering what treatments might or might not be indicated, there is a lot more we can do.

In relation to mindfulness and meditation practices, it's not surprising that meditation, which is attention training after all, improves attention in children and is therapeutic for ADHD — according to reviews of the research in the field.[17] Meditation helps to stabilise the areas of the brain, such as the frontal lobe, that are involved with attention and working memory. Although more and larger studies are needed, it looks as though meditation is probably as effective as the drug treatments for ADHD, but with positive side effects.[18] Meditation doesn't just help children to pay attention better; it also helps to develop their ability to be less impulsive. That little window of opportunity as far as choosing whether to act impulsively, or even to act at all, opens wider the more we practise paying attention.

Obviously, despite the potential role of meditation, it will still be important for a child with significant attention or behavioural issues to be assessed by a suitably trained health professional. In some cases it may still be necessary for a child to use medications in the short- to mid term and to use other strategies along with attention training.

Managing ADHD is as much about parents learning and setting an example at home as it is about the child learning new skills. A patient and loving hand will be needed because making a child feel stressed over their inattentiveness will make the problem worse.

Jack was assessed by a paediatrician, who confirmed ADHD. Between Amanda, her husband Colin and the paediatrician they decided that the problem wasn't severe enough to warrant medications. They were given some advice along the lines mentioned above, which they put into practice. Amanda and Colin got as much out of it as Jack did.

Take-home tips for a mindful response to Attention Deficit Disorders

Not so helpful

- Watch TV for many hours at a stretch while also working on your computer and trying to relate to your family.

Helpful

- Be a positive role model (but if we can't be an example then at least we can be a warning!). As adults we need to be more self-aware, more able to self-regulate and more able to live attentively. There's no point in telling a child one thing and then doing the opposite. The child will learn from what we do rather than what we say. Avoid complex multitasking. Gently encourage your child to attend to one thing at a time and to slow down. This includes managing the environment and IT usage — switching off the mobile phone, working on one activity at a time, reducing unnecessary stimuli and interruptions.
- Engage interest, not anxiety. The most compelling thing for the attention is interest and fascination. Making a child anxious about paying attention will worsen the problem, not relieve it.
- Practise performing one task at a time. Begin with priority one and do one thing at a time until it's time to move on to something

else. Take breaks when needed and provide variety both in what you do and how you do it.

- Practise mindfulness (attention regulation). Practise mindfulness meditation and mindful activities — that is, activities that require attention. Start with a few minutes and then gently increase the time when you are acquainted with the practice. Make it light by not forcing it on your child.

- Optimise the environment. Avoid fast-paced or aggressive music, gaming or other media such as films. Have soothing or slower tempo music in the background while your child is playing.

- Limit screen time. Limit leisure screen time (TV, computer and gaming) to no more than 2 hours a day on average.

- Engage in regular physical exercise and sports. This can be a great way to work off energy and engage attention in a healthy way, and is especially good when your child is interacting with other children in team games. Choose physical activities that your child enjoys.

- Eat a healthy whole-food diet. Give your child a healthy diet, including things like omega-3 fatty acids. Avoid food additives and colourings.

- Look after ourselves. We should all practise all of the above ourselves so that we're coping as best we can and also so that we're part of the solution and not part of the problem. Above all, be patient.

CHAPTER 11

Pain

Marie had experienced the pain of Irritable Bowel Syndrome (IBS) for a long time. She was 35 and couldn't remember when she didn't have it, although she would probably have been in her teens. Being highly strung didn't help but nor did the many and varied anti-spasmodic medications, laxatives and painkillers she had taken over the years. Marie spent much of her day on the lookout for any indication of her pain. When she noticed it she tended to get quite emotional about it, anticipating whether or not it was going to go on all day. The more she tried to do something about it, the more it didn't go away and the more helpless and despondent she felt. Marie was just getting sick of being sick and in pain and was coming to the conclusion that she needed to learn to cope with the pain better, if it wasn't going away.

The problem of pain

If we are experiencing constant or regular pain, or if we are close to somebody who is, then statistics showing what a huge global problem it is might not seem very meaningful, but a few stats may at least help us realise that a lot of other people are experiencing pain too.

The distinction between chronic pain and acute pain is fairly arbitrary, and has been variously described by different experts as pain that lasts over three months, six months or twelve months.[1] It has also been described simply as pain that lasts longer than it reasonably should. A large Pain in Europe survey was undertaken simultaneously in fifteen European countries in 2010. This revealed that almost one European in five over the age of eighteen had suffered from pain for at least six months at some stage in their life.[2] Well over half of these pain sufferers were affected to the extent that they were less able to work, and almost one in five had lost a job because of their pain. The survey also showed that almost one person in five was depressed as a result of their pain, and that almost half of the pain sufferers considered that their pain management was inadequate and only about one person in 50 with long-term pain attended a pain clinic. The real problem of pain of course is far deeper than its statistics can demonstrate. Pain affects the lives of many millions of people worldwide who are experiencing it, and the many more millions of people to whom they are connected. Basically chronic pain is common, it commonly leads to depression and it is uncommon for people to get optimal treatment for their pain.

The pain experience

Pain can be a great challenge to our ability to live our life enjoyably, peacefully and mindfully, especially when our pain is constant. Maybe, however, there is more to pain than meets the 'I'. You might already have an inkling of how it can be easy for people who *aren't* in pain to tell people who *are* in pain how they can improve their life. Mindfulness, however, can help us all realise that what other people experience may not be all that different from what we are experiencing, and that pain is pain, whether it's physical, emotional or spiritual. Pain is a fact of life, as is pleasure, but the issue may not be so much about the presence of these pleasant and unpleasant experiences, but how we relate and react to them.

Many wisdom traditions have recognised the simple truth that suffering and adversity happen, but have worked hard to find a way to transcend that suffering. The first Buddhist noble truth states that there is suffering. This doesn't mean that it's right and proper to suffer. It also doesn't mean that suffering is unavoidable, although acting unmindfully is a pretty good way to multiply the suffering in our life. What this actually means is that a good place to start doing something positive about our suffering is to recognise that it's there, and to realise that other people suffer too. If you have a painful tooth or appendix it's unlikely that you'll do anything constructive about it if you don't first acknowledge that something is wrong. A greater challenge, of course, can be dealing with pain that's been there so long it feels like part of us, but the same principle applies: first, recognise it. This can lead to the happy ending or at least happy-ish ending of the four Buddhist noble truths:

1. There is suffering.
2. The origin of suffering is attachment.
3. The cessation of suffering is attainable.
4. There is a path to the cessation of suffering.[3]

A very important point is being made here about the way we relate to pain and suffering. If we can remove the pain then that looks like a pretty good first option, but often we can't, so what do we do then? It might be easier to fix our idea that we are alone in our pain than it is to fix the physical aspect of pain.

One of the authors told somebody experiencing chronic pain that the condition didn't have to make her unmindful. This made her angry, which is possibly an indication of not having dispensed that little piece of wisdom in a mindful way.

'How can you say that, you don't know what it's like!'

Actually he did know what it's like, because he has been experiencing ongoing intense physical sensations relating to nerve degeneration that developed after a trivial dental problem was 'treated' about fifteen years ago. He has also experienced intense physical sensations relating to a spinal condition for about 35 years. *We all know what pain is.* None of us, that we're aware of, is so physically, mentally or spiritually perfect that we can't empathise with others who suffer. In fact, when we empathise with someone who is experiencing pain then we experience it too and our brains respond in just the same way.[4]

One of us once worked for seven years in a research institute linked with a hospital specialising in geriatric medicine. There was a pain clinic there. Something became very clear after observing many people's pain experiences and treatments — there is primary pain and secondary pain. Primary pain is directly linked with physical conditions such as nerve damage or arthritis. In these cases something is damaged and pain is the body's way of telling us and inviting us to look after the damaged part. Although we might dislike pain, if we were unable to experience it we wouldn't actually know when we were injuring our body and so couldn't look after it. Quite often these underlying chronic conditions cannot be treated or even managed by drugs without sacrificing some awareness and therefore quality of life. So what's the alternative? More and more painkillers until they become a problem in themselves? Well, the alternative is to improve our mindful acceptance of these sensations, and therefore our life.

Secondary pain is extremely common, and this is where mindfulness can be especially useful. Secondary pain comes from a tensing of our body in response to a primary pain and also an associated anxiety or anger or other negative mental state of non-acceptance. This is where the suffering comes in. Physical sensations are one thing; mental and emotional responses are another. We might have noticed that even before the dentist starts injecting or drilling we are already suffering enormously. We might have even suffered for days leading up to the appointment, if we have a sufficient fear of dentists. There can be suffering with no physical sensation — just an anticipation. We only have to notice the effect of anxiety, fear, depression, tiredness or anger on pain to realise that our mental and emotional state can greatly impact how we experience physical sensations.

It's common to see people in pain clinics who no longer have the condition that led to their original pain, but they still have pain. This pain is caused by the tensing habit that gets so ingrained that it's unconscious. There are millions of people with pain conditions who don't realise that they may be adding insult to their injury, and much of this may be taking place through the unconscious ways we relate and respond to pain. Secondary psychological pain may even be caused by exactly the same mechanism that leads to secondary physical pain.

Distraction is a method commonly applied to dealing with an acute pain, and it can work, but it doesn't tend to work well for chronic pain. Our mental and emotional response to pain (let's call it stress for now) may actually accentuate it in a number of ways. Firstly, stress increases the output of inflammatory chemicals, so if there's an inflammatory component to the pain then we have poured fuel on the inflammatory fire. Secondly, we may be very physically tense when stressed, which only adds to any muscle spasms that may be present at the site of the pain. Thirdly, when we become hyper-vigilant for the pain (always looking out for it) and emotionally reactive to it, as soon as we notice it we sensitise the pain circuits of the brain to fire off more pain messages with less and less stimulus. Evidence suggests that neural loops in the brain are literally sensitised and maintained by 'sustained attention and arousal.'[5,6] Over time it's like the brain is being wired for pain as our attention becomes monopolised by constantly looking for pain. This may be a significant reason why mindfulness is so therapeutic for chronic pain, because it helps to unhook attention from the preoccupation about the pain and reduces the emotional reactivity to it when it's noticed. Fourthly, stress seems to change the chemical composition of the nerve endings, making them more liable to fire off pain messages even in the presence of relatively little damage.

All of this may be why chronic pain syndromes are far more common and severe in the presence of stress (life stress, anxiety, depression). This doesn't mean we advocate saying to a person in pain, 'Your pain is in your mind!' The person with the chronic pain syndrome isn't making it up — although there is the occasional malingerer — it's just that the unconscious way we anticipate, react and respond to pain will change our experience of it enormously. Thankfully, this situation can be reversed and that's why the practice of mindfulness seems to be so helpful for chronic pain.

In summary, the reasons why the 'relaxation response' is associated with greater pain tolerance is because it:

- enhances the brain's responsiveness to endorphins, which are the body's own painkillers and are about 100 times stronger than morphine;[7,8]
- has an anti-inflammatory effect, which is important in conditions where inflammation is a part of the problem;
- causes a reduction in muscle spasm;
- desensitises the pain pathways in the brain; and
- enhances mood and coping and reduces emotional reactivity.

Pain and wisdom

Many wisdom traditions, including those associated with mindfulness as a practice and therapy, have recognised the pain principle: blindly reacting to what our mind doesn't like is what turns physical pain into psychological suffering. The principles of managing pain through mindfulness are simple, but it's definitely not easy. A big part of it is to learn to observe the pain in a more impartial way. When we do this it starts to become apparent that there's an aspect of ourselves experiencing pain — the body — and another part watching — our consciousness or awareness. The two are different. It's exactly the same principle for being able to observe mental and emotional pain such as anxiety and depression without getting involved in it.

One of the authors — the other one this time — remembers doing an experiment as a teenager on the side of a basketball court after a rather major ankle sprain in a match. It hurt, a lot, but what was interesting was when he identified with his ankle it hurt a lot more. It was like being consumed by the pain. When, on the other hand, it was just observed as a sensation at the end of the leg, with no desire to make it go away or change it, it was just a sensation that caused little suffering. He sat there for a number of minutes flipping the way of experiencing the pain from the one to the other. It became apparent that it was the resistance to the pain, the ideas about it and the personal relationship to it that made all the difference as far as causing suffering was concerned. The remedy was openness — observing without thinking — and objectivity. (A firm bandage was also useful when it became available!)

Obviously, the stronger and more chronic the pain, the higher the bar goes in terms of the challenge. The principles of managing it mindfully don't change but the courage, patience and perseverance required to apply the mindfulness practices do. In Jon Kabat-Zinn's initial research in this field, participants were asked to practise body scans and mindfulness meditation for 40 minutes a day; a significant but necessary commitment. It takes time for our underlying attitudes and reactions to pain to change, especially when some unhelpful ones have become engrained for some time. What was important, though, was that after the eight-week mindfulness course 80 per cent of people had significant and ongoing reductions in their pain and the suffering associated with it.

The English philosopher Alan Watts moved to California in the 1960s, where he helped popularise Eastern religions such as Buddhism and, to a lesser extent, Taoism. In his last book on Taoism, *The Watercourse Way*, he pointed out that our unconscious and unnatural tensing of our body makes our life more painful than it needs to be.[9] To summarise a venerable and ancient Chinese wisdom practice in a catchy modern phrase: 'Go with the flow!' To translate the untranslatable Tao: the Tao is simply life. Once we're fully aware that we're alive, unarguably alive, mindfulness and everything else worth having arises naturally.

The ancient Greek philosopher Socrates was noted for his capacity to cope with pain and adversity, as well as his capacity to remain impervious to the seductions of pleasure. He endured pain when he needed to and enjoyed the pleasures of life when they came his way without trying to hold on to them. He said it all had to with whether or not we get attached to pleasure and pain — it doesn't matter if our chains are made of gold or iron, they are chains nonetheless. Just as happiness isn't dependent on pleasure, so is unhappiness not dependent on pain. If we get attached to the one we will be attached to the other, and our happiness will go up and down accordingly.

The pain clinic that one of us was once familiar with based its treatments on mindfulness principles, even though at that time virtually nobody used the word 'mindfulness' or, even less likely, 'meditation' in a medical context. Patients in pain clinics were and are encouraged to be aware of the intense sensations in their body that they usually describe as pain, without reacting to them or labelling them, and to simply accept them. The patients who do this most conscientiously are often the ones who realise soonest that they are tensing, and that this is caused by their thoughts rather than their condition.

'Just be aware of all of your sensations,' was the eventual response to the angry mindfulness and pain questioner, 'including the ones that you normally think of as painful. Just allow them to be as they are, and let them come and go, without commenting or reacting. Just observe what happens.'

Her expression of cynical hostility softened after a few minutes of practising this non-habitual but natural response to pain, and this woman now looked a lot more receptive to life's opportunities. She also looked more compassionate and gentle — with herself and therefore with others. It was as if this brief foray into the mindfulness adventure was at least the beginning of an experience of pain as a phenomena that doesn't have to mean suffering.

There is a small but important issue related to bringing acceptance to pain. Practising acceptance in order to make pain go away isn't acceptance — it's non-acceptance pretending to be acceptance. People sometimes say, 'Oh, I tried mindfulness for my pain but it didn't work. It didn't get rid of the pain.' Well, they weren't practising mindfulness. Acceptance — impartial and unconditional — is just what it says: acceptance. Mindfulness works on softening the thoughts, attitudes, reactions and anticipation related to the pain; it doesn't work on making the pain go away. The pain may change, in fact it invariably will, but that's something that we allow to take its own course. Through mindfulness we become more aware of the pain and there may even be times when the pain and our reactions to it intensify, but we can welcome that, as unpleasant as it may be, as an opportunity to cultivate a different way of being with pain, and a different way of being.

Treatments for pain

Modern Western medicine commonly treats chronic pain with pharmaceuticals and surgical procedures designed to fix physical causes. Examples of this range from pulling out a rotten tooth to performing highly intricate microsurgery on a damaged spinal cord. Sometimes these procedures work — it's great when they do — and sometimes they don't. Pain is also commonly treated by the administration of painkillers, ranging from aspirin to morphine. Pain-relieving drugs tend to be more effective for short-term conditions such as toothache than for more serious and chronic conditions such as arthritis. Drug administration can be a problematic response to pain, however, because of its side effects and also because our body tends to get used to any external substance, so that we need more and more of it to get an effect. Addiction or dependency can become a significant problem in chronic-pain syndromes, particularly when the pain is mixed up with other psychological issues.

Drug treatments for pain can kill the messenger, so we don't get to know about something we should know about. Pain, like everything else, has a purpose. The purpose of pain is to alert us to something that's wrong that we need to attend to — to wake us up. This is true of all types of pain: physical, mental and spiritual. Pain, like everything else, can get out of balance and eventually out of control if we respond to it mindlessly, rather than mindfully. Although counterintuitive, paying attention to it helps us to learn about the pain — and ourselves.

There are more subtle treatments of pain that are commonly used, such as Cognitive Behavioural Therapy (CBT). This involves helping people understand how their negative thoughts can make their pain worse, and even cause their pain. There are also relaxation techniques such as Jacobsen's Progressive Muscle Relaxation (PMR), which has had some success in reducing pain. Relaxation techniques, however, somewhat force relaxation, by directing people to try to relax, body part by body part. This misses part of the point of the meditation techniques that it's based on — that it's about the mind as well as the body. Mindfulness involves encouraging easy and natural awareness and acceptance of whatever sensations and thoughts are experienced — *as they come.*

Mindfulness and pain relief — the evidence

A key early scientific study of the ability of mindfulness to help people with pain was undertaken by mindfulness pioneer Jon Kabat-Zinn and colleagues in 1985.[10] Ninety chronic-pain patients participated in a ten-week mindfulness course. There was a clear demonstration that these people improved in their present-moment pain level, body image, activity levels and mood disturbance including anxiety and depression. There has been much research since then that shows that mindfulness benefits pain sufferers. A recent example is a study performed in response to the increasing popularity of mindfulness therapies for a range of conditions, including chronic pain. These researchers gave 150 people who were seeking treatment for chronic pain a measure of mindfulness, and the results showed that the more mindful they were, the more likely they were to be functioning well emotionally, physically and socially.[11]

A recent Australian study of 104 outpatients of a multidisciplinary pain clinic showed a relationship between rating low on mindfulness scales and rating high on pain catastrophising.[12] Pain gets worse when we think about it and are scared of it and of what we associate with it. Think of the last time you went to the dentist! Generally you will have suffered enormously even days before the actual appointment. Mindfulness, therefore, can reduce pain. An experimental study that used some intrepid volunteers provided direct and powerful evidence for this. These researchers simply subjected their volunteers to pain, caused by 'electrical stimulation'. (Obviously the researchers hadn't done much compassion-based meditation at this stage!) Then they tested the volunteers' pain tolerance again after giving them mindfulness training. Pain levels decreased substantially.[13] Incidentally, one of us once volunteered for pain research that involved a series of 'electrical stimulations', although no mindfulness or even jellybeans were offered. He suffered enormously as a consequence — of the lack of mindfulness or jellybeans.

Mindfulness and pain — the benefits

Mindfulness can help us live our life more enjoyably, peacefully and naturally, no matter what mental or physical condition we're experiencing. Mindfulness can restore our natural awareness and our acceptance of what we are aware of. This process starts at the level of the connection between our mind and body, and then connects us with what is deeper than our mind and body — our awareness of them.

We think that we experience things *out there*, in the world of our senses, which is why we often crave stuff that we don't have and crave to get rid of stuff that we do have. Think for a moment about chocolate, as we briefly interrupt this chapter to remind you about just how delicious chocolate can be. The deliciousness of chocolate and every other experience that we have actually takes place in our body. This starts in our chocolate-appreciating sense organ — our taste receptors — and then something happens at the level where these sensations introduce our body to our mind: 'That tasted great, and I think I like the hazelnut ones even more than the strawberry ones!' Chocolate and other experiences actually don't take place *out there*, they happen within us. If we realise that our sensations and our reactions to our sensations are the key to our life happiness or otherwise, we're moving towards allowing mindfulness to help us overcome some of life's great challenges, including pain.

The philosopher Nietzsche famously said in his *Twilight of the Idols*: 'What doesn't kill me makes me stronger.' This statement has been misinterpreted by some to mean that we ought to be uncaring about problems and pain and even to actively seek it out — because it is character-building! Nietzsche was actually saying that we can overreact to suffering and that trying to blot out pain before we see the colour of its eyes, as it were, can prevent a great opportunity to deepen our understanding of ourselves and of others and to grow accordingly. This is similar to the idea behind some lines from Shakespeare's *As You Like It*, when he says that pain and adversity can help us to understand ourselves better if we pay attention to it: 'This is no flattery. These are counsellors that feelingly persuade me what I am.'

Examples of mindlessly blotting out pain by denying its existence abound. These include over-prescribing antidepressants or giving people so many painkillers that they don't feel alive anymore. This is an enormously common cause of unhappiness, and not just in officially diagnosed pain sufferers. The principle that the unmindful desire to escape pain can be far more destructive than the pain itself is contained in the first Buddhist noble truth — there is suffering. This principle is more recently elaborated in Russ Harris's *The Happiness Trap* — we can so easily become neurotic about the idea of wanting to be happy, and wanting to be pain-free, that we can want it so badly that it hurts — us and others.

Marie was referred by her GP to a pain clinic that specialised in mindfulness-based approaches. She had a caring, attentive teacher who taught her how to be less preoccupied with the pain and less reactive to it when she noticed it. Marie took on board the message that she would have to put in effort and learn to be patient with the process. It didn't make sense at first, but she found that as she became more accepting of the pain the less it seemed to hurt and the more she could get on with her life. Marie no longer felt trapped by the pain nor did she continue to define herself as a 'chronic pain patient'.

Take-home tips for a mindful response to pain

Not so helpful

- Try to shut out pain with denial or the overuse of drugs.
- Blindly react to pain by getting angry with others or ourselves, or cutting ourselves off from them, or doing things in response to the pain that will make things worse such as drinking too much or eating too much.
- Wait until the pain stops before we start living.

Helpful

- Practise being aware of and accepting the sensations we might normally think of and respond to as pain.
- Realise that no sensation — not even pain, not even pleasure — is permanent. This too shall pass.
- Accept whatever sensations we are experiencing and don't catastrophise about them.
- Avail ourselves of effective therapies.
- Realise and constantly be aware that pain isn't the same as suffering.

CHAPTER 12

Weight management and eating disorders

Kirsty was nineteen and doing her second year of university studies. She was intelligent and well liked but always in the back of her mind was an incessant insecurity about being attractive enough. Much of this insecurity was to do with her weight. Although she wasn't overweight, Kirsty always felt horrible that she wasn't like those 'beautiful people' she saw in the magazines that were so popular with her friends. Kirsty didn't really like herself and it didn't take much to set off a flurry of self-doubt and self-loathing. The solution? Her emotional ups and downs were often compensated for by comfort eating. The kinds of foods she preferred at such times were those that led her to put on weight, which she hated. If one chocolate biscuit was comforting, then it didn't seem unreasonable to expect that a whole packet would provide enough comfort to last her for weeks. The effect? All it did was to make her loathe herself even more.

The next solution? Kirsty felt she couldn't stop herself from eating, so it was better to eat faster so it was over more quickly. The effect? This just led her to eat more and get more emotionally agitated. The next solution? Eat and then induce vomiting so she could avoid putting on weight and not feel so guilty. The effect? Kirsty just felt worse about herself as the behaviour felt more compulsive and she had less control of it. Thinking of how ashamed she would be to tell anyone about what she was doing — how she wasn't coping when all her friends were so cool, calm and collected — meant that Kirsty spent her life living in a kind of miserable but solitary confinement. What she didn't realise was that two of her friends were having similar issues.

Eating and life

Eating, like breathing and sex, is one of those physical necessities that is wonderfully essential for life. As such, nature fortunately makes such things pleasurable, so that under normal circumstances we won't be in two minds about whether or not we want to do them. It wouldn't make much sense, after all, to make something unpleasant that is essential for our survival because as a species we would then be extinct in no time.

Unfortunately, for a whole range of reasons, we have messed with food and eating so much in affluent countries that we have created the kinds of circumstances where we actually hasten our demise, whether by over-nutrition, under-nutrition or poor nutrition. Collectively we have cultivated the kinds of conditions in which eating has become disordered in a whole range of ways. Many of us manage to mainly steer clear of trouble, but an increasing number of us are vulnerable and suffering the consequences.

In this chapter we will explore some of the issues around food and eating and how mindfulness might help bring some sanity into our modern-day love–hate relationship with food. The main topics that we will explore here are food choices, weight management and eating disorders.

Food choices

Being mindful of choosing healthy whole food when we shop is a very useful thing to do. If we don't pay attention we will just choose the habitual items we have always tended to eat. To make a conscious and more discerning choice requires that we pay attention. Nature evolved us to eat whole, unprocessed foods, but somewhere along the line humankind thought it would be a good idea to take the nutrition out of food and put in empty calories. Maybe it seemed like a good idea at the time, but this process messes with our genes and metabolism. Our 'everyday foods' need to be basically whole and healthy, and what experts call the 'sometimes foods' won't do us much harm if we only eat them sometimes.

Notice also that if we go food shopping at the supermarket when we're hungry, every form of calorie-dense (too much fat and sugar) food looks so appetising we just can't resist it. 'Hmm, a kilo tub of lard. That looks delicious!' And then there's all that clever advertising that can be so hard to resist or downright deceptive: 'Diet Lard: 1 per cent fat free!' If we shop on a full stomach it makes it much easier to walk past the things we may later regret purchasing. If the unhealthy food item isn't in our house in the first place then we don't have to practise nearly so much mindfulness-based impulse control to avoid eating it, which is what happens when the thing that we crave (as opposed to really want) is sitting in the cupboard just waiting for us to hoe in.

Making the wrong food choices is a habit that often starts early in our life, as do many of our habits. In fact, our metabolism, food choices and tastes start to get wired into the brain even while we're still in the womb. Governments are starting to become more mindful of the extent of the problem of obesity in young people and the need to do something to help reduce it. In Australia the Victorian state government has recently commenced developing a Jamie Oliver-style 'Ministry of Food' whose duties will include offering food-choice advice to early childhood services and schools. This is in response to figures that show that about a quarter of Australian children (and almost half of Australian adults) are overweight or obese. This is a similar picture in most affluent countries around the world. Given the relationship between being overweight and being unhappy as well as unhealthy, Ministries of Food might be as good an idea as Ministries of Happiness, which the small Asian nation of Bhutan has successfully created as a potential world model. It's becoming clear that poor nutrition is associated with more depression whereas healthy nutrition — a varied whole-food diet — is associated with better mental health.

Weight management

In principle, weight management is a simple thing: 'calories in' (food) needs to not exceed 'calories out' (energy expenditure). In practice, weight management is a complex issue for people living in modern, affluent countries, and we have to make sure that we balance our body books so that we don't end up out of our comfort zone.

We expend most of our energy in our metabolism (just generating our body temperature and keeping the motor running — staying alive), also some in exercise (depending on how active we are) and some in digesting food. Due to increasingly sedentary jobs, labour-saving devices and the prevalence of calorie-dense foods, most of us don't do enough physical activity to balance what we eat. Then when we go on a crash diet we trick our body into thinking it's in the middle of a famine and so it holds on to all the calories it can by reducing our metabolic rate. We really have to punish ourselves to lose weight quickly like this, and nearly all of us who do it will be back to our previous weight — and some — within a year or two. That's why harsh weight-loss diets are not a good long-term strategy. In fact, such diets can increase the risk of developing eating disorders particularly in children and adolescents. Much better to make smaller, gentler but more sustainable changes that will work slower but be much better for us over the long term.

This is one of the main messages of Dr Rick Kausman, the author of the award-winning book *If Not Dieting, Then What?*[1] He recommends a range of commonsense strategies that focus on understanding the thinking behind our eating, and are complementary to mindfulness-based principles.[2, 3] We have adapted a few of the main messages here but if you want to read more, then look at the book or website.

- Positive attitude towards food. Mentally labelling food as 'bad' or 'junk' can make us feel bad about ourselves or guilty, which can reinforce unhealthy eating, particularly when we're eating as a way of helping us deal with uncomfortable emotions. Kausman recommends that we use more neutral terms and think about food as 'everyday' food (fruit, vegetables, cereals) and 'sometimes food' (chocolate, chips).

- Eat slowly and enjoy. Slowing down the speed of our eating, and eating more mindfully, makes it much easier to recognise when our body is telling us we are full, therefore allowing us to stop before we've eaten more than our body needs. When we are mindful — connected with our senses — we are more in touch with what our body is experiencing. This also allows us to experience the flavours, textures and smells of the food we are eating. This can help us derive more satisfaction from eating because we will enjoy our food more, it will taste better and the sensations will last longer. This also helps us to eat foods more aligned to what our body needs rather than to the tastes we habitually want. If, for example, we have never eaten a chocolate bar with attention we may never have really noticed how sweet it actually is. If we eat more slowly and taste it with more attention, then we may surprisingly find that we are satisfied with less. If we eat a sometimes food, we need to savour it so that we enjoy it and then move on. What's the point in doing the 'guilt meditation' afterwards?

- Our body knows best. We often eat when our body isn't physically hungry. For example, we might eat because we're bored, it's time to eat, we're being polite, it's a celebration. This is what Dr Kausman calls 'non-hungry eating', but when it happens too often our eating gets out of balance and we get out of touch with our body's normal hunger signals. (This also happens with eating disorders, but for a different reason such as over-riding hunger messages.) It's therefore good to pay attention to the body and ask whether it needs food or not.

- Nurture ourselves. Eating, particularly comfort foods, helps to cover unpleasant emotions for a short time, but if we're not looking for other ways to care for ourselves and live a satisfying and enjoyable life then we will soon make a problem out of eating, to add to the ones we already perceive we have. Eating too much, like drinking too much, doesn't solve problems, it creates them.

In recent years research has looked at how mindfulness can help with weight management. For example, a study looked at the effectiveness of a six-week mindfulness program for obese individuals, called Mindful Eating and Living (MEAL).[4] The program included mindfulness meditation, mindful eating, group discussion and awareness of body sensations, emotions and triggers to overeat. The study followed changes in weight, Body Mass Index, eating behaviour and psychological distress as well as markers of risk for heart disease. Participants in the mindfulness program became — surprise, surprise — more mindful! They also found it easier to manage the impulse to eat, especially when not hungry. They also had significant decreases in weight, eating disinhibition, binge eating, depression, perceived stress, physical symptoms, negative mood and some of the biochemical markers of heart disease. Possibly the most important issue is that the weight was easier to manage but at the same time the people felt better mentally and emotionally. That's a win–win situation.

When mindfulness meditation is used as a core component of lifestyle management — say, for those at risk of heart disease — then it makes the process easier and more effective. The first to do this was American researcher Dr Dean Ornish, but other programs have confirmed the benefits he showed for heart disease and cancer. One of the main reasons that such programs produce benefits is that they help with healthier food choices and facilitating weight loss.[5, 6]

Eating disorders

Eating disorders are becoming increasingly common and are appearing in younger and younger age groups. There are many reasons for this, including pictures of unrealistic body images being presented to young people as normal or desirable, a body-focused culture, developing poor and irregular dietary patterns and a rising rate of mental health problems in the young.

The two main eating disorders are anorexia nervosa (a tendency to eat too little to the point of dangerous levels of weight loss) and bulimia nervosa (a tendency to binge eat often with induced vomiting afterwards). These disorders are far more common in young women and adolescent girls than in young men and boys, although the rate among males is on the increase.

It has become apparent that people suffering from anorexia nervosa (AN) have a distorted image of their body and a morbid fear of putting on weight. This often leads to their eating too little, choosing an unbalanced and calorie-deficient diet and exercising to excess to burn calories. For women this often leads to amenorrhoea (periods ceasing). Soon the normal hunger cues get distorted or don't even register and, when eating, the stomach feels full with minimal food in it. What they see in the mirror and what registers in the brain are two different things. These attentional biases tend to also be associated with difficulties with emotion recognition and regulation.[7] A background of poor mental health makes a person more susceptible to AN, whereas anything that helps a person improve their mental health and helps with their attention and self-control, such as mindfulness, is likely to be beneficial for AN. There hasn't been a lot of research to date on mindfulness-based strategies for AN, but it is likely to prove to be a useful strategy when used in conjunction with specialist care and other therapies.

Bulimia nervosa (BN) and binge-eating disorder (BED) are more common than AN. BED is marked by difficulty in managing emotions, behaviour and physiological regulation of food intake and self-identity. Guilt and self-loathing are common and often mean that a person is very unlikely to speak about the problem, especially to those whose respect the person desires, such as close friends and family.

A review paper on mindfulness-based eating-awareness training (MB-EAT) for treatment of BED and related issues found that it helped in:

- controlling responses to varying emotional states;
- making conscious food choices;
- developing an awareness of hunger and satiety cues (when one has had enough); and
- cultivating self-acceptance.[8]

Evidence suggests that MB-EAT decreases binge-eating episodes, improves one's sense of self-control with regard to eating, and reduces depressive symptoms. An eight-week mindfulness program for university-age women with bulimia nervosa reported 'transformation from emotional and behavioral extremes, disembodiment, and self-loathing to the cultivation of an inner connection with themselves resulting in greater self-awareness, acceptance, and compassion.'[9] There was less emotional distress and improved abilities to manage stress.

This is what Kirsty applied to her problems and this is what she found: that mindfulness works is encouraging — how to apply it is the important thing.

Take-home tips for a mindful response to weight management and eating disorders

Regular mindfulness practice helps us to:
- Improve our emotional health and stress management.
- Get in touch with our bodies and what they need.
- Pay attention to the act and experience of eating.
- Slow down eating but increase savouring.
- Notice our attitudes and emotions around food.
- Learn to recognise and unhook our attention from unhelpful thoughts and emotions, particularly in relation to eating.
- Move on by unhooking our fixation on guilt and self-loathing when an apparent slip-up occurs.
- Make conscious food choices.
- Remember to enjoy food and eating — it's natural! We wouldn't be here long without it.

CHAPTER 13

Heart disease and stroke

Ken was 52 and had a full life, with his work and home life including a wife and three children aged between sixteen and 23. He worked hard as an executive but didn't enjoy his work and was noted to be on a short fuse most of the time. He also loved his food — the richer the better — loved his wine and loved putting his feet up after a busy day. He didn't smoke but he did carry some extra weight and had a family history of heart disease. Despite the exhortations of his wife Amanda, Ken didn't have the time to go to the doctor and didn't feel the need; not that he felt well, it's just that he didn't feel acutely unwell.

Well, one day Ken did suddenly feel acutely unwell. On Monday morning at 6.30 while lying in bed thinking about the week ahead, Ken felt some chest tightness, clamminess and nausea. Ken just waited for it to go away but the tightness turned into a strong pain. It had been going on for about 20 minutes before Amanda came into the bedroom after her morning walk and noticed Ken not looking good. She didn't hesitate to call the ambulance and have Ken taken straight to hospital. The doctors diagnosed a heart attack and he was admitted to coronary care for monitoring. Ken made a fair recovery and was home after ten days, with another couple of weeks off work. This was time enough to reflect on what he wanted to do next to avoid the same thing happening to him again.

The problem of heart disease and stroke

In simple terms, what we call cardiovascular disease (CVD), which leads to heart attacks and strokes, is a narrowing and eventual blockage of the blood vessels that lead to the heart and brain. If the blood supply gets blocked off to regions of these organs for long, then there is death of some of the cells in that region. This can lead to the heart failing or going into a chaotic rhythm (a heart attack), or to death of brain cells leading to paralysis or other loss of brain function (stroke). Bleeding into the brain can also cause strokes.

Our risk of CVD is affected by our genes, lifestyle and emotional state. The busy, tense life many of us lead, especially in developed countries, along with an affluent lifestyle of 'too much of a good thing' prime us for CVD, which explains why it is the most common cause of death in developed — affluent — countries. Nearly 30 per cent of people will die of heart disease and 15 per cent of stroke; they also cause major loss of quality of life. So let's look at what's behind all this and how mindfulness might help us. The first thing we need to appreciate is that the mind is a central player because it can affect us directly — by its effects on our genes and physiology — and also indirectly — because of how it impacts our lifestyle.

Stress and our genes

We discussed this to some extent in Chapter 4 but let's elaborate a little further here. Put simply, if we have a genetic disposition to CVD, then the way we deal with stress can have a significant effect on how strongly that genetic disposition expresses itself. This affects how rapidly our genes age in response to our daily life and work-related stress, which predisposes us to CVD.[1] Links between our genetics, brain activity and emotional states such as depression are being established to try and help us understand how all these things are interrelated.[2] We can also have a genetic disposition to the risk factors for CVD like diabetes, high blood lipids (fats) and inflammation, and it looks as though emotional stress also makes it more likely that the genetic tendency for those risk factors is going to swing into action.[3] All of this just might get a little depressing, as if we weren't depressed enough already! The positive story, though, is that when we learn to switch off the unnecessary activation of the stress response through meditative types of techniques it doesn't just drop our blood pressure and heart rate, it also quietens the stress centre in the brain (the amygdala). Research at Harvard University has shown that this also 'turns down the volume' on the stress genes in our DNA.[4] This is all very useful. But wait, there's more!

Emotional stress and our cardiovascular system

In an average life our heart pumps 70 times a minute, 60 minutes an hour, 24 hours a day, 365 days a year for 80 years without missing a beat — well, maybe missing the occasional one. That's 2,943,360,000 (nearly 3 billion) beats in a lifetime. Makes you exhausted just thinking about it! If we're lucky our heart never asks for a day off. What a work ethic! What do we give it in return? We give our heart heartache, worry and stress and it doesn't enjoy it one little bit.

The upshot of all the stress we place on our mind is that it goes straight to our body and our heart bears the brunt of it. Activating the stress response while we're running from a tiger is fine — we need our heart to be thumping to get us out of the situation quickly, but long-term stress produces allostatic load, which we discussed in Chapter 4. That's the physiological wear and tear we place on our system in excess of what is needed. Activating our (stress) sympathetic nervous system unnecessarily leads to a range of changes that are not good for our heart, or for our whole cardiovascular system — or for anything else for that matter. To summarise, it increases heart rate, blood pressure, cholesterol, blood sugars and inflammation. These are all the kinds of risk factors that the GP checks for. The stress response also increases the stickiness of our blood and makes it more likely that our heart will go into an arrhythmia (an irregular heart rhythm). This, over years, adds up to a heart attack waiting to happen.

Stress isn't so much about the events that happen around us, but the way that we respond to those events. It has been found that those of us who respond to events with big surges in emotional and physiological activation (such as spikes in blood pressure or increases in adrenaline) have a greater risk of heart attack and stroke than those who experience the same events but are less reactive (those of us who stay cool).

This happens not just in anxiety, stress and depression but also in anger and hostility, which are also risk factors for heart attacks and strokes. Research has shown that males in their twenties who already show signs of cardiovascular disease were ten times as likely to have high levels of anger and hostility.[5] Suppressing anger doesn't help, nor does letting it rip. Learning what's behind the anger and not getting taken in by it does help.

An acute major stress (for example, extreme emotional or physical exertion) can trigger a heart attack. Just to illustrate, we know that in the two days following an earthquake there is a large spike in the number of heart attacks. Even more of a concern was a study on Germans done during the FIFA World Cup in Germany in 2006.[6] The researchers found that on football days the number of major cardiac events increased by 326 per cent in men and 182 per cent in women, compared to non-football days. Take a lot of care then over which football team you support and how mindfully you support it! If you're watching a close game use mindfulness to develop the mental flexibility you need to switch teams whenever you need to. We also know that more heart attacks and strokes occur among the working population on Monday mornings close to the time of waking than at any other time of the week. So, all this shows us that acute stress matters, but it's the long-term effect of our emotional health that predisposes us to being at risk in the first place.

That's the bad news. The good news is that all of these effects are reversible if we learn how to recognise and switch off the unnecessary activation of the stress response and to improve our mental health.

Mindfulness, heart disease and stroke — the evidence and the benefits

A study on meditation looked at whether it had an effect on the level of blockage of the arteries to the brain and therefore the risk of stroke.[7] Interestingly, the researchers found that it had a significant and beneficial effect even without making any other changes to lifestyle risk factors. Anything, in fact, that improves our emotional health has a side effect of reducing our risk of cardiovascular events. It seems to roughly halve the chance of having further events in those who already have CVD. A review of the 23 studies on including psychological and social support in the management of heart disease clearly showed that this led to major reductions in disease progression and the number of deaths.[8] Those with no such support were 70 per cent more likely to die from their heart disease and 84 per cent were more likely to have a recurrence. If a drug did that we'd all take it!

Changing our lifestyle for the better

We will discuss this issue at length in Chapter 17 but it's also worth mentioning here. As we have mentioned, our state of mind has an indirect effect on our risk of developing CVD because of its impact on lifestyle. When we're not feeling so good about ourselves we're more likely to eat poorly and too much, smoke, consume alcohol and other harmful drugs, be sedentary and not have supportive relationships, all of which increase our risk of CVD. Therefore, when we improve our state of mind we are better able to make healthy changes in all these areas.

This is one of the reasons why highly regarded researchers like Dean Ornish incorporate meditation into their cardiac rehabilitation programs. He said that if we don't get the stress–mind (and the social support) bit right we won't be able to make and maintain the other lifestyle changes needed to reverse heart disease. His research in *The Lancet* and the *Journal of the American Medical Association* was the first to demonstrate that the body can reverse heart disease, given the right conditions.[9] Follow-up over five years showed that patients with heart disease who had the usual care alone compared to usual care plus the Ornish program were two-and-a-half times as likely to have further heart attacks, need cardiac surgery or die from their heart disease.[10] The program also demonstrated massive improvements in quality of life and huge cost savings compared to usual care. We think that's what you call a win–win situation.

Neuroplasticity

We discussed the science of neuroplasticity in Chapter 4, but basically it means that our brain can adapt depending on our experiences and how we train it.

An interesting new area being investigated that involves the mind and focused attention has to do with rehabilitation after stroke. Strokes commonly affect an area of a person's brain that controls the movement of the leg and/or arm of one or other side of their body. Rehabilitation such as physiotherapy is aimed at helping a person get some level of function back into their affected limb. A series of studies have shown that if a stroke-affected person has their physiotherapy supplemented by 'mental practice' they regain more function and recover more quickly compared to those who don't.[11] Mental practice (in this study this was for 30 minutes three times a week) is when a person focuses their attention on mentally doing the movements and exercises they can't yet physically do. What seems to be happening here is that thinking about the exercises actually stimulates people's brains to make new connections in the injured regions or to find a way around their injury. The full therapeutic and human potential of this process has hardly even begun to be explored. This phenomenon might be similar to the performance benefits that sportspeople get when they mentally go through the actions they need to perform before they perform them.

A lot of people who have not suffered strokes, such as couch potatoes, will be immediately thinking of all the potential exercise they now don't have to physically do, and they can save on gym fees too!

Coping with CVD

There are no absolute insurance policies against getting CVD. We can, however, reduce our risk of suffering CVD by improving our lifestyle and mental health. But if we do get an illness, then how we cope with it is the next most important thing. Applying the strategies discussed in the chapters on lifestyle, anxiety and depression will go a long way to improving our wellbeing, even in the presence of CVD. This is confirmed by studies on people with heart disease — showing that mindfulness significantly improves quality of life and coping.[12]

Ken had lots of reasons to have a heart attack, and now he has lots of reasons to make some healthy changes to his life. Ken decided to stay with his current work but to try to improve his attitude to it and reduce his irritability. If this didn't work he was comfortable with looking for a new and less demanding career. He found a six-week mindfulness course at a local venue and got into it. Ken also started to make time for exercise in the form of walking a new puppy. This really was as much an exercise in mindfulness as anything else because the puppy was a great mindfulness teacher by spreading unconditional love everywhere he went and seeming not to have too many hang-ups about the past or future. Ken also started to improve his diet. Mindfulness was helpful here also by minimising the trauma associated with eating more fruit and salads and eating fewer pies and burgers.

Take-home tips for a mindful response to cardiovascular disease

Not so helpful
- Catastrophise about work or other issues in daily life — especially early on a Monday morning!

Helpful
- Learn to manage stress and reduce reactivity to life events.
- Learn how to manage anger better, without suppression.
- Use mindfulness as a way of bringing about healthy lifestyle change.
- Choose our football team very carefully.
- Have regular check-ups with a doctor who has a holistic approach to the prevention and management of chronic illnesses.
- Know the early signs of heart attacks and strokes, and practise mindfulness meditation if we are having one, but do it in the back of an ambulance on the way to hospital!

CHAPTER 14

Cancer

Mario was 58. He owned a pizza shop and probably ate more pizzas than he should have. He particularly loved the salami, the cheese, the olives and the anchovies. He didn't keep himself very fit and carried a significant number of those pizzas around his midriff. One day Mario saw some of the annual promotional activities urging men to go to their doctor and have a check-up for prostate cancer, and thought at his age it was probably about time he had such a check, particularly in light of the fact that Rosa, his wife, had been on his back to do this since he turned 50. Well, Mario had the physical examination and PSA test (of levels of a biological marker specific to prostate cancer), which came back high. A biopsy was organised, which confirmed that he had early prostate cancer.

Now Mario had to decide what to do: to have the surgical and drug treatments that were being recommended, which had their risks; to watch and wait and see which way his tests went in the future; to change his lifestyle; or to do nothing. Mario's son gathered some reading material for him from the web to help him make his choice. Thankfully, his GP was open to questions and helped Mario and Rosa to sift the wheat from the chaff as far as the quality of the information he had been given. Mario was generally of a cheery disposition, but he felt down like he never had before. A friend of his who had had cancer some years earlier called and recommended that Mario attend a lifestyle-based support group that he had found helpful in his recovery. He could do this while he made his other decisions about what to do next.

The thought of actually being able to do something himself was enormously empowering for Mario — he felt a little more in control again. Mario signed up for a live-in self-help program to be followed up with a twelve-week support group once home again.

The problem of cancer

As our community ages and our lifestyles become less healthy, we are seeing an increasing incidence of cancer. Skin cancer is very common (largely due to sunburn and excessive sun exposure in pale-skinned people), but fortunately most cases are not life-threatening, although melanoma is more aggressive. The most common cancer among men is prostate cancer, and the most common among women is breast cancer, with bowel and lung (most commonly due to smoking) cancers also very common. Virtually any organ or tissue in the body is a potential site for cancer.

A cancer is basically a group of cells that rapidly divide and spread in a way that doesn't recognise the normal checks and balances that the body places on dividing cells. It's when a cancer enlarges and starts to invade and destroy other healthy organs and consume more and more of the body's resources that it becomes life-threatening. Some cancers are of very low-level malignancy, meaning that they are unlikely to spread far or early and are therefore unlikely to cause death, whereas others are much more aggressive. A cancer that's hard to find can be quite advanced by the time it's picked up, either by examination or on screening tests. GPs are generally well placed to advise about what sorts of cancer screening would be useful, and if you ever have any symptoms such as sudden inexplicable changes in your body, or questions of concern, it would be good to speak to your doctor.

Many things contribute to cancer. We can have a genetic disposition to a particular type — depending on our family history — so genetics play a part. But it's our lifestyle and our environment that really determine if our risk goes up or down. The way that our lifestyle and environment affect genetics is the important and emerging field of science called epigenetics, which we explore in Chapter 6. Eating a poor-quality diet, consuming excess calories and/or alcohol, being inactive, obesity, exposure to toxins such as tobacco smoke, poor mental health and excess radiation (from the sun or from high-voltage powerlines) are just some of the risk factors for cancer.

Mario's case illustrates some important issues around the management of cancer, many of which are important from a mindfulness perspective. These include improving mental health, coping, lifestyle change and the direct physical benefits of undertaking mindfulness. Although the studies mentioned below are based largely on breast and prostate cancer, there's no reason to believe that the benefits found here wouldn't apply to other forms of cancer.

Lifestyle change

In Chapter 17 we deal with some of the details and how-tos of using mindfulness for lifestyle change, but there are a few points to make here. Firstly, lifestyle matters for cancer — a lot! This is both in terms of getting it in the first place and the progression of the cancer after we get it. For example, the World Cancer Research Fund in the United Kingdom makes the following lifestyle recommendations for the prevention of cancer.[1]

1. Be as lean as possible without becoming underweight.
2. Be physically active for at least 30 minutes every day.
3. Calorie restriction: avoid sweet drinks and limit energy-dense foods, particularly processed foods high in added sugar, low in fibre or high in fat.
4. Eat more of a variety of vegetables, fruits, whole grains and pulses such as beans.
5. Limit red meat, for example, beef, pork and lamb (maximum of 500 grams per week) and avoid processed meat.
6. Limit alcoholic drinks to two for men and one for women a day.
7. Limit consumption of salty foods and food processed with salt.

A series of studies by renowned American researcher Dean Ornish and his team have revealed the importance of healthy lifestyle change after the time of cancer diagnosis. He had already demonstrated that healthy lifestyle change helps reverse the progression of heart disease, but his original study on cancer was for men with early prostate cancer (biopsy positive and raised PSA) who chose not to have treatment (the watch-and-wait option). That's not unreasonable for prostate cancer because many of these are very slow-growing and will never become a major threat. In such an instance a man would be monitored regularly and if the cancer markers go up then he would be advised to have the surgical and other treatments. In Ornish's study, 92 men were randomly allocated to either the lifestyle change (experimental) group or the usual treatment (control) group with no advice to change lifestyle.[2] (It's a little bewildering and concerning that most cancer patients are still not advised, and sometimes are misadvised, about the importance of lifestyle change for cancer.) The Ornish lifestyle intervention was:

1. Vegan diet: fruits, vegetables, whole grains, legumes and soy; 10 per cent calories from fat (low in saturated or animal fats); supplemented by soy (tofu with plentiful phyto-oestrogens), fish oil (3 grams daily — a good source of omega-3 fatty acids) and antioxidants (vitamin E: 400IU daily), selenium (200 mcg daily) and vitamin C (2 grams daily).

2. Exercise: walking for 30 minutes six times weekly.

3. Stress management including gentle yoga, meditation, breathing and progressive muscle relaxation.

4. One-hour support group weekly.

The level of lifestyle change for the patients already with cancer is probably more rigorous than would be generally recommended for preventing cancer. Ornish emphasised the importance of the meditation and stress-management components of the program, because to him it was central in being able to make and maintain the other necessary lifestyle changes. This is also because making lifestyle changes can be stressful in itself, at least in the initial stages until the benefits start to kick in, so mindfulness will be very helpful in staying focused and on track in these early stages. It's hard to make effective lifestyle change without managing our mental health better.

What Ornish and his team found over the following two years was very interesting. The PSA readings and other cancer markers for the lifestyle group, particularly for those who complied strongly with the program, were tracking down, whereas those for the group that did the usual thing — no lifestyle change — were tracking up, on average. The more lifestyle change, the better the outcome. After two years, 27 per cent of patients in the control group have gone on to require cancer treatment because of progression of their cancers, whereas only 5 per cent of patients in the lifestyle group have gone on to require cancer treatment because of progression.[3] Even more interesting was the effect of the lifestyle change on the genetics of prostate cancer. In the lifestyle group the prostate cancer genes were being down-regulated or switched off.[4] Furthermore, genetic damage to telomeres (see Chapters 4 and 6) is associated with a greater risk of cancer. These telomeres are repaired by the enzyme called telomerase, and comprehensive lifestyle change in the Ornish program was associated with increased telomerase activity and genetic repair.[5]

Nobel Prize-winning Australian researcher Elizabeth Blackburn and her team have been working on the cancer and lifestyle research program, along with Dean Ornish. If their positive outcomes were drug-producing they would have garnered a massive amount of publicity, and it would be prescribed instantly — but there's a strange lack of interest in such simple, commonsense therapies from the greater part of the cancer establishment. Maybe this is because you can't patent lifestyle improvement.

Now, this isn't a chapter purely about lifestyle and cancer, but it's worth emphasising how much it matters and why mindfulness will help us make the conscious and informed changes we may need to. More lifestyle research has gone into breast cancer than any other, and here are some of the findings from studies reported in the world's leading cancer journals. Women in the highest quarter of intake of vegetables and fruit had a 43 per cent reduction in risk of recurrence of breast cancer over five years compared to women in the lowest quarter of fruit and vegetable intake.[6] A high intake of phyto-oestrogens reduced the risk for breast cancer recurrence by 32 per cent.[7] High soy intake reduced death rates by 29 per cent.[8] A study on 2437 women with breast cancer found that a low-fat diet (particularly saturated or animal fats) was associated with a 24 per cent reduction in recurrence and a 19 per cent improvement in survival after five years.[9]

Exercise matters too. More than 30 studies have shown a protective relationship between physical activity and colon-cancer mortality.[10, 11] The reduction of bowel cancer risk is around 50 per cent. A large-scale Norwegian study in the *International Journal of Cancer* showed a 30 per cent reduction in the risk of breast cancer in women who exercise regularly, particularly in those aged under 45.[12] This is confirmed in a recent analysis of the Nurses' Health Study.[13]

What about the effect of exercising after the time of diagnosis? A study on 2987 women with stage 1–3 breast cancer followed them for up to 18 years and found that the risk of death from breast cancer halved for those women who engaged in exercise roughly the equivalent of walking 3 to 5 hours per week.[14] This was confirmed in another study over a nine-year follow-up on women with breast cancer: regular exercise was associated with a 44 per cent reduction in death rates.[15] A study on 47,620 men followed them for more than 14 years and found that approximately 3000 had developed prostate cancer over that time. In men older than 65, the risk of getting advanced prostate cancer was a third less if they exercised regularly.[16] Another study followed 526 patients with bowel (colorectal) cancer for over 5 years and found that the risk of death was halved in those with stage 2 and 3 bowel cancer if they exercised regularly.[17] And the side effects are good. If exercise was a cancer drug and you had cancer, would you take it?

Mental health and coping

Does stress 'cause' cancer? Yes and no, depending on how you measure stress and on the person experiencing it. Again, more research by far has been done on breast cancer than on any other malignancy. A large review of studies in the area came up with the following conclusion about whether 'stressful life events' and primary breast cancer incidence are associated. Between 1982 and 2007, 618 studies looked at the topic, and most weren't of sufficient detail in themselves to provide an accurate answer. The ones that were of good quality found that things like widowhood and divorce were not associated with an increased risk. They also found that the self-rated intensity and frequency of stress was associated with a 73 per cent increased risk of developing breast cancer over the following few years.[18] Why the conflicting results? Well, it may all have to do with perception. A researcher may assume that an event is stressful but that may not be how another person, such as a study participant, sees it. Is divorce inherently stressful? Well, for many it is but for others it may be a blessed relief. So, one wouldn't expect there to be a strong relationship between divorce and cancer. But if a person reports that they have experienced ongoing and stressful events in their life then they do seem to be at greater risk, because of all those changes discussed in Chapters 4 and 6.

Depression when severe and prolonged (lasting more than six years) looks to be an even more significant risk factor for cancer because it nearly doubles the risk, independently of all the other risk factors the researchers controlled for.[19] That's almost worth getting depressed over but, optimistically, if the same case holds for cancer as for heart disease, then improving our mental health through psychological strategies such as mindfulness can reduce the increased risk. That's why effective cancer-support programs that improve mental health, coping and quality of life have a happy side effect — of increasing survival — whereas ineffective ones don't. All of the effective programs had some sort of meditative practice as an essential part of them, which makes sense when people are trying to deal with such challenging emotions.

Mindfulness and cancer — the evidence

Mindfulness programs specifically for cancer patients clearly improve depression, anxiety, distress and the ability to cope.[20] [21] To date there are no studies that have looked at whether mindfulness therapy by itself improves chances of cancer survival, although some have looked at factors that do point to a better prognosis. For example, a twelve-month study on the effects of mindfulness-based stress reduction (MBSR) on quality of life, stress, mood and endocrine (hormone), immune and autonomic (stress) measures for breast- and prostate-cancer patients showed that the enhanced mental and emotional wellbeing was accompanied by reductions in inflammation, cortisol and stress reactivity.[22] All of these are good prognostic signs for cancer patients. Another study found that improvements in emotional wellbeing through mindfulness were associated with reductions in inflammation, making it more difficult for cancer cells to multiply and spread.[23] There were also improvements in the activity of Natural Killer Cells, which are our immune cells that go around gobbling up cancer cells when they see them. As we mentioned above, the studies that have shown longer survival and included mindfulness-type skills have all included a whole lot of other things, so it would be difficult to say from that research how much mindfulness contributed to the survival benefit and how much other things did.

Mindfulness and cancer — the physical benefits

We have already discussed some of the physical benefits of mindfulness for cancer treatment in this chapter, and we detailed others in Chapters 4 and 6, so we won't go into them in great depth here, other than to summarise. Mindfulness-based therapy leads to:

- reduced inflammation,
- improved immunity,
- reduced cortisol,
- increased melatonin,
- reduced metabolic syndrome,
- improved genetic repair and fewer genetic mutations,
- slower genetic ageing, and
- better pain and symptom management (see Chapter 11).

Living mindfully with cancer

We outlined mindfulness-based principles for managing stress, anxiety and depression in Chapters 6, 7 and 8, so we won't repeat them here — but there is something worth adding in this chapter. Basically none of us knows how long we have to live, even if we fool ourselves into thinking we do. The big question is whether we are really living — consciously and in the present moment — or just going through the motions, either distracted by the busyness of life or living under a cloud of concerns about the future or recriminations, regrets and ruminations about the past. Is a longer life really a gift if we're not mentally there to appreciate it? It's not just the preoccupation about life expectancy that is an issue, but the anticipation related to the illness, symptoms, pain or treatment side effects that can really take the edge off living, even if we're not experiencing any of those things at the moment. Much better to save our attention, resources, time and energy for dealing with the things that are going on, rather than wasting them on dealing with an endless stream of what-ifs and maybes.

Whether we die one day from cancer, or something else, death is probably the ultimate test in acceptance and letting go, and according to some wisdom traditions at least, we can't be truly at peace unless we accept our mortality, because all fear is the fear of letting go of something that we don't want to let go of. The principles of letting go of our fear of death are no different to the principles of letting go of anything else; it's just that the bar is higher.

Mario went to the cancer support group. He never saw himself as being one to sit in a circle and discuss emotions, nor to learn meditation, but he was coming to grips with it. Pretty soon he kind of liked 'doing nothing' for two 30-minute periods a day. In fact, any time Rosa asked him to do something at home he protested that it was time to meditate, but she was on to him! Mario and Rosa actually enjoyed each other's company much more now. They noticed that although they always used to talk, often quite loudly, they didn't tend to listen. Making the changes to his diet was pretty hard initially and when he had a pizza these days it was one of those ones with lots of vegies lightly cooked in olive oil and with some greens and salmon. One of the greatest benefits, however, was that now he could cope far better when his beloved soccer club — AC Milan — lost a big match. The trauma of another close call in the UEFA Cup had once been more than he could bear.

A take-home tip for a mindful response to cancer

For dealing with cancer, probably 40–60 minutes of mindfulness practice a day (in one or two sittings) will be useful as a means of coming back to the present — no matter how many times our mind wants to go somewhere else. Even when we need to plan for the future we can only do that from the present moment.

CHAPTER 15

Dementia

Alice was a 73-year-old woman who lived alone and was worried about her memory, which she said had always been poor. Alice was worried about her risk of developing dementia and asked whether there was anything she could do to reduce this risk, and whether taking a course in mindfulness would help. When asked about her lifestyle and day-to-day life, Alice said that since her husband died three years earlier she spent much of her time watching television, had few hobbies other than buying her weekly lottery tickets, went outdoors irregularly, exercised little and ate a diet of largely processed foods. As well as recommending a check-up with her GP, it was suggested that there was much she could do to reduce her risk of developing dementia and also heart disease, because the lifestyle risk factors for these conditions are the same. She was also told that yes, mindfulness would help.

Alice was told that our brain is like our body — it needs exercise — practising paying attention and having things happening in her life that demand her attention would be helpful. Turning off the television, getting outside, engaging with people, rekindling her interest in dancing and foreign languages, and improving her diet would be a great start.

What is dementia?

Dementia is a broad term given to a group of related conditions that all lead to a loss of brain function including memory. The word dementia comes from the Latin word for 'without mind' (*de*: without; *mentia*: mind). The word dementia was first used in English with its modern meaning — described by the *Macquarie Dictionary* as 'impairment or loss of the mental powers' — in about 1812.[1]

The first symptom of most dementias is usually forgetfulness, and this usually worsens until there is a widespread loss of mental function. Don't worry unnecessarily, however, if you can't remember where you were living in 1987, or even 1997! Forgetfulness is common, especially as we age and especially when we're not really paying attention to what we're doing, but it can also be a symptom of a range of conditions including depression, or even just of tiredness or stress.

There are times in our life when it can seem like a blessing to be able to forget. Fortunately, however, there are ways of remembering what is good to remember, and of forgetting what is not so good to remember, without resorting to the unnatural and temporary forgetfulness of substance abuse, or the more permanent forgetfulness associated with the unnecessary loss of mental faculties.

The course of most dementias is slow, and they typically start off with very mild symptoms such as problems with short-term memory — forgetting where you left something or forgetting somebody's name. As they progress, dementias usually end up causing far more serious memory problems including with long-term memory, where people affected by the condition may forget once very well-known information such as where they live, or even who they are married to. Over time the condition generally also causes the loss of lower- as well as higher-order mental processes, including the control of physical processes.

Many people think of dementia as a mental problem that only affects old people, which isn't quite true. Almost two-thirds of people with dementia have Alzheimer's Disease (AD), and the next most common form is what is now called Vascular Dementia (VAD), which was previously called Multi

Infarct Dementia (MID). These dementias are certainly age-related, and the number of people who develop them roughly doubles with every five years of age over 60. However, even these forms of dementia aren't developed just by older people. In 1988 the well-known Australian journalist Claudia Wright was diagnosed with AD at the age of only 54, and there have even been (very rare) cases of people developing AD and also VAD in their thirties. Other forms of dementia include the increasingly common — or commonly diagnosed — Lewy Body Dementia, and the alcohol abuse rather than age-related Korsakoff's Syndrome. What characterises all dementias is their profound human cost for the person with the condition and also for those close to them.

As we have seen, there are many different types of dementia (see also the box below), but what's common to them all is progressive damage to the brain. Dementia and Alzheimer's Disease are often confused, in that there's a widespread idea that people have *either* dementia or Alzheimer's Disease. In fact, people can and often do have both, because AD *is* a dementia.

Types of dementia

- Alzheimer's Disease (AD), which is responsible for about two in every three dementia cases. The causes of AD still aren't fully known, but the condition is characterised by a gradual build-up of toxic substances in the brain known as senile plaque proteins, and tangles in the connections between brain cells. AD typically develops very slowly, with a gap of about ten years between onset and obvious symptoms.

- Vascular Dementia (VAD), which is responsible for about one in six dementia cases, and is often associated with Cardio Vascular Disease (CVD). This condition is similar to stroke and is also caused by minor blockages of blood supply to the brain. VAD results from a series of mini strokes that progressively damage the brain and cause dementia.

- Frontal-temporal lobe dementia, which is responsible for about one in ten dementia cases and is characterised by personality changes.

- Alcohol- and drug-related dementias, which are responsible for about one in 20 (and rising) dementia cases. These include Korsakoff's Syndrome, which is caused by a lack of thiamine in the brain and is often associated with alcoholism.
- Other types of dementia: these include Lewy Body Dementia, which combines aspects of AD and Parkinson's Disease. This is coming to be regarded as more common than was previously supposed, and typically involves a more rapid onset of symptoms than does AD. Symptoms include visual hallucinations.

The problem of dementia

Dementia is an enormous and growing global health problem. In dollar terms alone the cost in the United States is close to $100 billion a year, and in Australia over $6 billion a year — in lost economic production and health care. Dementia, however, costs far more than dollars, and dramatically affects the lives of the many millions of people who have to live with one of its many forms, or to live with it through an affected family member or friend. One of the most difficult things about dealing with dementia is that it can seem like it isn't as well understood as many conditions are, and in many cases there seems to be no effective treatment or prevention.

Almost one person in ten over the age of 65 has some form of dementia, and more than one person in six over the age of 75 has it. There are over 3 million people who have some form of dementia in the United States, and in Australia there are over 250,000 afflicted people. As our population ages over the next 30 years these numbers are expected to more than double. Does this mean that we have a dementia epidemic? The short answer is that although there are far more people diagnosed with dementia now than there were 50 years ago, and their number is increasing dramatically, the prevalence of the disease is increasing, but not the incidence. This means that there are more people now who have dementia than there ever were, but the percentage of people in the population who develop the condition in any one year has remained constant.

The reason why there are so many more people with dementia now than there were in the past is that people are living longer today, and therefore have more opportunity to develop age-related conditions, such as dementia, and also some forms of cancer. There's even a theory that if we all lived long enough we will all eventually develop Alzheimer's Disease. If this is true then it might be an even stronger reason to avoid immortality than is the fact that the human nose keeps growing for as long as we live ... Whether or not the theory that we will all develop AD if we lived long enough is true, it is vital that we do what we can to mindfully avoid this modern plague and mindfully respond to it.

The causes of dementia

Risk factors for developing dementia are similar to the risks for developing heart disease. These include genetic predispositions for some forms of AD, but mainly these conditions aren't genetically determined. Dementia involves damage to the brain and therefore anything that destroys brain cells, including substance abuse, head injury and CVD can increase our likelihood of developing dementia. Just how much a head trauma will increase the risk of dementia isn't fully understood. Aluminium is thought to be a common cause of dementia, but the evidence for this isn't strong. Exposure to any heavy metals or environmental toxins may, however, indirectly contribute towards later development of dementia, by destroying brain cells. Chronic mental ill health including depression has also been shown to increase our chances of developing dementia.

There are also risk factors for dementia that fall more directly within our personal control than do genetic factors, head injuries and mental ill health. Apart from avoiding substance abuse and untreated mental illness, it's also important for us to avoid less obvious lifestyle choices that can increase our risk of developing dementia, including social isolation and passive leisure activities such as watching TV. A study published in *Neurology* in 2001 found that people who engage in passive leisure activities such as TV watching are nearly four times as likely to develop dementia over a 40-year period than people with active and attention engaging leisure activities.[2] For example, occupations that exercise the brain, such as being bilingual, also seem to delay the onset of AD by around five years compared to people who are mono-lingual.[3]

We are social and clever creatures (mostly!) and we need to follow up on our natural inclination to seek out social and mental stimulation. This will help us prevent dementia, and respond optimally to it if we do develop it, as well as to achieve our full potential. We can compare our brain to our muscles — including our heart — which may wither or at least not perform at their best if we don't use them enough. It's important then to follow the basic brain-health advice offered to anyone who would listen by the professor of geriatric medicine who ran the National Ageing Research Institute at North West Hospital, where one of us spent a decade working on developing an earlier diagnosis of dementia: 'Use it or lose it!' Long-term stress is an undesirable and potentially dangerous modern lifestyle factor that can dramatically increase our chances of developing many physical and mental problems, including dementia. The specific mechanism involved here is that stress causes the activation of stress hormones, which is fine if the stress is short-term — such as for the 2 minutes or so that it takes to escape from a tiger or an inconvenient ex-boyfriend or girlfriend. If we are stressed for longer periods, though — such as for two decades instead of 2 minutes — the long-term activation of stress hormones can accelerate age-associated brain-cell loss. We also know that learning to manage our stress better through techniques such as mindfulness decreases the levels of these stress hormones, and seems to protect our precious brain cells, particularly in the learning and memory centres. So why then do we so often maintain our stress and our stressed physiological state for so much longer than is natural and good for us? What do you *think*? In the words of the receptionist in the emergency spiritual ward in an ashram in Rishikesh with whom one of us chatted: 'You Westerners think thinking is solution! Thinking is problem!'

Why do some people get over a traumatic life event quickly and others develop post-traumatic stress disorder in which the causal event is just as real 20 years later than it was the day it happened? Some people keep on thinking about what happened, whereas some don't. This kind of distracted mental activity goes by many names. When it's associated with depression we call it rumination; when it's associated with anxiety we call it worry; when we're just distracted without knowing what by we call it daydreaming. An overall term is 'default' mental activity. Areas of young people's brains that are involved in all this distracted default mental activity are the same as the areas that are affected by AD in later life.[4] An interesting coincidence! Although the dots are still being joined by research it seems that this unmindful default mental activity flogs our brain cells, whereas mindfulness gives them rest and rejuvenation.[5]

Mindless and circling thoughts can wear you down so quickly that you develop an instant physical or mental affliction — such as an anxiety disorder — or they can wear you down so slowly that you eventually develop an extremely gradual affliction that you probably won't see as related to your stress — such as dementia. A study conducted at the University of California looked at data from over 180,000 Vietnam War veterans.[6] Almost twice as many of them who were diagnosed with post-traumatic stress disorder developed AD during a seven-year follow-up period than those without this diagnosis did.

The Transcendental Meditation wisdom tradition offers us a saying: 'What you give your attention to grows.' This means that if we give our attention to our circling thoughts about what we 'shoulda done' or 'coulda done' or 'gotta do', then we're nurturing and growing our stress. This is likely to make us sick in some way, and to increase our chances of developing or not best dealing with dementia. If, instead, we give our attention to what's actually happening — the reality of what's right in front of us, here and now — then we're nurturing and growing our ability to be mindful. This will be especially beneficial in the case of dementia, because healthy regulation of our attention will result in us stimulating and therefore nurturing and protecting our brain cells.

Treatment, prevention and management of dementia

There is currently no effective drug treatment for most forms of dementia, including AD. This is despite the huge incentive of a multi-billion-dollar bonanza for drug companies if they can develop a drug that can cure, or more realistically, slow down the neurodegenerative processes of dementias. There have been some promising drug treatment candidates, such as THC, which is a drug designed to help AD-affected brains manufacture acetylcholine, a neurotransmitter depleted by AD. Clinical trials in the 1990s showed that people taking this drug did better on tests of mental function after six months than did people given placebos (sugar pills). More objective researchers later showed, however, that these benefits disappeared after twelve months. The drug merely tapped the brake pedal in the progression of AD; it didn't change its destination.

So, given that there's no effective drug treatment for dementia, is there an effective prevention, or a reliable way of improving or at least managing its symptoms? The answer may lie in the link between lifestyle, attention and dementia. Doing anything that stimulates your brain by encouraging you to give mindful attention to what you're doing, rather than to mindlessly dwell on what you're not doing, will help you prevent dementia, and respond to it if you do develop it. Formal and informal education are great ways of stimulating our brain and avoiding dementia. There's a demonstrated association between length of formal education and likelihood of developing dementia, with better-educated people less likely to develop it.[7] There's also evidence that any form of ongoing stimulation of the brain, including informal education and mentally engaging leisure activities such as reading books, chess, gardening, doing crosswords and learning languages — especially if it is for at least six hours a week — can reduce our chances of developing dementia.[8]

There is strong evidence that a healthy lifestyle that includes appropriate exercise and diet (plenty of fruit, vegetables and omega-3 fatty acids), as well as environmental stimulation, and stress-reduction methods, reduces our chances of getting dementia. Exercise will not only be protective because of all its physical benefits, but also because we tend to be far more attentive and in the moment when we are exercising, and also afterwards. There is also evidence that certain healthy substances can be useful in reducing the risk of developing dementia — folic acid, Vitamins C, E, B, carotene, omega-3, and antioxidants, which have all been shown to reduce the effects of ageing and the likelihood of developing dementia. Developing a healthy lifestyle and avoiding stress are keys, then, to responding mindfully and successfully to dementia.

Mindfulness and dementia — the evidence

Anything done with attention, whether it's our favourite hobby or just really tasting our food, is an exercise in mindfulness. There's strong evidence that mindfulness treatment and practice improves wellbeing, reduces stress and may even slow the ageing process all the way from our heart to our brain and our genes. Early evidence suggests that mindfulness may reduce the risk of developing dementia, and reduce its ill effects, although longer term studies are needed to confirm this. The key to allowing mindfulness to lessen the potential life devastation of dementia is to live mindfully and to practise mindfulness daily. This process begins and ends with awareness. This means being aware that there's a link between our lifestyle and our likelihood of developing conditions such as dementia. We also need to be aware that there's a link between our level of awareness and our chances of developing dementia. If we tune out of our life potential by indulging our cravings for substance abuse or passive leisure activities then we're not living life with full awareness — we're not being mindful — of our full potential for health and happiness. A review in the *Postgraduate Medical Journal* commented that, 'A healthy life physically and mentally may be the best defence against the ageing brain.'[9]

In 1984 Harvard researcher Ellen Langer undertook a key pioneering study of the relationship between mindfulness, ageing and dementia, by investigating their relationship in a nursing home.[10] Dr Langer used a form of mindfulness therapy she called a 'mindful memory-enhancement procedure'. Her experiment showed that nursing-home residents given her mindfulness intervention were significantly more likely to be alive and healthy at follow-up than those who weren't given it. AD was interestingly described by Dr Langer as an attempt to adapt to an 'overly routinised' environment, and therefore one where people don't get much of a chance to pay full attention. It's almost like the environment was conditioning people into automatic pilot. AD may be an unfortunate but logical process of switching off our brain to help us cope with institutions or other forms of chronic boredom. Approximately two-thirds of nursing-home in-patients suffer from some form of dementia. This might be the cause of many of them being admitted, but it might also be the *result* of admission. People in such environments need activity, engagement and stimulation, not television, to maintain their cognitive capacity, let alone improve it.

Mindfulness and dementia — the benefits

As we have discussed, most forms of dementia are age-related, and therefore anything that we can do to age gracefully, mindfully and healthily will help. Mindfulness can increase the positive stimulation of our brain cells and reduce or even reverse the harmful effects on our brain of substance abuse, anxiety and boredom. These negative brain influences will all make our body, including its brain, age faster. The non-judgmental and highly focused state that mindfulness produces will slow down and possibly even reverse the ageing process, and can reduce and improve age-related conditions such as dementia. Mindfulness offers increased awareness combined with acceptance to people with and without dementia who are getting older, but not necessarily wiser. This fast track to wisdom can help us accept what we can't change, and change what we can't accept.

Alice has not developed dementia. We don't know if she will eventually develop it, but what we do know is that the mindful changes she has made to her life have greatly improved her chances of remaining dementia-free.

Take-home tips for a mindful response to dementia

Not so helpful

- Live unmindfully, drifting unconsciously through situations and conditions that we don't want to be in — always reacting (usually too late) — to things that have happened to us.

Helpful

- Start informally practising mindfulness by giving our full attention to everything we do. We can live our life so that we're always awake to its full possibilities. We can live fully consciously and in the current moment so that we are living our life, rather than our life living us.
- Start formally practising mindfulness. Mindfulness classes and programs are widely available.
- Engage in activities that will stimulate our brain and that will encourage us to be mindful by requiring our full attention. We can easily drift off to unmindful fairy land watching TV, but this is more difficult when we're hang-gliding! We can enrol in a course or start a stimulating hobby such as chess, reading, crosswords or philosophy.
- Stimulate our brain to be mindful via stimulating our heart, such as by opening up to people and the life-expanding opportunities they offer. We can join a club, volunteer, connect with the neighbours.
- Stimulate our brain to be mindful via our body, such as eating nutritious foods, getting outside and exercising.
- Get referred by a GP for a thorough mental-status examination such as at a memory clinic, if we think we might have dementia.

And finally, if you do have dementia or if you're close to somebody who has it:

- Get in touch with a local dementia-related support organisation.
- Patiently make peace — with others and with yourself.

CHAPTER 16

Sleep

Sally was a politician who didn't particularly like being a politician. The constant scrutiny of her political actions by the media and her political opponents made her feel stressed, and made it hard for her to sleep — which in turn made her feel more stressed. She eventually realised that her lack of sleep was starting to affect her job performance as well as her life performance, so she decided to make some lasting changes to her life.

To sleep or not to sleep?

Have you ever tossed and turned for much of the night, churning over everything that happened the day before, or anticipating everything that might or might not happen tomorrow? Have you ever managed to blow every problem under the sun out of proportion at 3 a.m.? Well, if you have, then you have experienced the singular joy of how unmindfulness impacts sleep. Poor old Macbeth had it bad, although it also took a few pretty unmindful decisions to put him in that situation in the first place:

> ... *the innocent sleep,*
> *Sleep that knits up the ravell'd sleeve of care,*
> *The death of each day's life, sore labour's bath,*
> *Balm of hurt minds, great nature's second course,*
> *Chief nourisher in life's feast.*

> Macbeth, *William Shakespeare*

Sleep is important. You've probably already realised that not getting enough of the stuff can lead to symptoms that can be as serious as those caused by not getting enough of our other basic physiological needs, such as food, water and laughter. Sleep is like many things that we often don't really value until we feel that we're not getting enough of them. Then, all of a sudden, we appreciate how important they are, and how they can make a big difference to our health and the quality of our life. Lack of sleep causes many physical and mental problems, and can lead to psychosis and even death. Sleep deprivation is even an effective form of torture. Lesser levels of sleep deprivation — often called insomnia — are also associated with health problems.

A decade-long research study of over 70,000 nurses in the United States produced a popular media headline: 'Too little sleep — or too much — may raise the risk of developing heart disease.' The study found that nurses who slept on average fewer than 5 hours a night were almost 40 per cent more likely to develop heart disease than were those who averaged 8 hours of sleep a night.[1] Medical science still doesn't fully understand why we need sleep and the dreams that it usually includes, but it seems that sleep gives us a vital mental, emotional and physical de-bugging and re-charging, which we need to realise our full mental, emotional and physical potential.

Most of us take sleep for granted, just as we take breathing and interacting with others for granted. That's as it should be because all of these things are natural, as well as good for us. Sometimes, however, our circumstances — and our thoughts about our circumstances — can get in the way of our natural ability to sleep. This can make our life a lot less peaceful and happy than it has the potential to be, and often we don't even realise that something has gone wrong, or how. Sometimes we just get into a habit of not sleeping and just take it to be normal.

Interruptions to our sleep can be short term, such as when we're studying late for an exam the next day, or even when we're getting married the next day. Interruptions to our sleep can also be longer term, such as when we have a new baby to look after, or a book deadline to meet, or both, or if we're working night shifts, or if we have chronic pain … We may also have noticed that the harder we try to get to sleep the worse we make the problem. It can be a vicious cycle. As with stress, short-term sleep problems usually aren't serious, but when they become long-term problems — habits — that's when we really need to do something to restore our natural balance. Firstly, we need to recognise that we have a sleep problem, and that this has a cause and a solution.

The problem of lack of sleep

Scientific studies have shown that most of us don't get enough sleep. These studies include a large one undertaken on American adolescents, which showed that 80 per cent of them don't get enough sleep — as recommended by the US National Sleep Foundation.[2] It has even been reported that people in our modern age sleep approximately an hour a night less than people did a century ago. This might simply be because our minds are more active and our bodies less active than they once were. Sleep deprivation can result in serious psychological and physical problems, and it's far more common than we might think it is.

We can be suffering from sleep deprivation even if we don't know we are. Waking up too early is a form of insomnia, as is waking up constantly, and just not enjoying good-quality deep sleep. Studies have shown that the sleep we get at the end of our sleep cycle is vital for achieving optimal mental alertness and memory performance, and this is something we can easily miss out on if we're constantly relying on alarm clocks, or are otherwise prioritising something other than enough sleep, like being online late at night. If we want to upset our body clock and the hormone melatonin that regulates it, then that's a pretty good way to do it.

The psychological symptoms of sleep deprivation include increased stress levels, concentration difficulties, memory problems, distractibility, irritability and lassitude. Lack of sleep is also strongly associated with an increased risk of depression.[3] The symptoms of sleep deprivation can resemble the symptoms of serious chronic physical conditions. Because it affects our immunity, physiology and hormones — such as melatonin — chronic and severe insomnia can greatly increase our chances of developing real and serious physical conditions such as heart attacks, strokes, high blood pressure, cancer, diabetes and obesity.

Lack of good-quality sleep also greatly increases our chance of having accidents. Studies have shown that driving while sleep deprived can be as dangerous as driving while drunk or drug-affected.[4] This suggests that there are thousands of road and other accident fatalities happening globally each year that are directly caused by fatigue. In 1979 a minor technical problem at a nuclear power plant in Three Mile Island, Pennsylvania, wasn't resolved because an operator was fatigued due to sleep deprivation; the situation then worsened until it turned into a major nuclear disaster. Hospital medical interns are often seriously sleep deprived and this dramatically increases their risk of making diagnostic and drug-prescription errors. Contrary to what many of us might think — that we 'get used to' sleep deprivation, even if we're shift workers or insomniacs — we don't.[5] We just get used to feeling sleep deprived until we don't notice it anymore.

When is inadequate sleep a problem? When we feel constantly tired, sleep at inappropriate times and when our lack of sleep affects our health or capacity to function.

Causes of insomnia

Insomnia afflicts almost one adult in three in the modern Western world, with a greater proportion of women and older adults affected.[6] The causes of insomnia are varied, and can include physical problems such as sleep apnea, chronic pain or larger psychological problems. Insomnia and short-term sleep deprivation, however, are mainly caused by stress or a temporary increase in demands on our time. We do ourselves a disservice if we don't look after ourselves — having too many stimulants such as coffee late in the day, or trashing our body clock with irregular hours, or sitting in front of bright lights (and computer screens) late at night, or not understanding a few principles of how sleep works. But the most important reason for our chronic inability to sleep properly — and the mental and physical problems that this can lead to — is going to bed with the agitated mind associated with stress. It's far better for us to go to bed with something much nicer than stress, such as a warm cup of tea, or a good book.

The basic cause of stress in general is our habit of getting so fascinated with the lifelong running soap opera playing out in our minds — the *daze of our lives* — that we forget that we're actually calm and peaceful beings, deep down.

Our mental soap operas are actually just our idea of reality that our minds are addicted to. This is mindlessness and it's not good for us.

Treatments for insomnia

There are treatments for insomnia that are based on classical conditioning. According to these approaches we should associate our bedroom with rest and not associate them with work, eating or entertainment. If we have trouble sleeping, we should either read with a low light or get up and go somewhere else and do something other than try to sleep until the next wave of sleep comes — this is so we don't associate our resting place with our restlessness. Trying to sleep before the wave has come — they come about every 60–75 minutes and last for around 10 minutes — is futile and frustrating. Chill out until it comes and when it comes, don't miss it. This principle can be taken further, to suggest that we don't populate our sleeping room with things that we don't associate with sleep, such as a TV. There are competing theories to this one, of course, which state that we should just stay in our bed and rest if we can't sleep, because prowling around our house to distract ourselves from our sleeplessness can just add to our problems, such as by increasing our power bill.

Cognitive behavioural therapies are based on the idea that it's the usual cognitive suspects — our negative, personal and catastrophic thoughts — that cause our sleeplessness: 'I can't sleep! I can't do anything! I'll probably develop a 40 per cent higher chance of heart disease by morning!' According to these therapies we need to re-program our thinking habits to cure our sleep problems.

There is also a drug option for treating insomnia. In the days before modern medicine, some particularly desperate or innovative parents gave their infants spoonfuls of gin to help them sleep. Medical science has progressed from such barbaric and ignorant practices to a point where it can now offer the sleepless a wide range of modern equivalents to gin, including the benzodiazepines, the most common family of sleep medications. A serious problem with relying on medications, or gin, to help you or your family sleep, however, is that their efficacy tends to wear off after a few weeks, and the sleep that they help induce is of a lower quality than natural sleep. They also can be addictive and have unwanted side effects including poor health, memory and performance, and accidents. In the long run they can be as bad as the problem they were prescribed to treat. There are other remedies for sleep problems, including melatonin and natural therapies, which may be a little safer, but what makes more sense is to get to the heart of the problem.

Mindfulness and insomnia

The mindful solution to the problem of being sleepless in Seattle, or anywhere else, is to respond mindfully to the mindless circular thinking that can cause insomnia. It's very easy for our habitual overactive, over-reactive, overwhelming mind to come up with a thought circus such as: 'The clock just chimed again! That probably means that it's about 3 a.m. and I have to catch my bus for work in only four hours. Even if I got to sleep right now I'll only get 3 hours' sleep at best before I have to get up and start getting ready and I don't particularly like the bus that I go to work on or the job that it takes me to and I'm sure I'd be happier if I stayed in bed, except I can't sleep! I'll undoubtedly therefore become psychotic as a result of my continual sleep deprivation and lose my job, which actually doesn't seem that bad now that I realise I'll soon be too psychotic to be able to do it or to get on the right bus!'

Familiar? W.S. Gilbert knew all about the mindless games that our insomniac minds like to confound their owners with, if we're not mindful enough to recognise what's happening and to realise that there's always a conscious alternative. Gilbert described his own recurrent bouts of insomnia in 1882 in the wonderful Gilbert and Sullivan light opera *Iolanthe*. In doing so he created an accurate and funny word picture of what millions of other people have experienced before and since. This song incidentally is meant to be sung fast and then ever faster:

> *When you're lying awake with a dismal headache, and repose is taboo'd by anxiety, I conceive you may use any language you choose to indulge in, without impropriety; For your brain is on fire — the bedclothes conspire of usual slumber to plunder you: First your counterpane goes, and uncovers your toes, and your sheet slips demurely*

from under you; Then the blanketing tickles — you feel like mixed pickles — so terribly sharp is the pricking, And you're hot, and you're cross, and you tumble and toss till there's nothing 'twixt you and the ticking.

Then the bedclothes all creep to the ground in a heap, and you pick 'em all up in a tangle; Next your pillow resigns and politely declines to remain at its usual angle! Well, you get some repose in the form of a doze, with hot eyeballs and head ever aching. But your slumbering teems with such horrible dreams that you'd very much better be waking...

A mindful response rather than a mindless reaction to not being able to go to sleep can put the punctuation back into our thinking. We can recognise that we're responding to what our mind sees as terrible problems mindlessly, when we lose our natural mental punctuation — the little pauses or moments of silence that make our sentences and life reasonable rather than desperate.

Mindfulness and sleep — the evidence

Mindfulness is a highly useful way of preventing and treating sleep deprivation because it simultaneously increases our awareness and our acceptance of what we're aware of. This very effectively reduces the circling thoughts that can interfere with our sleeping and also our waking life, and helps us to get restorative rest even when we're not sleeping.

Recent studies have demonstrated the value of mindfulness as a treatment for insomnia. A randomised control study in Minneapolis showed that mindfulness is clearly effective for improving sleep levels of people diagnosed with clinical insomnia.[7] A study in Chicago investigated mindfulness within the broader context of its being a promising new approach to emotion regulation and stress reduction, that has several important health benefits.[8] The results of this study showed that mindfulness is very effective at helping people with chronic insomnia to work successfully with their nocturnal symptoms and their waking consequences. Another study showed that the benefits of mindfulness for helping the sleepless sleep are maintained at twelve-month follow-up.[9]

Mindfulness and sleep — the benefits

The key to achieving a mindful response to sleep problems is to just be aware of our sleeplessness: to observe it without reacting to it; to accept it without comment or judgment. This will take practice because it is highly likely that we are well practised in being reactive and angry when we don't sleep, which only activates our stress system, making the whole situation worse. We could even say that it *isn't* our inability to sleep that causes the psychological and physical problems that sleep deprivation can lead to, but that the real problem is our *worry* about our inability to sleep. It may seem like a paradox, but mindfulness can help us to stop trying to go to sleep, which will make it easier for it to come when it's ready to come.

If we practise mindfulness during the day — if we're really attentive to the reality in front of our nose — then chances are that we will naturally also be mindful at night, and that we will therefore sleep better. If we practise rumination or worry during the day, then we shouldn't be surprised to see it pop up at night. It's also highly likely that if we develop greater mindfulness, then our life priorities will change and this will also help us sleep. As we become increasingly mindful we're increasingly likely to prioritise peace, live a more balanced and regular lifestyle and to therefore enjoy more of it — right now, right here. This will work much better for us than will prioritising what gets in the way of peace, such as irrelevant ideas about how we're going in life or in bed, or all the things we think we need to be happy, or about how we can improve things that don't need improving, such as our natural ability to fall asleep.

We can practise mindfulness meditation on going to bed. We can also practise it at night when we don't sleep or, if we're really getting frustrated, get up and give our attention to something restful until the next sleep wave comes.

If our mind isn't content with making us mindless and exhausted all day and wants to force us into night shifts as well — we shouldn't fight it. We should just be gently aware of what our mind is trying to do *to* us, not *for* us, and not get caught up in its drama. We should just be gently aware of the thoughts in our mind, and not react to them. We should just be gently aware of the actual sensations in our body as we lie in bed. This will connect us with the reality of the present, and short circuit the unreality of our mindless day and nightmares. Above all, we should realise that we don't only get rest from sleep; we can also get it by resting our minds while we are awake.

It seemed to Sally that the worse her sleeplessness became the less time she had to find a solution. She eventually asked one of the authors if he knew of anything that might help her sleep better and be less stressed. He gave her a simple mindfulness exercise to practise when lying in her bed late at night or early in the morning, thinking about not sleeping. The practice consists of concentrating for about half a minute on each of our five senses, one by one, and if any thoughts come just letting them come, and go, returning our attention to whichever sense we were attending to. This worked and Sally now sleeps well enough to do her new job well and happily.

Take-to-bed tips for a mindful response to sleep disturbance

Not so helpful

- Worry if we can't sleep, or can't get to sleep as quickly as we want to.
- Engage in unrestful activities such as TV watching or snacking where we sleep because this will condition our mind to associate our resting place with restlessness.
- Get so engrossed in some meaningless activity that we miss our sleep train.

Helpful

- Be mindful enough of our body and its needs to go to bed when we feel tired. We have periodic rhythms of sleepiness that we need to respond to rather than ignore.
- Recognise if we have a sleep problem, and realise that this problem has a cause and a solution.
- Practise a simple mindfulness exercise before going to sleep, such as being non-judgmentally aware of each of our senses for half a minute or so each.
- Practise mindfulness as much as possible during the day, so that by the time we get to bed we will have turned our practice into perfection, even if only slightly more successfully than we did yesterday.
- Consider the benefits of attending classes in mindfulness.
- Don't worry about worry. If we're tired enough we will eventually sleep. Most insomniacs sleep a lot better and longer than they think they do.
- Be patient and gentle with ourselves. Effective strategies will take four to six weeks to work deeply into our system.
- Seek help from a suitably trained health professional if we feel we need it.

PART 3

MINDFULNESS AND PERSONAL DEVELOPMENT

CHAPTER 17

Lifestyle enhancement

Have you found it as difficult to make lifestyle change as the authors have? Have you ever known that something wasn't good for you but done it anyway? Have you ever known something was good for you but used every means available to avoid doing it? Is there anything more annoying than when your doctor just tells you to change your life for the better, as if there were nothing to it, but neglects to give a little guidance as to how to put those little pearls of wisdom into effect?

We have discussed the importance of lifestyle and health in a number of chapters including the ones on heart disease, cancer and mental health. We've also mentioned studies such as those by Dean Ornish and his team, who used meditation as a cornerstone to helping heart disease and cancer patients reverse their conditions through making healthy lifestyle change.[1,2] The more lifestyle change they made the better was their outcome. Well, this chapter will explore the 'how to' of lifestyle change through mindfulness.

Motivation

Earlier in the book, we referred to a quote from Israeli politician and diplomat Abba Eban: 'History teaches us that men and nations behave wisely once they have exhausted all other alternatives.'

We can relate to that. As far as health is concerned, it's amazing what lengths we go to in order to make ourselves ill or avoid getting well by following an unhealthy lifestyle — and all in the name of increasing our happiness, which is the strangest thing. Why is this so? What's going on?

As we've discussed previously, there are three main aspects of our psyche vying for control, and they each have quite different criteria to decide what's good or not good. The higher or executive centre (which works through the prefrontal cortex of the brain) judges according to what's reasonable, healthy or moderate. It's the boring bit of our brain but it's the bit trying to keep us healthy, happy and functioning well. It's also the bit of our brain that other animals don't have, or at least only in a rudimentary form. Then there's the middle part (related to the limbic system), which has to do with emotions, including courage, determination or resolution. That's the part of our brain that we want working for us when we want to have the 'courage of our convictions', or when we need to deal with a challenge. Then there's the lower centre (sometimes called the mesolimbic reward system) — the one we share with animals from sloths to slugs — that is the appetite centre. It decides what's good or not so good on the basis of what's pleasurable or not. Things that are necessary for our survival tend to be pleasurable — just to give us a bit more motivation to do them — but if the little pleasure centre rules without a little guidance from the higher centre, then we wind up with pain, illness and unhappiness. The pleasure of eating, for example, will be followed by the pain of indigestion when we overindulge.

Over the long term most of the things that kill us in developed or wealthy countries — such as obesity, diabetes, heart disease, alcohol abuse and cancer — are the diseases related to lifestyle and excess, and the avoidance of the effort required to moderate our habits. The joy of sex is followed by the discomfort and embarrassment of gonorrhoea, herpes or chlamydia when we become a little too joyful with a few too many people. The pleasures of wealth can easily give way to greed, excess and crime if we mistakenly think it will buy us happiness. Pleasure is pleasant, but it has a sting in its tail for the unwary.

There are very few people on the planet who can take the moral high ground in all this because we all know what the internal battle feels like. But if you're so lucky as to be a paragon of virtue in relation to living healthily all the time, then be a shining example to all who come before you, and don't nag or brag! If, on the other hand, you've slipped up now and then, then don't worry about being an example, be a warning instead!

The first big challenge in making healthy lifestyle change is to be aware of what's motivating us and what's sabotaging us. Mostly this goes on in the dark, meaning that we're unconscious of it because we're not good at paying attention. All we are conscious of when we're not very conscious is a sense of feeling conflicted or dragged in two directions at once. The things that motivate us tend to be habitual and are therefore not often consciously examined. We're often hardly even aware of why we do the things we do. To see what's going on in the dark we need a light; mindfulness is the way to turn on the light. When we turn the lights up a little we might find, for example, a little kid stomping their feet in the corner of our mind demanding, 'I want it and I want it now!' With some luck there's an adult somewhere in there too saying, 'Not just now, dear. Maybe later.'

Children, by the way, don't have an executive centre fully wired up until they're adults, so they rely on the adults to provide that for them. Women wire it in late adolescence and men a bit later than that — hence the problems with impulse control that some of us males might have observed or experienced in the past.

The child in us, driven by desire, doesn't go away as we age, it just gets sneakier. It screams, charms, cajoles, threatens, justifies and has even been known to lie in order to get its way. If we're not awake, we'll be taken in by it. We recognise it more easily and objectively once we can stand back from our mind and all its chatter. Don't worry, it will pop up during meditation practice or as we go about our day-to-day life. 'I want a coffee!' 'I want lunch!' 'I don't want to …!' 'I'm tired!' If we really pay attention we might notice that we aren't really hungry but are bored, or we don't really need a coffee, or we're not really that tired. Much of it is about avoiding what we need to do. Welcome the opportunity to practise not reacting to or getting involved with it when it arises. If we consistently don't get involved with our unnecessary internal promptings, then they will start to quieten. If we keep gratifying them in order to shut them up, then they will get more vocal. How we respond will get hard-wired into our brain, for better or for worse.

So, to change our life for the better we need to be motivated. The core principles of motivation include that the motivation must come from ourselves, not from someone else no matter how well-meaning. If we're doing it for someone else, but don't really see why, then the old behaviour will revert as soon as we aren't under scrutiny or if a little adversity comes along.

To be motivated we have to consciously examine why we need to make the change we need. What are the costs and benefits of changing? What are the costs and benefits of not changing? Consider all of them. Then sit with that for a while — see what makes sense. Try filling out the following grid if that helps.

	Behaviour/ habit	Costs	Benefits
Change			
No change			

For a therapist, friend or family member wanting to help someone make healthy change (we're talking about those with some executive functioning to call their own), then we need to resist the temptation to tell the person what to do. Far better to ask questions so that the person's own answers convince them out of their own mouth. This helps strengthen reason through the dialectic process, a method of inquiry that has been popular since the ancient Greeks. There is in fact a whole form of psychotherapy based on mindfulness called Dialectical Behaviour Therapy (DBT). For example, what are we looking for when we do X? What do we really find when we do X? What gets in the way of us changing X? Afterwards, are we happy when we do X? Does it give us peace of mind? Is it always good to get what we want? Is it always bad to not get what we want?

Enabling strategies

An enabling strategy is something that enables us to act more effectively on the things we know or on the advice we get from a trusted source. One of the main reasons that a doctor's lifestyle advice isn't more effective for patients is because the information given is either too general to be of much use or, more commonly, isn't supported by motivational support and strategies to translate the information into action. Medical courses haven't always given much attention to training doctors in how to help people make effective lifestyle change, and the healthcare system hasn't really supported doctors with the time and resources for helping patients in this way. In order to learn how to help our patients, we as health professionals need to learn to help ourselves first.

Since 2002 the core curriculum at Monash University has included a six-week mindfulness and lifestyle program called the Health Enhancement Program, based on the *Essence of Health*[3] and aimed at addressing these oversights. ESSENCE is an acronym that stands for Education, Stress management, Spirituality, Exercise, Nutrition, Connectedness and Environment, because these are the essential elements to consider in the prevention and management of any chronic condition along with the best that modern medicine has to offer. The key enablers are learning about mindfulness, motivation and behaviour change. A study on the program published in 2009 showed that it significantly improved student wellbeing and quality of life even in high-stress pre-exam periods.[4] The program is currently being taken up by other universities and faculties in Australia and elsewhere.

We need to feel empowered, motivated and involved in order to act on what we know. Our key disablers are stress, despondency and pessimism — and if we don't deal with them, then it will be very hard to stay on course or to pick ourselves up quickly if, and when, we stumble.

Another big enabler is working in a group, with like-minded individuals. We don't have to sit in a group for too long to realise that all the things we thought were only problems for us are also issues for others. We gather a lot of strength, insight and resolve from working with others towards a similar goal. That's why support groups rather than individual forms of therapy are often far more effective.

Cycle of change

We often assume that changing a behaviour just happens. Well, it does, but generally it does after a whole process that's has gone on before. Many experts agree that behaviour change takes place in a cycle with the following steps.

1. Pre-contemplation: We haven't even begun to think about it or recognise a need to change. Often it takes a shock or other event to bring it to our attention.

2. Contemplation: We start thinking about the need to change. It's important here to consider the things that really motivate us to change.

3. Preparation: We begin to put in place the things we need to successfully change, such as informing others, noting the places or people we might need to avoid, getting the resources or equipment we might need.

4. Action: We start out on the new behaviour. The early stages — generally a few weeks — are the most difficult as the new behaviour gets established. Our old patterns attempt to reassert themselves and others around us as well as ourselves might try to sabotage the new behaviour.

5. Maintenance: Here the new behaviour is easier to maintain and the old habit isn't asserting itself so hard. Complacency and adversity can be the main threats.

6. Relapse: If it happens, then we learn from it and move on. Beating ourselves up is a good way to prolong the relapse. The most important thing is to pay attention and learn something from the experience. There is no failure, there's only a learning opportunity taken or missed. As Thomas Edison is reported to have said, 'I have not failed 700 times. I have not failed once. I have succeeded in proving those 700 ways will not work. When I have eliminated the ways that will not work, I will find the way that will work.'

It is important to appreciate from the outset that change takes time, but every time we make the effort it gets easier the next time as the brain slowly rewires itself for the new and, hopefully, healthier behaviour. As Shakespeare said:

> *Refrain tonight,*
> *And that shall lend a kind of easiness*
> *To the next abstinence: the next more easy;*
> *For use almost can change the stamp of nature.*

Hamlet, William Shakespeare

How can mindfulness help us with all this? Well, it can help us to be more conscious of the need for change. It can help us to contemplate why change might be needed. It can help us to stay focused and not be side-tracked by internal and external barriers. It can help us to remember what's important when change is established. It can help us to get back on track if we go bush-bashing for a while. It can help us to learn from our mistakes by paying attention to them in a more impartial and objective way.

Distress

Distress isn't particularly comfortable or attractive. The authors would like to avoid it as much as anyone else would, but it does have its uses. A positive motivator is like a carrot — moving towards something we want — whereas distress is like a stick motivating us to move away from what we don't want. Carrots are good but sticks will always have their place. Uncomfortable as it is, distress can motivate us in a way that complacency won't. Constantly numbing ourselves to our distress with distractions and substances won't help us to learn anything useful from it. To learn from distress and use it well we need to pay attention to it and not just rail against it.

Just to illustrate, in studies on cancer patients with malignant melanoma, the patients who felt most distress at the beginning were the ones who actually had the best outcomes at the end, because they were the ones who most engaged with the self-help therapies offered, which included meditation. When followed up six years later, there was a halving of recurrence and death rates for those who had the psychological support as well as the standard surgical care, compared to those who had the surgical care alone.[5] Over the following ten years as complacency crept in, those benefits started to erode.[6]

Distress may look black but, like oil, it contains within it an enormous amount of emotional energy. Accepting distress combined with the conscious and intentional use of all that raw energy can get an enormous amount done. Otherwise, used unmindfully, it will just burn us up.

Urge-surfing

With practice we can learn how to ride our brain waves rather than drown in them.

When we have 'got it together', as it were, we work as one. We make decisions that have the stamp of approval from the executive area of our brain, and the emotive area draws up the resolve to carry those decisions into action — without the appetitive area protesting too much. Even when our lower centres are in competition with our higher centres we don't lose focus and we follow through on our better intentions. So there we are, having enjoyed a piece of chocolate cake and our lower mind is howling for more even though we're so full we're about to burst, but inside there is that quiet voice that says, 'That was lovely but that's enough; time to stop!' Depending on the level of intestinal fortitude available to us at that moment we either stop or keep going. This kind of thing goes on all the time in just about every situation. Are we awake to this — and everything else — or not?

The appetitive area of our brain doesn't need to be suppressed, but it does need to be regulated. Self-regulation is different to suppression. One is a simple choice of whether or not to do something; this doesn't require tension and allows us to feel in control. The other is all about tension — internal conflict and an uneasy kind of control — like wrestling with a lion that will eat us if we let it loose for a moment. Learning how to manage and work with that internal tension is one of the most, possibly *the* most, important thing we can learn from mindfulness in making better lifestyle choices.

Stopping smoking, for example, isn't easy, and we have to learn to deal with the cravings. The habitual way is to suppress them, but this comes at a cost as far as our mental health is concerned and soon, when our guard is down or we are in a vulnerable moment, the vast majority of us go for the cigarette packet. A study on the effectiveness of suppression versus mindfulness for coping with cigarette cravings reported that smokers who used mindfulness to help them stop were able to quit without any cost as far as negative affect (mood) and depressive symptoms were concerned.[7]

Why? Well, it may have something to do with learning to 'surf' rather than 'fight' the urge to smoke, or do anything else for that matter. (We explored this to some extent in Chapter 9.) When a big wave comes we will probably struggle and drown if we try to fight it. What we can do instead is let the wave pick us up and float on the surface of it, like surfers and body surfers do. There's no need to do anything other than not get involved with it. When we sit and practise mindfulness meditation, or when we go about our day-to-day life trying to be mindful, we will notice urges, emotions and impulses coming and going all the time. If they arise it's a waste of time and effort wishing they weren't there, because they already are. But we can practise letting them flow in and out without reacting, fighting, suppressing or judging them in any way. Just notice the urge, the response, where the attention goes and gently escort it back to the body or breath or whatever other thing we're practising being mindful of.

There's not even any need to wonder when they will stop coming because we are only likely to get despondent about that. The only urge we need be interested in not getting involved with is the one happening now. Even if we get drawn into fighting with the urge, we can just look at the effect of that. We can see it as an experiment in the way that Thomas Edison did. It takes practice, patience and a considerable amount of self-compassion. Bit by bit the urges come and go more and more easily until they create little disturbance on the way through. Doesn't urge-surfing sound like a whole lot more fun than urge-wrestling? We might even learn to enjoy it.

Take-home tips for a mindful response to improving our lifestyle

Not so helpful

- Fight with our less-than-healthy urges.
- Criticise ourselves.
- Brood over the things we are trying to give up.

Helpful

- Savour the things we experience.
- Learn to 'surf' urges.
- Gently unhook our attention from the things we might otherwise brood over.
- Stay present rather than allow our mind to project into its exaggerated imaginings about a future life full of deprivation.
- Unhook our attention from internal rumination about things such as self-criticism particularly if we ever slip up.
- Practise and realise that healthy change takes time to establish itself.
- Take comfort from the realisation that every time we make a healthy choice it is wiring itself into our brains, making it easier next time.

CHAPTER 18

Education and academic performance

Is teaching mindfulness to a child teaching them a new skill they never had, or is it helping them to either maintain or rediscover a skill that was natural to them from birth? Consider looking into the eyes of a six-month-old baby. Do you have a sense that they are really present and looking straight at you, or are they distracted, perhaps by concerns about future career prospects, or where interest rates will be 30 years from now? Consider watching a two-year-old child play. Are they in the moment with what they are doing or are they preoccupied, concerned and burdened about the sheer volume of play they need to get through by the end of the day? No, without even trying, children have a natural disposition to mindfulness. In the normal run of things, we don't learn how to be mindful as we grow up — we forget.

In Chapter 3 we shared an example of a mother — who was also a health professional — who went to the beach with her daughter with the aim to be mindful and to consciously experience what was going on around her. It wasn't easy and she spent much of the time wondering if she was really present or not. Then her five-year-old daughter came over and wanted to play. They started playing and had a ball as about an hour went by. Suddenly the mother realised that, without even trying, she had been far more present and mindful while playing with her daughter than she had been all morning doing 'intense' mindfulness practice. Like a child, mindfulness is simple, easy, innocent and un-self-conscious.

There are a couple of important lessons here. Firstly, we don't think our way into mindfulness; in fact, if we're thinking about whether we're mindful, then we're not. Secondly, like the child, the mindful state is not a self-conscious state; in fact, when we're mindful we lose our usual sense of self-consciousness — we stop thinking about ourselves — and just respond spontaneously to life as it unfolds.

So, mindfulness, for all the reasons outlined in this book, is a life skill and one that we need to help maintain as we age. It's a skill that the environment and the example of the adults around a child can either foster or obliterate. Mindfulness is a skill that can easily be, and should be, taught and modelled in schools right from the beginning. As far as education is concerned, mindfulness matters. It helps to foster creativity, improves academic and sporting performance and is vital for developing mental health and emotional intelligence in children — the science of mindfulness is starting to change the way we think about education.

Primary, secondary and tertiary education

Mindfulness can be easily taught to children of any age, but teaching mindfulness requires a different skill set depending on the age of the child, adolescent or young adult, and the context in which they are being taught.

For a young child — say, up to the age of ten — simple, brief and playful is the order of the day, without the need for too much explanation or justification for why it's being taught. Any explanation needs to be in a language that makes sense to a child of that age. Janet Etty-Leal's *Meditation Capsules: a Mindfulness Program for Children* is a great example of the methods and style for introducing mindfulness to young children.[1] Any formal practice doesn't go for any longer than a few minutes. It can be incorporated with games and other educational or creative activities. One art teacher, for example, likes honing the children's powers of observation in the process of learning art, such as taking the time to notice with interest the colours, shapes, textures and proportions of things they're about to draw. In creative writing a little exercise in connecting with their senses in a natural environment can be a great way for a child to begin describing the world around them and their experiences. In such examples children are learning to explore with a depth and richness of perception that modern life is almost always conditioning them to just skim over as we hastily rush from one thing to another.

For older children, say ten to sixteen, we are getting into an age where the reason for practising mindfulness might need to be made a little clearer. We may have noticed how adolescents don't necessarily do what they are told to do — let's face it, we didn't when we were that age — so it is most important for learning mindfulness that it is an invitation to practise; an inquiry, an exploration.

Interest naturally draws attention, so whatever is put in front of a child will foster learning especially if it is creatively put and made relevant to the individual or group. What's important to them? Then explain it in such a way that the mindfulness is clearly relevant. If the teacher is not interested in the content then the children won't be either.

A mother asked how she might interest her fourteen-year-old son in mindfulness because he was becoming anxious and hard to live with. Well, the anxiety is one point of connection — helping to unhook his attention from the stream of worrying thoughts — but she was also asked what he was really passionate about. She said football, so we mentioned some of the footballers and other elite athletes who practise mindfulness and why they do it. The mother had wanted to interest her son in inner peace and tranquillity, which is not so attractive for a fourteen-year-old male, but sporting prowess and the ability to perform under pressure was. For others it will be about getting a good night's sleep, or it may be just the chance to enjoy some rest and relaxation. For older children a little more explanation is helpful, and mindfulness can be practised for a little longer, say up to ten minutes at a time, supplemented with many short pauses.

For older children, who aren't really children because by sixteen they are becoming young adults, the case for practising mindfulness can be made a little more fully with perhaps more background about the relationship of the mind and body, and the impact of stress on the body, brain and performance. It can even be incorporated into their science or biology studies to help them understand from the inside through experience what they are trying to learn from the outside in the form of information. All of the same things apply here as above in terms of relevance, but by this age one of the big drivers will be academic performance and dealing with exam stress. Students will have noted how much study time they waste because their attention wanders, how much they catastrophise about the future, and how much their memory and performance drops when they are anxious and tense.

There are also likely to be a significant number of students, whether they tell you or not, who are experiencing anxiety and depression, or are having problems with anger management, for whom mindfulness will be very helpful. Another topic of interest at this age is practising impulse control, which is not a particularly attractive option for a sixteen-year-old male who thinks risk-taking behaviour is the order of the day, so it might be best expressed in other language such as 'being able to stop and think before we do something stupid and/or dangerous that we might regret later'. Mindfulness is a great way to provide that little bit of space, and it doesn't need to be much, in order to choose whether or not to do something. If there is no awareness then it is stimulus, impulse and unmindful reaction — before we can even say 'damage control'. Students of this age can practise mindfulness for longer and can be encouraged to punctuate their days with formal mindfulness practice as well as informal, for example starting and finishing a study session with some mindfulness, or practising as they go to sleep.

In the tertiary setting, issues related to mental health, academic performance, wellbeing and development of potential are all to the fore. For it to be integrated into the core curriculum, as it is at Monash University, then mindfulness needs to be connected to or integrated with other content in the course. Preferably the core knowledge should be examinable, although the personal practice will be an individual choice. No one should be compelled to practise mindfulness (although we have perhaps provided a case why it should be put in our water supplies!), but it can be explained and made relevant in such a way that the desire to learn and practise is natural. 'Preaching to the unconverted'[2] isn't best when heavy-handed or imposed, rather when inviting inquiry, self-exploration and discovery.

The mindful teacher

There is a lot of obvious interest in helping a child to become more mindful, but before doing this a very important point needs to be emphasised. A teacher can't authentically teach mindfulness unless they have explored and experienced the practice of mindfulness themselves.

A mindless teacher is not a pretty sight — ranting, raving and reacting their way through the school day. A more mindful teacher is not so reactive and can model a little more impulse control for their students — which will be good for them personally and also for all those around them. Furthermore, a mindful teacher hears more of what their students are communicating to them, some of which will be in words but much of which will be in postures, gestures and grunts! This opens the door to a more measured, empathic and creative response, remembering that sometimes the best response may be no response.

A mindful teacher also needs to learn to manage the often hyperkinetic and time-pressured environment they are immersed in by learning not to multitask and to deal with priorities one at a time — from most important to least important — not to mention saving the time commonly wasted while marking or preparing for a class by constantly getting distracted by the thought, 'Why am I doing this job?'

Attention, memory and learning

Unfortunately we are building a world that trains inattention in children. Creating stress and anxiety is one part of the problem. Children will unconsciously soak up the anxiety and unhelpful habits of the adults around them. Another problem is all the chemicals that children are exposed to such as food additives and colourings, which have been found to increase problems with hyperactivity and attention.[3]

Another issue concerns the methods and content of children's play, which has changed to incorporate far greater time spent in front of screens, and a bombardment by faster and faster media. Added to this is the interaction with IT children are undertaking from a much earlier age than in the past. Does this help a developing brain to grow and wire itself in the optimal way? It seems not, as indicated by a growing number of studies. The world's leading paediatric journal, imaginatively named *Pediatrics*, has reported on a range of studies clearly indicating that higher than average amounts of screen time (largely television viewing and video games) are associated with a roughly doubled risk of attention problems such as Attention Deficit and Hyperactivity Disorder (ADHD).[4] The maximum recommended screen time for children is two hours a day, as we mentioned in Chapter 10, but the average amount of screen time for the modern child is about four hours — and growing.

Experts suggest that the effect of the rapid and ever-changing input of sensory stimulation — associated with much of what children are exposed to —makes it difficult for them to pay attention when they are performing a task, like school work, that does not stimulate the sensory centres in the same way. When the input is rapid-paced, it conditions inattention and impulsivity into the child's brain. To illustrate, a study found that a fast-paced TV show negatively influenced children's executive functioning such as self-regulation, impulsivity, processing information and working memory.[5]

TV content matters too, as another study concluded. 'Viewing of either violent or non-violent entertainment television before age three was significantly associated with subsequent attentional problems, and the magnitude of the association was large.'[6] In an even more recent study, 60 four-year-olds were randomly assigned to three groups to either watch a fast-paced TV cartoon (*Spongebob Squarepants*) or a more moderately paced educational cartoon, or draw for 9 minutes. They were then given four tasks measuring executive function, including following instructions, tests of memory, ability to delay gratification and impulsivity.[7] Children who watched the fast-paced TV cartoon performed significantly worse on all executive-function tasks compared to the other children — the tasks tested included following instructions, memory, the ability to delay gratification and impulsivity. It wasn't that the children who did the other tasks gained an advantage that the others didn't — it was that 9 minutes of the fast-paced TV cartoon made those children perform worse than they did before the cartoon. The producers of such shows justify it as being 'entertainment' and point to the fact that it is popular and children like it — like it so much that they get mesmerised by it. It's great that children are entertained, but it's a shame when that entertainment dumbs them down. As adults we need to select the input for young children a little more discerningly.

A child's brain needs interaction with their environment in order to lay down the connections it needs to develop. When a child is playing in a park, throwing a ball, wrestling with the family dog, or building something out of clay, the whole brain and sensory channels are open and active. This stimulates the brain to lay down the connections it will need for later life. When a child is interacting with a screen, the senses aren't engaged to nearly the same extent — in fact, they are being starved of sensory connection, and this makes it more difficult for the attention to stay where it is put because a screen providing virtual experiences is far less tangible than a real-life experience.

Add to this the tendency to multitask (which is actually just frequent task-switching) and we have the perfect storm, just made for creating the impulsivity, behavioural problems, learning difficulties and mental-health problems that are becoming so common in children today.

The area of the brain called the prefrontal cortex is vital for the development of all of our higher (executive) functions including working memory, also called short-term memory. This involves the brain structures and processes used for temporarily storing and manipulating information as it comes in. ADHD is associated with impairment of the functioning of this part of the brain, but practising attention helps to stabilise this area. Improving working memory helps to increase IQ and treat ADHD.[8] Stress, on the other hand, has a negative effect on memory and performance, largely because it hijacks the part of the brain we rely on for high performance. For example, one study found that high anxiety about being able to do mathematical problems led to smaller working memory spans and a pronounced increase in reaction time and errors.[9] 'Performance pressure harms individuals most qualified to succeed by consuming the working memory capacity that they rely on for their superior performance.'[10] That's why increasing children's anxiety isn't a particularly good way to help them to learn something. When a child's mind is packed full of anxious thoughts, there isn't much room for anything useful to get in. Much better to allay their anxiety and engage their attention.

Multitasking

As we have previously mentioned, multitasking is an illusion.[11] We switch attention so quickly between tasks that it appears we are performing multiple tasks at the same time, but the reality is that we are switching back and forth between tasks. Modern children are being drawn into multitasking far more than any generation before because of their exposure to media and IT. The modern myth is that we get more done when we task-switch, and that if we do it a lot we get better at it. The unfortunate truth is that we get less done and we get worse at it. This rapid task-switching is inefficient because we have to reboot data all the time as we go from one task to another and we lose chunks of data all the time. Multitasking leads to distraction, a disorganised memory and poorer performance on analytic reasoning. As Clifford Nass said, 'We worry that it may be we're creating people who may not be able to think well, and clearly.'[12]

We hate to be old fuddy-duddies (well, we usually do), but the old ways of doing things may actually be better. For example, reading from hard copy seems to help stabilise our attention. Research by Laura Levine and her team from Connecticut State University found that, 'The amount of time college students spent instant messaging had an increased effect on their levels of distractibility in performing academic tasks, and that the amount of time they spent reading books reduced their levels of distractibility.'[13] Heavy media multitaskers perform worse, not better, on tests of task-switching ability, due to a reduced ability to sift what is relevant data from what is irrelevant.[14] This is all linked with the 'attentional blink' discussed in Chapter 19. Just to reiterate, mindfulness looks to be the remedy for these ailments in that it reduces attentional blink and improves information input and the ability to deal with distractions.[15] Even four sessions of mindfulness training had beneficial effects on mood, the ability to think (executive functioning), verbal fluency and working memory. It also reduced fatigue and anxiety.[16]

There is no memory without attention. Let's face it, if we're not paying attention when we put down the car keys we don't remember where they are. It's no different for our kids. The advice given by UCLA psychologist and researcher Russel Poldrack, is, 'The best thing you can do to improve your memory is to pay attention to the things you want to remember ... [Complex] tasks that require more attention, such as learning calculus or reading Shakespeare, will be particularly adversely affected by multitasking.'[17]

Kids may assume that multitasking is good; in fact, that it is the only way to go. If they try not to do it after they have been doing it for some time then it will feel uncomfortable not to do it, and instead to focus attention on one activity at a time. Invite the kids to try an experiment in doing this and report how it feels. The younger a child, the easier it will be for them to develop the ability to focus. A child needs parents and teachers to help them to do this and, for young children, to have adults help them to manage their environment and exposure in such a way as to save them from themselves — or should that be to save the children from the things that we adults have unwisely put in front of them. Simple multitasking — such as walking and chewing gum at the same time — isn't such a problem. Complex multitasking, however — doing two activities that each demand a bit of mental grunt, such as texting and having a conversation at the same time — is not a good habit to get into.

For a teacher, helping children in the classroom to ration their sensory inputs at any one time will be a useful habit to get into. Having the laptop open when it's really useful may be fine, but having it open while they are meant to be listening will mean that they don't listen well. This will be most effective if the same strategies are being practised at home too, so helping parents to understand the importance of attention and how to practise it will help to reinforce rather than undermine efforts at school. Taking time for quiet as a way of breaking up the day — say, beginning and finishing a class with a minute or two of mindfulness — will also help children (and teachers) to be mindful and less reactive during the class. Peaceful music can also be used for this purpose. Children love to stop and be present; it's a lot closer to them than it is for most adults.

Social and emotional development

We have discussed this topic at length in other chapters, particularly on emotional intelligence, but this is one of the main reasons children need mindfulness at school. Paying attention to others is a prerequisite for good mental health but also for empathy, compassion and for understanding the impact our words and behaviours have on others. This is being confirmed with studies on children from primary- to secondary-school ages.[18] It helps with impulsivity and managing anger. We know that children and adolescents with issues around anger and hostility have their stress centre (the amygdala) firing off all the time, but we also know that mindfulness quietens this area of the brain. Bullies are generally more anxious and depressed than those they are bullying, but unfortunately they have not yet found a more constructive way of dealing with their emotional distress than making the life of someone else unpleasant. We all want control, and if we don't know where to find this in ourselves we may try and impose it on others outside ourselves.

Positive psychology and mindfulness training are increasingly being seen around the world as central pillars in the innovative approaches to education. Probably the world leader in this area is Geelong Grammar in Australia, which has spent considerable resources developing and making available a whole new approach called 'Positive Education',[19] and has worked with the positive psychology pioneer Martin Seligman.

Levels of performance

Karol Miller is an educator with an interest in the levels of performance of students and how to assess them.[20] The levels she identified in ascending order of importance are:

1. 'Knows': is easy to assess: most exam assessment is focused on knowledge as information, but it is least important in producing effective human beings.
2. 'Knows how': is a measure of a student's ability to apply knowledge to practical situations.
3. 'Shows how': is a measure of the ability to communicate that knowledge or skill to others.
4. 'Does': is most important. These are actions that have results. Knowledge without action is about as useful as a car without a key.

Knowledge isn't generally the driver of behaviour. We often don't do what we should do because of inattention, apathy, fear, being too busy, an unsupportive environment, a negative attitude or habit. A teacher can tell a student to do something a thousand times but unless these barriers to translating knowledge into action are seen and examined by the student themselves, and then stepped over, nothing will happen, or it will only happen while the student is being watched. They won't have any personal ownership over it. A simple example in medical education is teaching medical students to wash their hands after seeing a patient: they know, know how, could show how, but many don't actually do it — or not as often as they should.

Mindfulness is therefore an important skill in helping us to be more self-aware of our actions and the factors that influence them — for better or for worse — and thus help translate knowledge into action.

Rewarding process or outcome?

You can do a little experiment with your students (or with somebody else's if you don't have any) — with those who are old enough to do long multiplication anyway. Present them with the following student's answer to a mathematics exam question. Ask them to work individually, no talking, and after a minute or two to give the student a mark out of 10.

$$269x$$
$$23$$
$$787$$
$$5380$$
$$6167$$

Now, the student got the question wrong because they didn't carry a 2 on the first line of the multiplication — meaning that the answer should have been 6187. When a room full of medical students are asked to give a mark there's a relatively even spread from 0 to 9 out of 10. So much for validity and reliability in assessment! We like to think that mathematics is a reasonably objective and precise discipline, but it seems not. The mark awarded is largely dependent on whether the marker rewarded outcome or process. If it's all about the outcome then 0/10 — because the student got the answer absolutely wrong. If it's all about the process then nearly all of the steps were well performed and the student clearly knew how to do it so it's about 9/10. If you reward both then the mark will be somewhere in between, depending on how you weight their relative importance.

There's nothing wrong with precision and outcome. If you were going to buy a car, you would hope that there was a fair amount of precision in the design and construction of it if you plan for the car to safely take you where you want to go.

But are there implications here for the way we teach or learn? Does rewarding the process or outcome have an effect on where our attention goes and our capacity to persevere and learn more quickly? Well, it seems that it does — judging by some of the positive psychology studies on the subsequent learning of children who were praised either for outcome or for effort and process.

As a teacher, if you give a class a relatively easy task you can then observe what effect your response to the students has. If you praise a class for a successful outcome, they will be happy. If you then give them tasks that extend them, and they don't succeed quickly and therefore aren't getting the praise they want, most will get frustrated, won't persevere and will want to go back to the easier task. Making the outcome the main focus of attention isn't necessarily helpful and it can make a challenge appear as a threat. If, on the other hand, you give a class a relatively easy task and praise the effort the students put in and their capacity to make progress by learning from their mistakes, then students will tend to enjoy learning more. If you then give them a harder task, they are much more likely to enjoy the challenge, to want to learn through experience and to persevere. They are more likely to learn quickly and want to extend themselves. Challenge, in this case, is seen as opportunity and experiment, and mistakes are seen as learning opportunities.

Anxiety about the outcome distracts from focusing on the process and therefore impedes performance. Process takes place in the present moment — outcome is all about the future. A student who becomes very anxious about their upcoming exam results may find themselves unable to focus on the very study they need to do in order to prepare for those exams. Forgetting about the result but focusing on what needs to be done here and now can not only help the student to feel better, but also to achieve better in the long run.

Fixed and growth mindsets

Not unrelated to the above is the concept of 'mindsets'. Mindsets are a fascinating new area of interest related to learning. Carol Dwek is a psychologist who has done a lot of work in this field.[21] A 'fixed mindset' is characterised by thoughts along the lines of 'I can't do that' when confronted with a challenging task. A fixed mindset believes that talents and abilities cannot be improved even with effort. It's consistent with a notion that we are born with a certain amount of talent and so we wish to avoid challenge in order to avoid the possibility of failure. Challenge provokes fear and avoidance for the person with a fixed mindset because it is a potential threat to self-worth or self-esteem. Challenges are not seen as opportunities for personal growth. Fixed mindsets are not innate, they are acquired. Imagine if we were born with a fixed mindset. The baby would sit on the floor and just say, 'Mum, how many times have I told you — I can't walk! Don't even make me try.' A preschool child would say, 'Please, teacher, take those paints away. Look at what I've produced — it's hopeless. I'm no Michelangelo. You're just causing me stress!' No, we pick up fixed mindsets as we grow — from who knows where. It's therefore really important that as parents and teachers we are careful with our language because unconsciously we may be reinforcing a fixed mindset.

A 'growth mindset', on the other hand, believes that intelligence, talent and ability can be developed over time if we wish to put in the effort and perseverance required to develop them, whether it's in relation to sport, academic ability, relationships or any other capacity. For a growth mindset, obstacles give rise to a sense of challenge and opportunity. With such an attitude, a growth mindset doesn't fear failure but rather sees it as a learning opportunity or as a chance to improve oneself. High achievers all have growth mindsets as they learn to match their efforts to their vision of what's possible.

Mindsets tend to get taken on board early in life. We soak them up without even knowing it largely by modelling the adults and teachers around us. We can all change our mindset at any age — if we have the awareness to see it operating and make the effort to engrain a different attitude. Like simply crossing our arms a different way, it will feel uncomfortable and unnatural at first but with sustained practice it gets easier and easier. You may like to try this out as an experiment.

Mindfulness can help us to develop a growth mindset in a number of ways. Firstly, it helps us to recognise the telltale signs of a fixed mindset when it arises such as fear, avoidance, mental agitation and inattention. Secondly, it helps us to stand back from our thoughts and see them not as facts but just as thoughts. This gives us more choice about whether to act on them — and so reinforce them — or not to act on them — and so to loosen their grip. Thirdly, mindfulness helps us to focus our attention on the activity we're trying to learn about by unhooking it from the self-consciousness about outcome, performance and failure. Fourthly, by helping to reduce stress, it liberates the areas of the brain required for learning, which we spoke about earlier in this chapter. Lastly, for parents and teachers, we much choose language and responses that encourage a growth mindset.

Deep learning

John Biggs was an educator who investigated student approaches to learning and studying.[22] He looked at the literature on predictors of student performance at university and defined what personal characteristics within the students were associated with how they learned. He was interested in the motivations and strategies of students relevant to their performance, and came up with three learning styles.

Learning styles and strategies adapted from Biggs

Approach	Motive	Strategy
Surface	Surface Motive (SM) is instrumental: the main purpose is to meet the requirements minimally: to achieve a balance between working too hard and failing. (Main aim is to avoid failure.)	Surface Strategy (SS) is reproductive: the aim is to gain the bare essentials and reproduce them through rote learning.
Achieving	Achieving Motive (AM) is based on competition and ego-enhancement: the aim is to gain the highest grades, whether or not the material is interesting. (Usefulness for profession is not of concern, only for marks.)	Achieving Strategy (AS) is based on organising one's time and working; to behave as a 'model' student.

Approach	Motive	Strategy
Deep	Deep Motive (DM) is intrinsic: study is done to satisfy interest and maximise competence in particular academic subjects. (This approach is called mastery in other theories.)	Deep strategy (DS) is meaningful: students read widely and relate with previous relevant knowledge. There is an interest in the interconnectedness of subjects.

Deep learners are driven by interest and enjoyment and therefore find the process relatively effortless compared to those who are driven by other motives. The interest draws the attention, and where the attention goes interest follows, and where interest goes enjoyment follows. Einstein, the archetypal deep learner, wasn't driven by stress so much as fascination. Now that's a sustainable strategy for lifelong learning. Deep learners have the most flexible and creative minds because they are most engaged with the content for its own sake rather than for the sake of something else, such as avoiding failure or enhancing one's ego. Studies suggest that First or Second Class Honours students all used deep approaches whereas Third Class Honours students tended to use surface approaches.[23] Deep learners like to see things in context and note the interconnectedness between different topics — that is, they are more holistic in their approach and their knowledge isn't artificially siloed. The particulars are interesting here in so far as they point to big principles.

There are other interesting relationships as far as learning style is concerned. For example, for students whose motivation was achievement or failure avoidance (surface), there is a positive correlation between anxiety and performance on exams. Students who adopted mastery goals (deep) didn't show a correlation between anxiety and performance; that is, they didn't *have to be* anxious to do well. Furthermore, cheating and learning approach seem to be related. 'Understanding a student's academic orientation might be useful in predicting academic dishonesty ... Cheating and plagiarism were more common among students who desired good grades or simply wanted to gain a degree. Students who placed more emphasis on learning had less plagiarism ... Universities might be better off putting resources into developing [an emphasis on learning] in the students rather than just saying "we told you not to cheat".'[24]

So there's a good question for a teacher to ask themselves — what motivates my teaching? What strategies am I going to foster in my students? Am I really interested in the topic I am teaching? We might be thinking we're teaching students about a subject but, without us or them really knowing it, we may be teaching them far more about how to, or how not to, learn.

One of the authors was being interviewed by a PhD student about the factors that fostered lifelong learning. The reply was, 'The first thing is that the teacher should love their subject.' The PhD student turned off the recorder and said, off the record, that teachers virtually never acknowledged that. Well, maybe we should acknowledge that every time we take a class. If not, perhaps we should question why we're there in the first place.

The bottom line

Well, we've tried to make the case for mindfulness within the educational environment in a relatively short chapter — this could be the subject of a book in itself. The bottom line is that mindfulness is such an important life skill that it's a core part of education from the very beginning. It's such a valuable generic skill that has so many particular applications relevant to learning, growing up and developing our potential, that it needs to be creatively woven into the educational experience at every level — relevant to time, place, people and context.

Take-home tips for mindful education

Not so helpful

- Make students anxious while learning.
- Create a preoccupation about the outcome rather than focusing on the process.
- Foster surface learning.
- As a teacher or parent, be uninterested in what you are teaching.
- Spend lots of time in front of screens and less time immersed in real-life experiences.

Helpful

- Train attention in your students.
- Start a class with some time for mindfulness.
- Be interested in what you are teaching.
- Encourage a growth mindset.
- Praise effort more than outcome.
- Treat mistakes as opportunities to learn rather than failure.
- Encourage deep learning.

CHAPTER 19

Workplace performance and leadership

Work and health

When are there more heart attacks and strokes than any other time of the week for the working population? Monday mornings around 7 o'clock.[1,2] This is before the working person has even arrived at work. It's enough to make us not want to go to work on Monday! Better to just turn up some time on Tuesday — when and if we feel like it. The fact that weekends are associated with a reduced rate of heart attacks and strokes is as good an argument for the seven-day weekend as you will ever hear.[3,4] Why the heart attack before one has even got to work? Well, the effect of stress on the body was discussed in Chapters 4 and 6.[5]

That fertile imagination we have is probably already at work even before we've got out of bed to go to work and has dreamed up a thousand catastrophes before we've made it to the shower. For example, imagining things going wrong at work, or arguments with the boss, or the replaying of past stressful events will all activate the stress system even if we are in a totally stress-free situation at that moment, lying under a warm blanket with a soft pillow under our head and listening to birds singing in the trees. Thus, being mindful right from the moment we wake up is a much better way to start the day — let's deal with the catastrophes if and when we get to them. That's a better use of our attention and energy.

Because work can form such a big part of our life and can impact our emotions so significantly, it can affect our physical health as well as our mental and emotional health. We can also be exposed to many occupational hazards so it can affect sleep, immunity, our risk of heart disease and also cancer.

Although work is good for us, like anything else, too much or too little is not so good. Neither unemployment nor overwork is good for our physical, mental and social health.[6] For many people the workplace looms as a major source of stress, particularly as over recent years work demands have escalated, workplaces and employment have become less stable and workplace restructuring is a more frequent occurrence. Workplace stress makes itself known in many ways.

In the West we have come to value activity and productivity so highly that it's easy to get addicted to it, plus we may not realise that it's the quiet time that we spend that allows us the energy, clarity and creativity to be sustainably productive during our active hours.

A significant factor in whether or not work has a good or bad influence on our health has to do with our attitude to the work we're doing. If, for example, we practise an attitude of intense resistance to our work, then, unless we're able to avoid it, it will be stressful. An attitude of acceptance, on the other hand, particularly if we can't avoid it, can help us to not get overly stressed when things are not so good, at least according to our mind. If, of course, it would be advisable and possible to change our stressful working situation, then it would be helpful to accept the effort it requires to change our circumstances, rather than be passive victims of circumstance. Mindful acceptance isn't inertia. Feeling trapped or out of control of our situation is a good recipe for stress, which we will discuss later in the chapter.

Burnout, mental health and errors

Burnout is pretty common in tense, busy, demanding and competitive work environments. Burnout — as measured by Maslach's Burnout Inventory — is assessed as a combination of emotional exhaustion, depersonalisation (not feeling empathy or connected with people) and a lack of personal accomplishment. Among new medical graduates, for example, during internship 75 per cent of interns would have qualified as having burnout at eight months into the first year of their working life,[7] and 73 per cent would have qualified as having a mental illness (mainly anxiety and depression) at some stage in the year. What would the figures be for lawyers, teachers, counsellors, community workers, police or mothers? What does this say about the way we train (or don't train) people to do a job? Are we missing something?

To address such issues, medical students at Monash University are given what's called the Health Enhancement Program. Research has revealed that this leads to improvements on all measures of psychological and physical wellbeing, despite the pre-course evaluation being in a low-stress period and the post-course evaluation taking place in a high-stress pre-exam period.[8] The notion that we have to have stress to drive performance really has to be questioned.

Self-care isn't just for the benefit of the worker; it's also an investment in the wellbeing of the people the workplace is meant to be looking after. Take doctors again. Doctors are much more likely to make medical errors if they are experiencing poor emotional health. To illustrate, an American study found that 20 per cent of resident medical staff in hospitals met criteria for depression at any given time.[9] Even scarier was the fact that depressed doctors made more than six times as many medication and prescribing errors as non-depressed doctors doing the same job. The lesson here: never let a doctor treat you until you've done a mental-state examination on them!

What about mindfulness in the workplace?

In the hurly-burly world of the workplace, some would look on mindfulness or meditation as a touchy-feely kind of thing; something you do on a work retreat organised by a member of HR who, although well-meaning, has gone a little soft in the head and wants the executives to hug trees and do a little astral travelling to boot. At the very least, mindfulness would be seen by many as a time-waster designed by lazy people who want to make a virtue out of doing nothing. Well, nothing could be further from the truth. In fact, an increasing number of high-level organisations and corporations are looking to mindfulness as a core strategy for improving resilience, focus and performance and for fostering the kinds of qualities that make good leaders

— the kind of leaders that team members want to follow.

Some of the basics relevant to performance, stress management and wellbeing are covered in other parts of this book, but here is a summary of a few key points.

- Emotional states such as stress, anxiety, depression and anger negatively affect executive functions such as working memory, information processing, decision making, emotional regulation and impulse control. A large part of this is because the 'stress centre' — the amygdala — can hijack the prefrontal cortex of the brain.

- The practice of mindfulness quietens the amygdala and stabilises the working of the prefrontal cortex, which improves executive function.

- Some stress can improve performance compared to an apathetic state. Past a certain point however, more stress will diminish performance.

- Mindfulness practice improves our ability to receive and process information and enhances memory and executive function.

- The zone or flow-state is a low-stress but high-performance state. It's the most mindful state we can have while we're engaged in action. Therefore, as far as performance is concerned, alertness — which is good — needs to be distinguished from stress — which is not so good.

- Leadership attributes associated with EI such as self-awareness, self-regulation, motivation, empathy and social skills are a direct consequence of attentiveness and are therefore fostered by mindfulness.

The hyperkinetic workplace and multitasking

According to an article in the *Harvard Business Review*, the modern workplace is becoming more hyperkinetic, which is another way of saying busy and time-pressured.[10] For workers in such environments this leads to what the authors called Attention Deficit Trait (ADT), which is the tendency to be less and less attentive as we try to deal with too much input. This results in:

- black-and-white thinking; perspective and shades of grey disappear,
- difficulty staying organised, setting priorities and managing time,
- feeling a constant low level of panic and guilt.

The experts suggest that ADT can be controlled by engineering the environment, which influences the emotional and physical health of employees. Leaders can also help prevent ADT by matching employees' skills to tasks. Workers can help themselves by:

- making time for 'human moments',
- getting enough sleep,
- switching to a good diet,
- undertaking adequate exercise,
- breaking down large tasks into smaller ones,
- keeping a section of their work space clear,
- keeping a portion of the day free of appointments and email.

Training attention is a pretty good idea too, because we have to learn to manage the environment rather than feel we are being managed by it. One of the key enemies in the busy workplace is multitasking, although multitasking is something of an illusion.[11] When we appear to be multitasking we're not actually focusing on two things at once but one thing at a time; we are switching attention so quickly that we merely appear to be paying attention to two things at once. When we do this we are losing chunks of data as we have to 'reboot' data, and data becomes disorganised. If we don't have anything to compare it to we can easily deceive ourselves that multitasking (attention- or task-switching) is the most efficient way to work. It's not, but if we are heavily conditioned to task-switch all the time, then practising mindfulness will initially seem like quite a challenge, but it may allow us to become aware of how agitated our mind is.

Dr Glenn Wilson and his team report some interesting findings from a workplace-based study funded by Hewlett-Packard and conducted by the Institute of Psychiatry at the University of London. They found that 'workers distracted by email and phone calls suffer a fall in IQ more than twice that found in marijuana smokers.'[12] We don't think the message here is to smoke marijuana instead of attending to our emails and phone calls, but this just gives a comparison for us to mull over. Information Technology, as useful as it is, can be an enemy as well as a friend if it's not managed well and used moderately. Rather than the habit of task-switching enhancing our ability to function and process information, it reduces it, but this reduction is not necessarily apparent to us. 'Heavy media multitaskers performed worse on a test of task-switching ability, likely due to reduced ability to filter out interference from the irrelevant task set.'[13]

When we're not paying attention or are rushed or tired, it's even more important to have checks and balances to help pick up errors. For example, when checklists along the lines of what are used in the airline industry were introduced into the operating theatre it was found to nearly halve postoperative complications and deaths.[14]

Attentional blink

Attentional blink is a term used to describe our limitation in information processing. It's the time gap in being able to identify and consolidate information from our environment in our memory. It can take more than half a second before our mind is free to receive and record a second stimulus, so it's often not detected, as if we didn't even see it. The bits we miss are the attentional blink. When we're stressed the attentional blink gets longer and we're more vulnerable to being influenced by distractions (distractor interference), that is, our attention isn't able to sift relevant from irrelevant information. When a sportsperson is sledging or jibing their opponent so as to take their mind off the game, they are really empirically testing their ability to manage distractor influence.

Mindfulness training can help us process information better and more quickly, and feel calmer to boot. In one study, three months of mindfulness-based attentional training reduced people's attentional blink and improved their ability to select goal-relevant information, when it was mixed up with irrelevant information; that is, it improved people's ability to deal with distractor influence.[15] This may also be part of the reason why workers 'in the flow' or 'in the zone' are more able to make accurate instinctive decisions, whereas taking more time leads the mind to second guess, hesitate, get distracted and make more errors. This was demonstrated by a study that found that 95 per cent of instincts were accurate if given less than half a second to perform a computer-based pattern-recognition task. If people were given twice as long, they were only 70 per cent accurate, which means that they made six times as many errors.[16]

Of course, some issues may not be as appropriate for snap decisions and we may need to take time to gather more information, sit with the decision or bounce possible solutions off others.

Mindful practice

Mindful practice is a term coined by Ron Epstein, a professor of primary care at Rochester University in the United States. Mindfulness is important in medical practice: just imagine you have turned up at the emergency department — would like to see a multitasking doctor or one giving you their undivided attention? Epstein describes mindful practice as the 'conscious and intentional attentiveness to the present situation — the raw sensations, thoughts, and emotions as well as the interpretations, judgments and heuristics (learning by experience) that one applies to a particular situation.'[17] For a doctor, mindfulness fosters self-monitoring and avoids automatic pilot.[18] Among other things, self-monitoring leads to:

- early recognition of cognitive biases,
- avoidance of technical errors,
- awareness of emotional reactions,
- facilitation of self-correction,
- development of therapeutic relationships.

If we're not paying attention, we can't correct errors in real time (the present moment), but will have to do it after the event — generally when the consequences of our mistake have made themselves known. An article from the *Journal of the American Medical Association* explored the potential for diagnostic errors among unmindful clinicians and the need for mindfulness to help prevent such errors. When we're unmindful we are much less likely to take an objective view of what's in front of us, or be aware of how our own mood, assumptions or biases are affecting our judgments and decisions.[19] The article described two sorts of bias:

- Confirmation bias: the pursuit of data that support a diagnosis over data that refute it.
- Anchoring bias: a resistance to adapting appropriately to subsequent data that suggest alternative diagnoses.

This means that we have a preconceived idea and unconsciously misinterpret or select data to fit in with that idea, regardless of whether it fits or not. Although all this is being discussed in a medical context, it's an issue just as relevant for anyone, whether it be a scientist who prejudices the experiment and its interpretation before they have even done it, or a teacher who judges a child's behaviour or learning capacity according to their like or dislike of them, or a judge or judging employer who has judged the case even before they have heard the evidence, or an athlete who has a fixed idea about their game plan even when it isn't working well.

How mindfulness affects work

Eight-week workplace-based mindfulness programs for staff that have been run at the Monash University and the Australian National University have produced a range of interesting findings, including improved performance, wellbeing, meaningfulness and work engagement. This emphasises the important point that enhancing the wellbeing of a worker has the side effect of also improving their capacity to work effectively and sustainably. The energy often wasted in stress can be conserved and used for something more useful, unless we're working in a stress factory — in which case producing a lot of stress would be our main Key Performance Indicator (KPI). Maybe there are more stress factories than we realise.

A study from Rochester in the United States found that a mindfulness program for physicians was associated with a range of improvements for workplace burnout and other aspects of workplace performance.[20] Thankfully, practising mindfulness led to improvements in mindfulness, but the more mindful the physicians became the greater the reduction in burnout. There was also increased empathy and responsiveness to patients, reduced mood disturbance and increased conscientiousness in the presence of greater emotional stability rather than stress.

Control, support and demands

Research by Karasek and Theorell from the Karolinska Institute in Sweden suggests that there are three main dimensions of workplace stress: control, support and demands.[21]

One of the major causes of stress in the workplace, and life in general, is the desire to be in control. There are two aspects to control: control of the external environment (the external locus of control) and control of the internal environment (the internal locus of control). As far as wellbeing is concerned, the internal locus of control is generally more important than the external locus. This has to do with us having control over ourselves; that is, our responses and attitudes to the things going on around us. Modifying the external environment to increase control includes things like involving people in decision-making processes, developing systems that work on cooperation rather than competition, modifying workplaces to give variety or offering choice where possible over things like conditions and rosters.

Some of us might have noted that often we have little control over what's going on around us, and this is where control through choosing our attitude or response to the environment matters a lot. Internal means the level of control we have over ourselves, that is, our thoughts, feelings and attitudes. A key point mentioned previously that needs to be remembered here is that if we try to control our thoughts, feelings and sensations we will fight a losing battle. Mindful control has to do with being aware of the thoughts, feelings and sensations but not having to be controlled by them — through non-attachment. That makes it easier to choose the ones to which we would prefer to give our attention, time and energy. Changing an attitude from 'unwillingness' to 'willingness', for example, can have an enormous impact on how we experience a situation and on the level of mental and physiological stress we experience.

Building support in the workplace in order for it to be most effective needs to become a part of the workplace culture and include both employees and employers. Support becomes a rare commodity in very competitive environments. Spending effort and resources on building adequate support into our workplaces in the long run is really an investment — not only in the wellbeing of those doing the work but also in the ability for those working to be able to keep working efficiently. As the saying goes, 'There is no I in team.' Support can be built in as a formal process through debriefing, professional development and building effective communication strategies, but equally, if not more, important is building a workplace culture that will sustain and support people.

The third of the workplace stresses is demands. A mismatch between demands and performance can be rectified by three approaches: reducing demands, improving performance capacity and moderating the perception of the demands.

Reducing demands may be necessary, particularly where resources have been cut too far, but many find that demands are ever increasing rather than reducing as employers or shareholders want more return on their financial or time investments. We can moderate our demands by avoiding putting too much on our plate where we have that choice available to us. Sometimes demands are beyond our control, so how we meet demands becomes an important issue. Rather than hoping for more time, resources and energy, we can learn to make better, more focused and efficient use of the time, resources and energy we have. Thus, skills such as focusing attention, relaxation, training in time management and problem-solving can be very helpful. Another solution, which can be the easiest to miss, is the ability to discern between real and perceived demands. We often anticipate that jobs will be far more demanding than they really are and so feel overwhelmed before we have even attempted them. Avoidance often masquerades as an inability to meet demands. We can easily consume ten times as much time and energy in avoiding a job as it would take to complete it. There's no peace of mind in that. Mindfulness can be just the thing to help us be aware of the presence of such prejudicial ideas, to reserve judgment and to focus attention on the job rather than on all the thinking and worrying about the job.

Taking time for self-care or personal and professional development is what Stephen Covey describes in his *Seven Habits of Highly Effective People* as an 'important' but 'non-urgent' job, and as such it nearly always gets put on the backburner when competing with the apparently more important and 'urgent' needs of everyday work.[22] In fact we cannot, or at least not happily, sustain our everyday work without adequate time taken for self-care. To use the metaphor — if we don't take a little time to stop and sharpen the saw we will have to take a lot more time and energy to do the job.

Mindful leadership

There are a number of things that leaders need in order to be effective. Social skills, empathy and being able to self-regulate difficult emotions are the core personal skills of a person managing people — and emotional intelligence helps — which we will explored more fully in Chapter 21.

Being able to manage stress is also useful. As Rudyard Kipling wrote in his poem, *If*, 'If you can keep your head when all about you are losing theirs and blaming it on you; If you can trust yourself when all men doubt you, But make allowance for their doubting too.' The leader needs to be cool in the crisis for their own benefit and also to serve as a role model for their team members. The other thing is that we cannot perform sustainably at a high level unless we manage our stress well.

A leader needs to be able to listen, and when speaking must speak with attention. There is little gravitas in barking a command out of the corner of the mouth while thinking about something else. It doesn't engage the attention of the person we are speaking to, so the instruction or guidance doesn't go in with the same clarity.

Leaders often have very complex jobs, and they need to make challenging decisions and discern what's relevant from what isn't. The term 'executive functioning' is used in neuroscience, but it's a term well coined. We all have an executive decision-making part of ourselves, and it needs to work well, not be slumped in the corner because we're not paying attention, nor pulling its metaphorical hair out. In fact, there's a whole Neuroleadership movement now that is using the knowledge gained from modern neuroscience to inform us on how to perform at a high level — and develop effective leadership skills.

Take-to-work tips for a mindful response in the workplace

Not so helpful

- Avoid multitasking, especially complex multitasking.
- Avoid practising avoidance because we will only get good at it.
- Avoid haste and know how to pace ourselves.

Helpful

- Practise paying attention and being present.
- Manage our environment by: reducing and managing technology such as mobile phone calls, the Internet and email; reducing unnecessary stimuli such as sound pollution, Facebook and Twitter; managing interruptions so that the focus is on what it needs to be on; beginning with priority one, proceed with one task at a time and have the mental flexibility to change priorities when needed.
- Listen to work colleagues.
- Know when to take breaks and freshen up including getting away from the desk to eat lunch.
- Practise self-care outside of the working day to help keep ourselves healthy and fresh — it will save time, not waste it.
- Understand that knowing when to stop working is just as important as knowing when to start.

CHAPTER 20

Sporting performance

Sportspeople must train the mind as well as the body

These days elite athletes are spending nearly as much time training their mind as training their body. Why? Because it often makes the difference between being a talented athlete and being a great one. But training the mind is not just relevant for the elite athlete. Any social golfer who has stepped up to the first tee overlooking a water hazard between them and the green realises that they have a major test for their attention — is their focus on the ball or on the water? Mostly the water has a magnetic attraction for the mind and the ball follows suit.

Let's look at mindfulness and its usefulness in sport. We'll start by considering a few examples. Each of these situations illustrates an important issue related to sport and how mindfulness and unmindfulness affect enjoyment and performance of it.

Jo was 21 years old and a very good golfer — so good, in fact, that she had won a number of amateur tournaments and recently turned professional. So good, in fact, that she wanted to play on the US golf tour but she needed to gain her player's ticket by performing well enough in a four-round event for aspiring young golfers to be able to enter these lucrative tournaments.

After three rounds and 15 holes Jo was in a good position to qualify for her ticket and she just needed to come home over the last 3 holes in par to make it. Jo sliced the next drive into the trees. She then 3-putted from 20 feet. Finally she found the water hazard on the last hole. Jo missed the cut-off by four shots. Jo got very angry with herself, especially as the same thing happened again, particularly when she found herself in close contention late in a tournament. Jo never got her player's ticket for the pro tour and gave up her dream of being a professional golfer by the age of 25, feeling that she had never really reached her potential.

Jo experienced what nearly everyone experiences at various times, and not just in relation to sport: performance anxiety. But just what lurks behind performance anxiety? In the spirit of mindfulness we shouldn't simply hate the fact that it comes up, we should be interested to see what's going on. Jo fought with herself, which made the situation worse, until she gave up — but where was her focus when she found herself in a tight situation? If she had consciously examined the situation then she might have noticed that it wasn't on the process (which takes place in the here and now), it was on the outcome (which is a hypothetical future event). The more important the outcome, the greater the likelihood for distraction and nerves.

To prepare for a golf shot, a lot of information is required: the attention needs to be on the breeze, distances, contours and nap of the green. Then, having assessed the context for the shot we need to execute it — our attention needs to be on the feel of the club, the ball, the muscles, the smoothness and flow of the movement. All of this is present-moment stuff. If the attention is on our ideas and aspirations about the outcome — at the moment of assessment or execution — then we not only introduce the potential for anxiety, but also significantly reduce our potential to play the shot well. The more we want the outcome, the greater the potential for this interference. 'What if I get it? What if I miss?'

Strangely, we often interfere with the attainment of the very thing we want. We can do all the imagery and motivational thinking we like in the lead-up to the event, but in the moment of execution there is only one thing that matters and that's our focus on the task — here and now — our mindfulness. Paradoxically, although we may have a goal, it's letting go of the goal that allows us not only to feel relaxed again, but also to optimise our chance of reaching the goal. It's one of those Zen things.

Peter was a top-level shooter and was leading the biggest tournament of his life. He was three shots in the lead and had a score of 192 hits out of a possible 195 and was about to take the last five shots. The second-placed shooter was on 189 with five shots to go and had just scored five out of five with his last five shots to finish on 194. Considering that he hadn't missed three out of five for years, Peter felt supremely confident. He stepped up and missed three out his last five shots, thus finishing on 194. Peter lost the tournament on a count-back.

When Peter was approached by an incredulous reporter after the event he was asked what went wrong. Peter shook his head in disbelief. All day he had been so focused, so cool and calm. He had been in 'the zone'. In the lead-up to the last five shots, and being so far in front, Peter's attention turned to the most pleasant of dreams: standing on the podium, receiving the medal, being a hero, coming home to a hero's welcome, being 'the champion' for the rest of his life. The lesson here? Pleasant daydreams are just as much of a distraction as unpleasant ones. If he had been just one shot in front with five to go we can expect that he would not have let his mind wander anywhere other than on what it had to do.

Greg was 44 years old and had taken up running in the mornings again because he had become unfit, was putting on weight and felt like he was ageing faster than his years. The intention was just to get back to running a few kilometres a few times a week but, enjoying the challenge, over time he had been slowly increasing his distances and now his longest runs were up to 10 kilometres. When younger, Greg had intended to run a marathon but never did. It was an unfulfilled ambition, but while listening to a radio interview with someone about to run their first marathon in a couple of weeks Greg noticed the thought pop into his mind: 'I wonder if it's not too late to run a marathon?' There wasn't time to train for it this year, but what about next year?

Steadily and methodically building the distances, by the age of 46 Greg found himself fit enough to run the city's annual marathon. Everyone had told him how tough it was, and how those last 5 kilometres really hurt, so it wasn't surprising that when Greg made the final turn for home, still 5 kilometres out from the finish, the thought entered his mind: 'It's really going to get tough now!' It was as if someone put a 20-kilogram pack on his back — all of a sudden it was a whole lot tougher than it was a minute ago. 'Wait a minute! Just check in with the body. I'm tired but going okay. Just take one step at a time and we'll get there when we get there!'

This is the literal 'one step at a time' situation. Greg was just about to start telling himself a story — one that he probably didn't realise he had rehearsed — about how tough it was going to be. It was like there was a play button pushed at the 5-kilometre mark and off it went. He was about to filter his experience of what was happening in the present moment through this story. We do it all the time — tell ourselves how tough something is, how much something is going to hurt, how we can't do something. All this does is make a task more difficult than it needs to be, or increase our perception of the pain, or make us give up even before we've begun.

In Greg's case there was tiredness, sure, but it wasn't really painful. If he thought about how long another 5 kilometres was then it seemed like forever, but how much of a burden was just one step? It wasn't such a big deal, nor was the next one, nor the next ... This is mindfulness — just being in the moment and not focusing on the outcome; just attending to the journey and not being preoccupied about the destination. Checking in with the body by paying attention to what the senses are telling us — not necessarily what our noisy mind is telling us — is an act of mindfulness. If Greg did pay attention to his body and it was about to have a major meltdown or a heart attack, then the reasonable and mindful thing to do in that moment would be to say, 'Hmm, that's interesting, my body seems to be telling me it may be time to stop running and get some assistance from one of those helpful-looking people standing on the side of the road who enjoy telling marathon runners, "Not far to go, you're nearly there!"'

The zone and flow states

When we're performing at our peak, whether it's in sport or in any other activity, we tend to describe mindful states of a very high order. Athletes have a term for this: 'The Zone'. Others call it 'The Flow State'. This is a state that's widely recognised and described, and looks to be the same in whatever sport or activity in which it arises.[1] Mihály Csíkszentmihályi is the most widely cited author writing about flow states.[2] (If you can't pronounce his name, call him 'the flow guy'.) The kinds of things that athletes describe when in the zone or flow is summed up by Billie Jean King, one of the greatest female tennis players of all time:

> It almost seems as though I'm able to transport myself beyond the turmoil on the court to some place of total peace and calm ... I appreciate what my opponent is doing in a detached, abstract way. Like an observer in the next room ... It is a perfect combination of [intense] action taking place in an atmosphere of total tranquility.[3]

Many athletes later come to describe such experiences as spiritual, such is their transcendent nature.

So let's discuss some of the characteristics of the zone or flow state. We'll try not to get too Zen, but you just can't avoid a bit of Zenness when discussing such things. If you can recollect peak experiences in your own life, these tips will make a lot more sense.

• Deep but effortless concentration on the process.

The concentration is fully drawn by engagement and interest in the activity itself and not to some secondary goal, such as winning. Therefore, these experiences are the most alive, vivid, fulfilling and memorable. This also implies an ability to not be interested in anything irrelevant, including being heckled by opponents.

- A sense of self-control. The zone is a unified and integrated state. If there's no internal battle, then there's nothing to pull us off balance and nothing to fight against — because it's a state of non-attachment. There may be a hurricane of activity going on around us, but we are in the 'eye of the hurricane' — some call it being centred.

- An absence of self-consciousness or ego. When we're thinking about ourselves we're not on task, and when we're on task we're not thinking about ourselves. Although we're not self-conscious, the zone is the most self-expressive state.

- Enjoyment, relaxation, confidence and freedom. The satisfaction that comes when watching it happen with such effortlessness. Freedom of expression. What is there to be anxious about?

- Focus on the goal without feeling anxiety about it. The zone isn't an aimless state. We're able to set our course with clarity and unwavering resolve and yet not pin our happiness on the outcome. There's resilience here because we're no longer focused on the things that sap resilience — such as self-doubt — so losing holds no fear.

- Be in the present moment. The focus on the present leaves no room for preoccupation or anxiety about the outcome, and allows attention to engage fully — to optimise performance.

- The sense of time is altered. Although events may be moving fast, things seem to slow down (which is a sign of acute attention). Although a long time may have passed while engaged in the activity, it seems to be no time at all. Some describe the present moment as being timeless.

- Peak performance. Enough said.

The zone or flow state sounds pretty good, and we think most of us would live there if we could. For many of us, our desire to be in the zone is about performing well. For others it's about fulfilment and enjoyment — a much better motivation. For others, like rock climbers, it's about life and death — that's one way to bring ourselves into the joys of being present!

Mindfulness and cultivating the zone

Is being in the zone a matter of luck? Not really; it requires practice. Can we snap our fingers and transport ourselves into it whenever we like? Not really, because thinking about being in the zone isn't the same as being in it; in fact, it's quite the opposite. So what do we do? Well, according to Dr Jim Taylor from the Association for the Advancement of Applied Sport Psychology, this is how he sees the role of mindfulness in sport.

> *Mindfulness is vastly different than the way many athletes conceive it, and it offers many benefits to focusing and athletic performance. Mindfulness teaches athletes to focus on the present rather than dwelling on past mistakes or future results. This present focus enables athletes to be more alert to relevant performance cues and allows them to more easily disregard distracting cues.* [4]

The way to cultivate the zone is to learn to pay attention, to be present. It means 'keeping the eye on the ball', which doesn't make much sense if you're not playing a ball sport, but you know what we mean. If swimming — feel the water, the body's movements, the flow of the stroke. It's about connecting with the senses and letting the mind's innate intelligence work unimpeded. A famous Australian Rules footballer equalled a record for goals kicked in a season in 1971 that had stood for 39 years. When asked for the key to his success, he didn't mention a special secret diet or training drill or innate physical talent, he said that he gave his complete attention to the football — all the time, even when it was out of play.

The zone is a natural state, not an artificial one. We don't force ourselves into it, we just practise not thinking our way out of it. When we notice our attention is off task, we bring it back on task again. When we're practising worrying about the outcome before or during the game, we focus again back on process. The future is unknown and will not be known until it's the present — and then it will come to pass. When we're practising beating ourselves up about a past error, we can instead be present and reflect on what the experience can teach us — and then leave it alone.

One other little trick is to not try to hold on to being in the zone. Holding on is the exact opposite to what mindfulness is about. We can only rest in the state. Thinking about being in the zone when we notice we've been in it is also a good way to catapult our way out of it — like Adam and Eve getting evicted from the Garden of Eden. 'Look at me, I'm in the zone!' is a sign that the ego is about to pop up its head and it's as much a distraction as any other thought. In the zone the mind is quiet but very perceptive and not self-conscious, so we need to gently get our attention back on track.

Training is as much about the mind as it is about the body. It will not only wire the nerves and muscles to do tasks they couldn't previously do, but we can train attention — with training drills — especially when we 'don't have time to think'. If pain follows hot on the heels of being unfocused, we can learn focus very quickly. We need to practise fluency, rhythm and flow; this will help us focus our attention and shorten the attentional blinks.

Racing-car drivers have trained their reflexes by shooting tennis balls from a machine straight at their face. Thinking about lunch, or impending pain for that matter, is a great way to get one on the snoz.

Instinctive decisions

In 2007 a BBC news story reported on a recently published study. 'Trusting your instincts may help you to make better decisions than thinking hard, a study suggests,' said the journalist.[5] When participants were tested, the researchers found that 95 per cent of instinctive decisions were accurate when participants were given less than half a second to perform a computer-based pattern-recognition task. We might expect giving them extra time would reduce that error rate of 5 per cent. Well, the participants were only 70 per cent accurate if given more than twice as long.[6] That meant that the error rate went up from 5 per cent to 30 per cent with more time — that is, it was six times higher.

Why? Well, if we're paying attention we see and we recognise — it all happens pretty quickly. If we respond to what we recognise in the moment, then no further correspondence need be entered into. But having extra time to delay the response and double-guess doesn't lead to a better decision; it leads to self-doubt and a loss of flow. Sportspeople will say that when they are in the flow they just see, recognise and respond without thinking about it; the window of opportunity opens for a split second and they go straight through it. When we're not in the flow, then the window of opportunity opens and then we ask ourselves, 'Is that the window of opportunity? I'm not sure. If it is, should I go through it? How could I be sure? Maybe there are better windows somewhere else?' By this time the window of opportunity has not only closed but the crowd has already left the park.

Of course, some complex issues may not be as appropriate for snap decisions, and in these cases the mindful thing to do is to wait or gather more information. Being able to tell the difference between when we should act and when we should wait is one of the hallmarks of wisdom and serenity.

Teamwork

Sport is, of course, as much about the team as it is about the individual. Teams can be more or less mindful, more or less in the zone, more or less focused and working as one, more or less in the present rather than the past or future. Furthermore, many of the attributes of Emotional Intelligence we will discuss in the next chapter are attributes of good teams and leaders.

A team that learns and understands the principles of mindfulness is likely to do far better than one that doesn't. To illustrate, one of the authors much enjoyed hearing John Bertrand speak at a conference not so long ago. Bertrand was the skipper of *Australia II*, the first foreign boat to win the America's Cup from the Americans after 126 years of attempts — in 1983. Apart from having a great boat and support team, he said there were two things that helped them to perform under that kind of pressure. One was a sense of humour. The other was to train in his team a capacity to stay in the present moment. He knew that when the pressure was on, if the crew grew anxious about mistakes or misfortune, or concerned about the outcome, then they would lose focus on their tasks. Executing their tasks reliably, as one, and with precision and efficiency, was all they needed to do. He didn't call this mindfulness, but a rose by any other name …

Children and sport

For children, learning mindfulness as a part of how they learn to play sport will be a great advantage and should be the goal of any coach. Not only will mindfulness help them to enjoy their game more and play it better, it will also help them to display better sportsmanship. Unfortunately many adults, especially ones who are projecting their anxieties on to their children, train their children to be unmindful. If children learn to focus better because their enjoyment of the activity is the aim, then better performance will also follow in its wake. That's a win–win situation.

One of the authors still remembers playing in a Little League football grand final a hundred or so years ago, and being screamed at by footy fans including the parents of his team-mates for dropping the ball at a critical moment. This was an enduring lesson in the potential destructiveness of unmindfulness — on the part of parents and himself. Eventually there was an illuminating realisation that he dropped the ball because he was so lost in thinking about the outcome of the thrillingly/chillingly close game that he had forgotten his coach's earnest and simple instructions: 'Keep your eye on the ball!' What better lesson in mindfulness? Unfortunately, when we create anxiety about the outcome in the mind of the child we make them far less able to focus.

Very important also is fostering a growth mindset rather than a fixed mindset in relation to sport as well as to academic work. Read more about this in Chapter 18.

Sorry, but we just can't help ourselves: let's finish with another quote from that sage author, Rudyard Kipling, from his poem *If*, which he wrote for his son approaching his sixteenth birthday. The first two lines of the quote are placed prominently in the Wimbledon changing rooms for the players to read just before they enter the playing arena. These precepts would be valuable for any child's development in sport, and in life for that matter:

> *If you can meet with triumph and disaster,*
> *And treat those two imposters just the same ...*
> *If you can fill the unforgiving minute,*
> *With sixty seconds worth of distance run,*
> *Yours is the world and all that's in it,*
> *And, which is more, you'll be a man, my son.*

Tips for playing sport mindfully

Not so helpful

- Be so anxious about the outcome that we can't focus on the game.
- Put winning before anything else including our values.

Helpful

- Keep our 'eye on the ball'.
- Play hard but enjoy the game rather than get anxious about the outcome.
- Value sportsmanship.
- Cultivate the flow state.

CHAPTER 21
Emotional Intelligence

Emotional Intelligence (EI) is a hot topic in the psychology world these days. Even the driest cognitive scientists are having to move over in their beds and begrudgingly share the space with more free-flowing scientists for whom emotions are what it's all about. We won't get caught up in any hot psychological debates here about which is more important — thoughts or emotions — other than to say that the authors believe that thoughts and emotions are both very important, and that they are intimately linked.

Consider an example of two people walking in the forest in the early evening and due to the light fading they mistook a rope coiled on the path for a snake. What followed was extreme fear and a resulting big physiological fight-or-flight response. This is a cognitive error (a mistaken thought based on misinterpreting what one sees) that leads to an emotional response, which the body faithfully translates into a physical reaction. If there were no emotion generated by the thought, there would be no significant physical effect.

So, what is EI? Well, according to one definition, 'Emotional intelligence (EI) refers to the ability to perceive, control and evaluate emotions.'[1] Probably the best-known author on the topic, Daniel Goleman, breaks EI into the five elements summarised in the table opposite.[2]

Elements of Emotional Intelligence
(adapted from Goleman)

	Definition	Hallmarks
Self-awareness	Ability to recognise and understand emotions, drives and effects	Self-confidence, realistic self-assessment, self-deprecating
Self-regulation	Can control or redirect disruptive impulses, can think before acting	Trustworthiness and integrity, comfort with ambiguity
Motivation	Passion for work that goes beyond money or status, energy and persistence	Drive to achieve, optimism in the face of challenge, organisational commitment
Empathy	Ability to understand emotions of others, skill in interacting with others	Can build and retain talent, cross-cultural sensitivity, service to others
Social skill	Can manage relationships and build networks, can find common ground, rapport	Can lead change, persuasiveness, expertise in building and leading teams

Mindfulness and Emotional Intelligence

Does mindfulness have anything to do with EI? Well, according to evidence from renowned mindfulness researcher Ruth Baer, people who rate highly on mindfulness scales tend to have lower levels of neuroticism, symptoms of psychological distress, experiential avoidance (coping by trying to avoid problems rather than by addressing them) and dissociation (the feeling of being cut off or disconnected that sometimes happens in traumatic situations). On the other hand, more mindful people tend to rank highly for EI and absorption.[3] Absorption is a state in which a person feels in the flow — fully connected, energised, focused, inwardly calm and in control. Athletes talk about this in terms of being in the zone (as we discussed in Chapter 20).

Similar findings have been shown in other studies too. People with higher EI report fewer psychological symptoms relating to their traumatic experiences.[4] EI is inversely related to depression, that is, the more EI we have the less likely we are to get depressed.[5] For university students, higher EI is associated with less fatigue and stress.[6] For it to consistently have such effects suggests to us that this must be a very desirable and natural part of us. For it to map so closely with the benefits associated with mindfulness, they must be covering similar territory. Let's look at the elements of Emotional Intelligence, and at how they relate to mindfulness.

Emotional Intelligence and self-awareness

Self-awareness is the ability to recognise and understand emotions and drives and their effects on others. This requires the ability to pay attention to what's going on inside and around us and on how they interrelate. Just to illustrate, a study on university undergraduates found that low EI was associated with stress, expressed in emotional terms ranging from anger and frustration to hatred; and low-EI students were also more likely to engage in health-damaging behaviours. High-EI students, on the other hand, were more likely to adopt reflection and appraisal and self-management skills.[7] Adolescence and early adulthood is an important time for the development of EI.

If we're not paying attention, we don't see what's really driving us, and we then spend lots of time and energy trying to fool ourselves and others into believing that things are other than the way they really are. This is like trying to convince someone that we didn't mean what we just said when we actually did mean it. 'No offence, but …' Being self-aware also includes appreciating that sometimes we are ambiguous creatures with competing drives and motivations, all playing out at the same time. Without self-awareness there's little prospect for authenticity or choice. With self-awareness we might have a chance of getting to know ourselves better.

Emotional Intelligence and self-regulation

Self-regulation is sometimes also referred to as emotional regulation and relates to the ability to deal with and redirect emotional impulses. We have probably all had the feeling of experiencing anger that is destructive, or some other unhelpful impulse — and realising that expressing it in the way that we feel driven to may not be such a good idea. Being able to recognise it and either 'let it go through to the keeper' (which may mean something to you if you speak cricket) or express something that needs to be said but in a more constructive way, is very much a part of self-regulation. Practising being mindful may help, for example, to reduce the amount of anger we feel because we realise there's really not so much to get angry over.

This doesn't mean that anger will never arise if we're mindful, or even that anger may not be necessary in a given situation. A key element of self-regulation is that we're not trying to control the emotion by suppressing it — which tends to make it pent up and ready to explode at some inopportune time — but we realise that we don't have to be controlled *by* the emotion. This requires an ability to recognise it but not be attached to it.

All our minutes and hours spent in our chair practising mindfulness meditation will prepare us for this and therefore improve our Emotional Intelligence. Any emotion can and will present itself to us during our mindfulness practice and it's best that we cultivate an open attitude to this fact because then we can practise not so much trying to get rid of these emotions, but rather not engaging with them — reacting to them, fighting with them, suppressing them — or even criticising ourselves for having them. We can welcome them in if they knock on our front door, but just let them pass right out again through our open back door. If we react to them, we will amplify them and attach ourselves to them. That's when it all starts to get a bit complicated!

We should bear in mind that emotions such as anger or sadness aren't necessarily negative — they can have their place. Like a piano keyboard, we have a number of octaves of notes available to us, and 'being positive' isn't about playing just the high notes. Sadness could be entirely appropriate in a given situation and there would be nothing useful about suppressing it — in fact, it will be stressful, or at least inauthentic — not honest — to not express it. Mindful anger, if we could call it that, is different to the more common unmindful anger. Mindful anger arises as an emotional strength or conviction to meet the needs of a given situation. It's based on clear — undistorted — perception; it's not of harmful or venomous intent; we feel in control of it rather than it controlling us; it's supported by reason as well as emotion; and isn't over-expressed. With mindful anger we're aware of the effect of our words and actions on the people or events we're interacting with, and it dissolves quickly after the situation is over, without leaving agitation or bitterness in its wake. If we experience and express unmindful anger, then so be it — we should learn from the experience and then be better able to recognise it the next time it arises.

Emotional Intelligence and motivation

Motivation can come from all sorts of sources. We can be motivated by fear, courage, greed, compassion, altruism, the desire for fame or a million other things. In fact, our motivations are often mixed and competing, so if we're not cool-headed and paying attention, we might find ourselves being motivated by things that we would rather not be — if we really thought about it. We might, for example, be motivated by the desire for money — the more the better — such that we dedicate the whole of our life to it. But if we examined this a little more closely we may see that the real drive behind our desire for money is a desire for happiness, influenced by an unexamined belief that money leads to happiness. It could be a very sobering wake-up after 30 years of chasing the almighty dollar to realise that in the process we have made ourselves and everyone around us unhappy. There's nothing particularly wrong with money, it's just that it may not do what we think it will.

On the other hand, we might never have considered that we may be happier if we spent a little more time helping those around us, particularly those in need. We could try this as an experiment and see what we find. So, it's not too difficult to see that in being more awake, and learning from our experience, we might find that our motivations and values are different to the ones we unconsciously take on board from advertising and elsewhere. Being motivated by our deeper nature and core values is far more satisfying than the more superficial and noisy desires crowding our thoughts for much of the time, and this will sustain us in times of adversity. This naturally flows into the next element: empathy.

Emotional Intelligence and empathy

Empathy and compassion are natural but they can get covered up, mostly by ideas of difference and separation. So, for example, if as we watch the nightly news we think of a refugee as a foreign invader then we may be very insensitive to their plight; if, on the other hand, the same person turned up on our doorstep one rainy night, battered and starving, we might feel a natural outpouring of compassion and care for them. If we saw them drowning as we were sailing in the bay then we would feel strongly drawn to rescue them. Empathy and compassion strongly rely on relationship and attention. If we don't pay attention, then we won't feel compassion.

There have been some interesting discoveries on empathy and compassion arising from our eavesdropping on people's brains through brain-imaging techniques such as Magnetic Resonance Imaging (MRI). The centre of the brain that largely responds to emotions is called the limbic system. It sits very closely to the memory centre. There are specific areas of our limbic system that fire up in the empathic response to another's pain. We literally 'feel' the pain in much the same way as the person experiencing it. Interestingly, experienced meditators have more active empathic responses and activation in their limbic system than do novices.[8] The longer we have practised meditation, the more responsive or awake these areas become. Attention or mindfulness leads to empathy, whereas inattention or unmindfulness leads to a lack of empathy — callousness and even cruelty.

Other studies have also confirmed that increases in empathy are associated with improvements in emotional wellbeing.[9] To illustrate, a study on primary-care doctors published in the *JAMA* (the *Journal of the American Medical Association*) showed that when they are trained in mindfulness they become more emotionally stable, but also more empathic and responsive to their patients.[10] High burnout levels have also been found in nearly 50 per cent of surgeons. Lack of emotional control, emotional recognition and expression, and understanding of emotions are significant predictors of burnout risk.[11] In short, as EI goes down in the scales, burnout goes up, and as EI goes up, burnout goes down.

Why is this so? Empathy associated with stress and aversion to suffering often overwhelms health practitioners and leads them to experience carer fatigue or to become indifferent, whereas mindfulness training increases empathy and reduces carer fatigue. This may be largely because it helps us to be more comfortable and less avoidant in the presence of discomfort, whether ours or another's. This isn't a vital skill just for clinicians, but for anyone, particularly teachers, community workers and those caring for others such as parents and people with chronic illnesses and disabilities.

Emotional Intelligence and social skills

The last of the elements of EI is social skills. Leaders with stronger EI are better at communicating, being responsive to their team-members needs, bringing people together and resolving conflicts amicably. Again, it's not really surprising that greater awareness helps us be more responsive to those around us and to recognise the impact of our words and actions on others. We may find ourselves more able to appreciate the concerns or issues under the surface or better able to read cues if we are paying attention than if we're not.

One of the fascinating things that one of the authors has noticed when following people through mindfulness programs is how their emotional world and relationships start to change. People often report that they are able to see emotions arising, are able to discern which are more helpful and which not, whether or not to express them or how to express them in a better way. One of the most important benefits of these programs is that as we become more aware of ourselves and our emotions and motivations in a mindful and compassionate way, we also tend to start to be more understanding and tolerant of others. Let's face it: we're all in the same boat, even if it's leaking.

The bottom line

To paraphrase Shakespeare: EI by any other name would smell as sweet. It's not only for ourselves that we need to cultivate it but also for those around us. It will help us at home, at work, in teams and when dealing with life's challenges. Emotional Intelligence is a natural consequence of mindfulness, and it is just another of the many collateral benefits that we get when we practise mindfulness, even if cultivating them wasn't our original intention.

Take-home tips for mindfully cultivating Emotional Intelligence

Not so helpful

- Judge ourselves for experiencing emotions we don't like.
- Fight with the emotions we would rather not experience.
- Ruminate about why we are the way we are.
- Endlessly relive past mistakes rather than learn from them.

Helpful

- Learn to be more aware of our emotions without the need to criticise the ones we don't like.
- Learn how not be so attached to our emotions.
- Learn how to gently unhook the attention from the emotions that are not so useful.
- Give attention to the emotions that we would like to foster.
- Be patient with ourselves — change takes time.
- Cultivate empathy and compassion for others.

C H A P T E R   2 2

Mindful parenting

It's 3 a.m. in the maternity ward and my wife has been in labour since 8 a.m. yesterday, when her waters seeped rather than broke. I'm sitting in what would normally be a comfortable chair in what would normally be a comfortable, even luxurious, birthing suite, with an oil burner and a CD player. It looked like a holiday resort — yesterday. Now I'm recording the time between contractions on a small notepad that's rapidly becoming too small.

'Four minutes, again,' I call out, with no idea of why I'm counting. Days later I learned that this helped give my wife a sense of achievement, and me a focus to restore my contracting mindfulness.

'You both look exhausted!' announces our all-night midwife. 'You need a rest!'

Penelope [not her real name] and I look at each other quizzically.

'I'll give you some sedatives so you can sleep for a few hours and then you can start again. You've only dilated about 2 centimetres so far, so it looks like we might need a Caesar.'

Things are feeling so surreal now that we almost believe you can have a 'rest' from hard labour. Penelope takes the tablets, and I lie down beside her, until she throws up her sleeping pills and just lies in the bed for maybe an hour, quite possibly wondering just what I meant when I told her that this would be an ideal time to practise mindful childbirth, as a prelude to mindful parenting. This is an especially good opportunity because she isn't taking any pain relievers or other drugs that might interfere with her ability to be as fully conscious as possible, as fully mindful as possible during our first experience of childbirth. I'm wondering if mindful childbirth or mindful anything else is really possible.

Somehow Penelope realises that what she really needs is available in this moment, so she abandons her 'rest' to sit in a squatting position. She's also naturally mindful enough not to swear at me — awake or asleep! This practical response came from fully attending to what was happening to her body, without 'escaping' into negative and irrelevant thoughts and emotions. Miraculously she soon dilates another eight centimetres and our baby's head appears, followed eventually by the rest of her body. Phoenix [*not her real name*] looks at us, the medical staff and her wonderful new world with an amazed and amazing awareness, as if of the adventure of life.

Mindful *and* not-so-mindful parenting

The above story is a true life example from the true recent life of one of us (the generally less mindful one) and it demonstrates the choices parents can make between responding mindlessly and mindfully. Another real life example of the possibilities for either mindless or mindful parenting (or both at once) is that of the mother who took her eight children to The Show and bought them all ice-creams: when she had one ice-cream left she realised that one of her children was missing.

Mindless-parenting examples appear on the Internet every day. This demonstrates the potential mass mindlessness of the mass media, as well as mindless parenting. Dreams and drama are often chosen over reason and consciousness. A less-dramatic-than-usual Internet example was about a woman recently interviewed by a radio station about sending firefighters to her home to 'rescue' her baby. When she arrived at kinder to drop off her other child she realised she had left her baby at home. She told the mindful and understanding firefighters who managed to break into her house without waking her sleeping baby that she was 'sleep-deprived'!

We don't need to go further to find an example of how not to be a mindful father than the life of one of us (the same one). When bathing his baby one night he was distracted by a spectacular goal kicked by his favourite football team — he was being mindlessly simulcast to by a TV and a bath. In less than a second his baby had somehow slopped most of her bathwater on to the usually dry carpet and was trying to drink the rest of it. What mindlessness can teach us very quickly is that disasters can be instant.

An example of mindful fathering might be the baptism that the same baby attended as guest of honour. Her father managed to give her his complete attention before and during her first public performance as the recipient of some special and watery blessings. The baby responded mindfully, by beatifically giving her full attention to her baptismal duties. The MC remarked: 'That was a ten out of ten performance!'

A great literary example of mindless parenting is that of an exceptional children's story character called Mrs McCave, in a book called *Too Many Daves* by Dr Seuss. She took the wise precaution of calling all twenty-three of her sons Dave, presumably so that she would never forget who was whom. Do you still think you have problems? Keep reading!

The world's a stage, or going through one

If we're a parent or a prospective parent we might think that mindful parenting sounds like an oxymoron — like fighting for peace. If we've just spent the entire night feeding, changing and consoling our new baby, or waiting for our teenager to come home from a party, then mindful parenting might even seem like a particularly moronic oxymoron. Mindfulness, however, can offer us hope that things don't have to be as bad as they sometimes seem when we're unmindful. No matter what we're doing, we can do it mindfully.

When we don't realise that things come and go we can spend our life playing our part — but not our whole — as parents or as children of parents. In this incomplete state we can get attached to dangerous ideas of what we *should* be doing and our expectation of how it *should* turn out. We're far better off just doing our best, enjoying the show and simply being with rather than against our every experience. This realisation of impermanence works: it can make us happier and calmer and far better at doing what we do, paradoxically by allowing us to realise that it's not as desperately and grimly important as we think it is. This can even work for parenting!

The impermanence of our thoughts, feelings and experiences has been discussed in earlier chapters on how to cultivate mindful practices in general, and parenting is certainly a potentially wonderful applied example! Take thoughts, and the feelings they so often generate. It's not uncommon as a parent, particularly a first-time mother or father, to have self-hostile thoughts such as 'I'm a terrible parent!' Some thoughts are easy to let go of and others seem like magnets for our attention. A thought like this one is likely to attract a lot of our attention, and when we're feeling down or tired our mind will generally flail about trying to find things to support the harsh judgment we have made about ourselves. Just being mindful enough to notice our tired state will help us to be cautious in taking such thoughts as facts. Meanwhile, the very thing that really needs our attention — for example, *our child* — isn't getting it, or is only getting part of it, while our precious attention and energy is being diverted to our self-abusive self-talk.

Thoughts can, and generally do, distort a fair picture of how we're really going, and usually it's a lot better than what we think. If we can become aware of how often our attention gets diverted to repetitive and negative thought patterns and feelings, we can start to gently redirect it back to where it needs to be. This is good mindfulness practice and good parenting practice.

A woman participating in a mindfulness course with one of us (the mindful one) recently gave an example of a shift from unmindfulness to mindfulness from her own parenting experience. While breastfeeding one night her attention was fixed on her thoughts about when her baby would finish feeding, how tired she would be the next day and how disrupted her life was since becoming a parent. This grumbling, low-level resentment was a common experience for her.

Then she described having a moment of seeing what was happening in her own head and it prompted her to practise mindfulness. 'What did it mean to be mindful at this moment?' she asked herself. 'Pay attention!' What was in front of her now? As her baby was peacefully feeding she looked at her with undivided attention, not trying to have positive thoughts or to wish she was somewhere else; she just stopped and looked. The more that this woman was just in the moment with her child the more she noticed the exquisite beauty of her baby and the moment they were sharing; a mundane moment certainly, but beautiful and tender nonetheless. Love arose, not by trying to get rid of thoughts and feelings of anger and impatience, but simply because such thoughts and feelings were no longer the focus and seemed not to have any place. Her focus was the moment and not the ideas about past and future she had been projecting on to it.

Love is our natural and conscious state: all the other stuff in our head is what we create to eclipse that love. Resting in that experience and not wishing to be anywhere other than where she was gave this woman a refreshment and peace that surprised her. An interesting postscript to this experience is that this woman reported that the peace and joy was soon disturbed by a thought of being a terrible mother for having previously cheapened her love for her baby with such unworthy thoughts and feelings of resentment as those she habitually felt. This, however, is just the next subtle twist of the mind soap opera that can cunningly draw us back into our unmindfulness quagmire. We can just see this thought too, notice it, and gently let it go. Mindfulness isn't about tomorrow, nor about the past; it's no more or less than full realisation of our one true moment — now.

It would be easy to read about an experience like the one described above and then put pressure on ourselves to have the same experience, and then to put a burden on ourselves if it doesn't happen. But even looking at our baby and being aware that there's some low-level resentment and the effect that it's having on us tells us something. At least we then have the opportunity not to feed the resentment and also to not get caught in an unmindful and judgmental stream of thoughts.

The answer to how can we escape our thought circus is to realise that no matter how serious parenting might seem, it's all about things that pass, often in the night! What better way of proving this than to let our full attention be with what our child is doing, right now? This includes giving our total attention to our baby who's screaming with toothache at 3 a.m., or to our child we just dropped off at school for the first time, or to our teenager who's just woken us up at in the middle of the night yelling goodnight to their feral friends as they zoom off into the night like there's no tomorrow. Parenting is one of life's great challenges, and whether we do it mindfully or mindlessly is what will make it either a calamity or a blessing. Our greatest challenges are our greatest teachers.

Infancy

Mindful parenting of an infant can be as simple as really watching what they do, and learning a natural lesson in mindfulness from them. Infants are experts in mindful living. They naturally give their total attention to what they do, and they don't let reality be distorted and lessened by imposing judgments and filters on it that belong in the past and the future, such as: 'Hey, this rusk isn't nearly as nice as the one that I had yesterday, maybe she's trying to save money — at my expense — by getting me those cheaper imported ones! What's she going to do to me next?'

The smile a baby gives you when they see you for the first time in an hour or a minute isn't filtered by anything. A baby naturally beams its obvious delight with being alive, with being near you, with being part of a loving universe that's full of peace and potential, once a few little clouds like lack of sleep or milk have been taken care of! Even when a baby cries it's usually in response to an immediate event that's usually obviously temporary and reversible. A baby generally cries because it's hungry or because its hat has fallen over its eyes or because its doll has fallen out of its bouncinette. Such problems are usually easily fixed, as problems that aren't caused by thoughts usually can be. Babies are far too naturally mindful to indulge in such sophisticated and potentially painful mental gymnastics as: 'I'm just so worried about my behaviour at my mother's office party last night, when I cried to be taken home to bed even though it was only seven o'clock. What a *baby* they all must have thought me!'

Mindful parenting of infants comes naturally, if we let it. We just need to act in the same mindful way that our infants do, and only concern ourselves with what's actually happening. The trick here is to really tune in to what's happening, and not tune out. To be mindful is to really notice the smile on our baby's face, or the slight refinement in their ability to roll, which they are totally delighted with and want us to be too. We can miss such treasures if we're not mindful, if we only give our attention to our baby when they scream or when something goes wrong. Think of the life opportunities that both our infant and we will miss if we're not mindful.

Mindful parenting is ultimately about genuine communication, which can only happen in the here and now and with the person in front of us. Genuine communication with an infant is much the same as it is with anybody — don't tell them what you don't really believe yourself, or ignore them if something supposedly more interesting happens. Real connection starts with really listening to somebody, not only to our infant's obvious needs, but also to their more subtle statements of what's important to them — their triumphs and tragedies that they need to share with us. Connecting with others is about recognising that what makes somebody else the unique and wonderful individual they are isn't so very different from what makes *us* the unique and wonderful individual *we* are.

Mindful parenting is just a special case of mindful living, and this means giving our complete attention to it. Bringing a newborn baby home from hospital can be a wonderful as well as valuable lesson in mindfulness because it forces us to realise that this little person is something we have to look after for life. This means noticing when they are hungry and then responding to this; it means noticing when they are in potential danger and then responding to this; it even means noticing when they need a baby version of a conversation and then responding to this.

Part of the great value of parenting infants as a mindfulness practice is that they naturally direct us home from the modern psychological wilderness of 'What's in it for me?' to the much healthier 'What do you need?' This process is simple and natural and is a vital aspect of mindfulness — looking out for somebody else. Nothing makes us more mindless than getting lost in the complexities of our problems. A baby crying for milk in the middle of the night might seem like an ordeal, and it probably will be if that's all we see in the situation, but it can be a wonderful opportunity.

A crying baby can be our life wake-up call: it can make us realise connectedness to others, and our responsibility to listen to them and respond to them; and it can tell us of the happiness and peace that a mindful response to life can give us and others. A simple surrender to this fundamental truth — an attitude of acceptance — can make this process a simple joy. Resistance and resentment — non-acceptance — will fill the same situation with misery. Sometimes we wonder where we learned our unmindfulness: we should remember that we are teaching our children every moment, not so much by what we say, but by what we do and by our way of being.

Middle childhood

If an infant is naturally mindful and if parenting is naturally mindful, then what goes wrong? Psychology can be a wonderful source of complicated descriptions of simple processes, such as growing up, but in this case its complexity basically agrees with more ancient and simple wisdom traditions. The psychological 'theory of mind' is similar to the ancient idea of the problems involved in our ego development. Both explain how our sense of separation from everything and everybody else is the key to what can go wrong with our life.

What psychologists call the 'theory of mind' and philosophers call the 'birth of the ego' arrives at about the age of eighteen months, when infants start to develop language and the problems and potentials that this leads to. Some psychologists even did a study on the development of lying. This arrives soon after language does, when children realise they can avoid trouble if they lie. A problem with words is that we can use them to tell people they are separate from us; a potential of words is that we can use them to tell people we love them.

So, what do we do with a child who's just starting to get sophisticated enough to manipulate others with words and to be manipulated by them? Again, the key is deep communication, and this doesn't just mean trying to get our child to put down their chocolate biscuit or little brother or sister and listen to us. This doesn't even mean keeping them safe and stimulated and interested in things that are good for them, even though all of that's important. Communication reaches its full potential when we can just be with our child, when we can give them our full attention without any purpose in mind, when we can simply enjoy their company and they can enjoy ours and neither of us is playing a role of parent or child.

The great benefit of mindful parenting is that it frees us to be truly with and truly aware of our child. To mindlessly do things for our child but never simply be with them is to risk ending up putting off one of the most valuable things we can experience. In the potentially prophetic words of Harry Chapin's song 'Cat's in the Cradle', don't wait until it's too late. We can do it *now*, we can be it *now*.

This doesn't mean we have to pander to our child every moment of the day so there's no time or attention for anything else; it just means that when we're interacting with them we do actually pay attention. This is illustrated by another example from a woman's experience related in a mindfulness class. As a busy professional she found a recurring pattern to her mornings: she was forever trying to make the children's lunches, get them ready for school, get her own work together and get out of the house remotely on time. Every day the same experience of frustration and bellowing commands went on, made all the worse by her five-year-old daughter constantly coming up to her and wanting to show her things, but not putting on her socks and shoes. Usually the mother would say, 'That's nice, dear, now will you go and get dressed for school?'

One day, a few weeks into her mindfulness course, as this woman's daughter was trying to show her something, she found herself stopping and actually listening to what her daughter was saying, and looking at what she was trying to show her. To her surprise it was quite interesting and they shared an engaged conversation for a few moments. It was a simple, lucid moment but it was like a rest and the mother felt enriched by it. To her surprise, her daughter felt listened to and stopped nagging and went happily to get dressed for school. The woman realised that she hardly ever listened to what her daughter was saying, although she pretended she did.

Adolescence

Mark Twain said that when he was fifteen his father knew nothing; he was amazed to discover just how much the old man learned in the next five years! Part of the getting of wisdom is realising that other people can be wise, and that this even includes people as weird and unfashionable as our parents!

Adolescence, as we may have observed as an adolescent or someone who knows one, can be a difficult time. This difficulty comes from trying to refine our sense of being an individual self that was thrust upon us as children.

The adolescent's paradox comes from their development of a brand new shiny individual self as something completely separate from their parents' selves, with their dusty values and ideas. This means rebellion — against something that can seem to everyone else as unreal as Hamlet's classically dysfunctional family ghost. This rebellion has inspired many popular movies, books and plays including James Dean's *Rebel Without a Cause*. The teenager's paradox is that they often mindlessly conform to their rebellion: if everybody rebels in exactly the same way, and wears exactly the same rebellious clothes and listens to exactly the same rebellious music, then everybody is actually a conformist.

If everybody in a group wears a Mohawk hairstyle and a surly expression and tattered jeans, then they are actually in uniform. We can try telling a teenage rebel that they are actually as much of a mindless conformist as we once were, and we can see if they agree with us! We can try telling a teenage rebel that the cool things they 'invented' such as the word cool, drugs and sex, were actually invented by guys in caves, and we can see if they agree with us! Underneath the adolescent rebellion there's often a vulnerability and intense desire to be accepted. Mindful parenting can mean being courageous enough to just keep doing what we think is right, even if the person for whom we are doing it thinks that we are seriously uncool.

Neurophysiology, like philosophy and psychology, can also explain why adolescence can be difficult, to adolescents and to everybody else, as if we need any scientific proof. Adolescent brains are hard wiring themselves into their mainly final version, and like many transitions, it can be scary. It's now known that boys' brains don't reach full maturity until they enter their mid twenties, with girls' brains fully maturing about five years earlier. This partly explains why teenagers and even adolescents in their early twenties have been known to do the occasional odd thing, or even the occasional downright mindlessly destructive thing, often to themselves.

Spontaneity is one thing, impulsivity another. Impulsivity is a hallmark of adolescence and when this impulsivity isn't moderated by a certain level of awareness it can soon develop into risky behaviour. Mindfulness helps to develop those areas of our brain that can exercise some executive control. It can help to quieten those parts of our brain that are sometimes overly impulsive and aggressive, particularly in males. Psychologists like to use other words like self-awareness and self-regulation, but all these terms mean being mindful.

With mindfulness, it's not that someone else is telling the adolescent how to act, but rather that they are paying attention for themselves and choosing their words and actions in a more conscious way. And mindfulness certainly isn't about adolescents suppressing their feelings, but rather learning to stand back from them, like watching flood waters without getting swept away by them. As we may know from our own experience, when we make poor decisions we're generally not really aware of what we are doing at the time.

So, what do we do as parents of adolescents? Leave town until our offspring reach neurophysiological maturity? Tempting! In *A New Earth* Eckhart Tolle skilfully tells us what we already know, but sometimes don't want to acknowledge: many children harbour deep resentment toward their parents. According to Tolle a lot of this resentment comes because many parents are in his words 'inauthentic'. We can get so trapped in the role of a parent and trying to play it well that we don't simply develop genuinely human and mindful relationships with our children.

We need to treat our children, particularly our adolescent children, as people. This means interacting with them just as we interact with anybody else we like and respect — especially when they really need us to be accepting and mindful and authentic, not judging and panicking. This means not doing what we should do, or what seems like a good idea to do or what some person or book told us we should do. This means really listening to our child even if that child is an adolescent and looks in certain challenging moments more like something out of an alien movie than a family movie. This means really meeting the needs of our child rather than the needs of a theory or of our desire for self-protection, domination or revenge. This means treating adolescents as we would like them to treat us. This simply means being mindful — seeing what's actually there, who's actually there — no matter how downright awful this might seem. This also means acceptance — not necessarily of an ill-advised mistake, but of the person beneath all the tumultuous feelings and self-obsession.

Take-home tips for a mindful approach to parenting

Not so helpful
- Get distracted — by the TV, or by the idea that we're not a good parent — or by anything.
- Make parenting more complicated than it needs to be by judging ourselves or others.
- Panic!

Helpful
- Remember that mindful parenting comes naturally from love and that love comes naturally from acceptance — of what's happening here and now.
- Give our full attention to our children even if what they are doing seems mindless or addictive or even violent, and respond naturally, mindfully and with love.
- Make contact with other parents, or with our friends and/or relatives. If things seem like they are falling apart or even just not as smooth as we would like them to be, we can reach out and talk to somebody, or ask them for help.
- Attend parenting classes and/or mindfulness classes.
- Do what comes naturally, wonderfully, mindfully and enjoyably.
- Don't panic!

PART 4

MINDFULNESS AND SPIRITUAL DEVELOPMENT

CHAPTER 23

Mindfulness and self-actualisation

You may have heard that when a couple gets married there are actually six people getting wedded at the same time: there is who he thinks he is, who she thinks he is, and who he really is — marrying who she thinks she is, who he thinks she is and who she really is. There are enough permutations and combinations in there and also enough room for confusion to keep the average couple going for a lifetime — but if they are lucky they may actually get to know each other, one day.

Are you who you think you are, or who others think you are, or are you something else? Do you feel like you're playing the role you were born to play, playing someone else's role, or do you feel like you're making it all up as you go? Would you like to feel more fulfilled? Would you like a stronger feeling of being settled in yourself, being who you really are and of being guided in your life by this knowledge? Would you like to want less and have more? If you answered yes to any of these questions, would you like to know how mindfulness can help you better be yourself? If so, read on, but before you do, you might like to briefly consider what would most make you feel ultimately fulfilled. What would make you feel most alive, if you could do it right now?

Mindfulness and our true selves

Shakespeare's Hamlet was a fairly ordinary medieval Danish prince, except for his fondness for talking to ghosts and for soliloquising. He did, however, find an extraordinary way of learning that we don't usually attain fulfilment just from changing our life circumstances, or from agonising over their disreputable state, just as he was agonising over what was rotten in the state of Denmark. We attain fulfilment ultimately from accepting, and not by excepting — or taking exception to — what's going on in our life. What could have been Hamlet's ultimate and mindful answer to his question: 'To be, or not to be?' Hamlet was really asking himself, 'To practise mindfulness, or not to practise mindfulness? That is the question.' Well, he didn't practise it and that's why his story ended up a tragedy rather than a comedy with a happy ending. Perhaps another bit of advice that Hamlet didn't heed until too late, possibly because it was given by Polonius to Laertes and not to him, was: 'And this above all: to thine own self be true, and it must follow, as the night the day, thou canst not then be false to any man.'

Abraham Maslow was in many ways a fairly ordinary great twentieth-century American psychologist, except that he was really a philosopher. He created a bridge between psychology and philosophy. One of Maslow's bridge-building theories was his idea of self-actualisation. According to Maslow, we have a hierarchy of needs. We need to have enough to eat and drink, and we need to feel safe. As we move up our existential league ladder we also need to feel like we belong and we need to feel good about ourselves. Then right on top of the ladder is our need to be self-actualised — our need to feel like we're playing the role we were born to play, that we're living our life to our best ability and therefore being as useful to ourselves and to others as we can be. As we come to know ourselves better and feel more connected to ourselves we also come to better know and feel more connected to others.

So, ultimately we need to find and be our true selves, rather than what we can spend our forged life pretending to be while we wait for something better and more real. What's stopping us? It's the usual suspects. Our mind creates a preoccupation with who we think we are and with all the ideas we hold about ourselves. The further we separate who we think we are from who we really are, the less happy, the less fulfilled and the less self-actualised we become. We ultimately need to wake up to our true selves, and realise that spending our life making decisions based on fear, confusion and other unsuccessful forms of reality avoidance is making our life a lot less rewarding than it can be.

Living the mindfulness practices described in this book won't just help us overcome the difficult mental and physical conditions to which we have applied mindfulness, and it won't just help us improve the life pursuits to which we applied mindfulness. Being ever more mindful will also help us really feel like us, possibly for the first time in a long time. This is related to what some people call 'authenticity', which, when researchers measure it, relates to three factors: self-awareness, authentic behaviour and open relationships. Mindfulness programs in the workplace, for example, have been found to increase a person's sense of living authentically and maintaining authentic relationships with their fellow workers.

Feeling like we are finally living the role we were born to play might even be what gives some people a secret happiness weapon. To describe this idea slightly more scientifically, there is objective evidence that supports the idea that there is an aspect of personality that is highly protective against extreme forms of misery, such as anxiety and depression, and this is *resilience* — mental buoyancy. This idea might help explain why some people don't develop anxiety, depression or other psychological or physical problems even in response to what may be seen by many people as serious life difficulties. Examples of this include chronic pain, where 95 per cent of people with it develop depression, but 5 per cent don't. Why? What is it that that 5 per cent do or think that most of us don't? How do they respond in such a way that protects them from depression?

Other examples of being free from damage by life difficulties include the lives of people who could be unscientifically described as heroes or saints. There is the famous Australian example of Weary Dunlop, who heroically ignored his own considerable problems and helped his comrades survive a Japanese prisoner-of-war camp in World War II. There is the famous South African example of Nelson Mandela, who somehow wasn't destroyed by his long and difficult years in prison — he instead profited deeply from them. There is the famous Crimean War example of Florence Nightingale, who was inspired by human suffering to help reduce it, rather than be repulsed by it. There are also numerous less famous examples of people who were elevated rather than destroyed by their serious life difficulties. Maybe we should focus more on finding the active ingredient of why some people rise above their afflictions of body and mind and spirit, rather than on why so many don't.

Maybe it will eventually be officially discovered that the active ingredient of positive reactions to adversity is resilience, which is what we get when we are self-actualised — when we are mindful.

The bottom line

There was a movie made in the United Kingdom in 2003 starring Hugh Grant, Bill Nighy and others, called *Love Actually*. As with many good movies, songs and lives, it had a pretty simple take-home message, which was, to quote the Beatles: love is all you need. Maybe one day somebody will make a movie about Abraham Maslow's hierarchy of needs — perhaps it will be called *Self Actually*. Knowing who we really are can help us be happier, healthier, more peaceful and more fulfilled. It might just be that when we're mindful and conscious enough to know who we really are, we will finally realise that true self-knowledge and true love are our ultimate natural bedfellows.

CHAPTER 24

Mindfulness and happiness

Finding happiness is like trying to find the soap in the bath: it's elusive and if we try to hold on to it, it will slip through our fingers. Would you like to be happier? Would you like to know if being more mindful can help you be happier, and how? Would you like to have more and want less? If your answer to all these questions and more was, 'No thanks, I have all the happiness and everything else that I can stand, and I'm so mindful that I have disciples,' then perhaps you would be so kind as to send the authors some tips and also your autograph. If you answered, 'Yes' to any of the above questions, then you might like to keep reading.

In Bhutan there is a government ministry of happiness. This might seem a bit odd to those of us who live in countries who only have government ministries for things like education, agriculture, transport, defence and finance, but if you think about it, what good are any of those things if you aren't happy?

An interesting study on happiness was done at Harvard University.[1] The researchers gave each participant an iPhone. No, that wasn't to make them happier — although many people these days couldn't conceive of how someone could be happy without one. What the researchers wanted to test was whether people were happier when they were paying attention or not. So what they did was call participants at random times during the day and ask them three questions. One: Rate your happiness at this very instant, from 1 to 100. Two: What are you physically doing at that moment? Three: Where is your attention: is it wandering to unpleasant, neutral or pleasant topics, or is your attention on what you are doing right now? Most people assume we are happiest when our mind is wandering to pleasant topics, but the research confirmed that the participants were happiest when they were paying attention to what they were doing. Even if it's a mundane job, people are happier paying attention than not. Why is it so?

The idea of happiness

Do we need to think our way into happiness or stop thinking our way out of it? Well, experience with mindfulness might give us an answer to that question. When we sit down and pay attention to our body (the body scan, see Chapter 3) or breathing for a few minutes in a very accepting kind of way, and let the busyness of our mind come and go without getting involved in it, we tend to feel more at ease, less burdened and happier. It just kind of sneaks up on us without us trying. This indicates that it's just by being ourselves that we experience a contentment that must be part of us. If, on the other hand, we sit there trying hard to be at ease, unburdened and happy, then we're not paying attention; rather we are thinking about how we would like to be experiencing something in the future, other than what we are experiencing now. We might as well sit there trying to not think about pelicans. This indicates that our thinking, striving, wanting and doing actually gets in the way of our being happy — and of our being. This is covering up what's natural to us. So, mindfulness isn't a way for us to think our way into happiness; it's here to help us to stop thinking our way out of it.

The next question in what certainly isn't meant to be a happiness test is: Have you heard of a great twentieth-century Indian philosopher called Krishnamurti? There were actually *two* great twentieth-century Indian philosophers called Krishnamurti, but don't worry if you haven't heard of either of them.

Uppaluri Krishnamurti was once described as a 'spiritual terrorist' because he was noted for his fairly extreme philosophical views on practically everything, and also for his rather confrontational way of presenting them. Uppaluri Krishnamurti believed, as many philosophers and clinical psychologists also believe, that a certain type of thinking is what causes our problems. He went further than most, though, because he also believed that thinking systems, such as science and religion and philosophy, can also cause problems. This Krishnamurti believed that we can't find real happiness and peace by following a system, and that ultimately we need to turn inward, not outward, in our search for what we most yearn for.

The importance of our own experience has been emphasised in many religious and philosophical traditions — Islam, Judaism and Christianity all have mystical aspects — whose proponents basically follow their own experiences of an ultimate reality, of a permanently clear and peaceful consciousness, rather than following a system or doctrine. Taoism is a subtle Chinese philosophy that can be rather difficult to understand, if all you're using to understand it is your mind. This system of thought — or should that be a non-system of non-thought? — can't really be translated into words, Chinese or otherwise. The basic non-idea of Taoism is that life simply is, and therefore the more we think about it the further we lose contact with it. The paradox is that we want to understand ourselves using the mind but it is the mind that actually gets in the way. According to Taoism, knowledge systems can guide us to happiness and peace but they can't take us there. Eventually we have to get off our bus or elephant and walk — we have to find our own answer by experiencing it.

This brings us to the other great philosophical Krishnamurti — Jiddu — who once told a large and expectant audience that he would give them the secret of happiness at the end of his talk. Maybe he was worried that they would otherwise sneak off to a rival gig somewhere else. We will give you the secret of happiness at the end of this chapter!

So, how do we learn to ski? We go to a skiing expert and ask them to coach us. How do we learn to be happy? Why not ask an expert and get some coaching?

The 14th Dalai Lama describes himself as a fairly ordinary man, although many in the world see him as an icon and great spiritual leader. He happens to be extremely happy and at peace with himself and the world, despite some serious apparent obstacles to his happiness, such as being taken away from his mother as an infant and chased out of his homeland by Chinese tanks at the age of 24. One of his secrets to happiness and contentment is given away at the start of the book *The Art of Happiness* by Howard Cutler, who interviewed the Dalai Lama. The Dalai Lama suggested that when we focus on differences we separate ourselves from others and create the seeds of isolation, conflict and unhappiness. We have far more in common with other people than we generally acknowledge, and when we work from that understanding, there are the seeds of connection, peace and happiness. It's simple but it's profound.

The 14th Dalai Lama once gave an intimate gathering of a few thousand seekers of wisdom another universal practical happiness tip. What we experience as real — our life as we usually think of it; our victories, defeats and even our team's position on the football league ladder — *isn't* an illusion. According to the Dalai Lama, however, our life consists of something *more* than the mind stuff with all its partiality and labelling as good and bad. If, for example, we have a thought or feeling that we label as bad — not so much in a discerning way but in a vitriolic, personal and judgmental way — then we make an issue of it and bind ourselves to it. Our attention goes to it, we elaborate on it and we become preoccupied by it. If we just mindfully notice it, and note that the thought or impulse isn't helpful or relevant, then we just practise doing nothing about it other than being disinterested in it and letting it go.

According to many philosophies a wonderful way of increasing our connectedness, and therefore our happiness, is to give it away — or at least to share goodwill. Empathy and compassion are intimately related to what many a wise sage has said, but we now also know that one of the main reasons that mindfulness helps us to function better and be happier is because it helps us to care for others more and relate to them better. Paradoxically, the less happiness we think we have, the more it helps us to give it away. We connect with others by giving to them, even if it's the most mundane thing. One of the authors vividly remembers the first thing his baby gave him. It was a grain of rice, given with a love that made it a universe in a grain of rice, to paraphrase the poet and mystic William Blake. What better gift is there than happiness?

The benefits of volunteering have been clinically recognised, and there are community volunteering options offered in many countries specifically to people who suffer from psychological conditions such as anxiety and depression — disconnectedness. Acts of altruism, small or large, help us unhook our focus on ourselves and engage more with life around us.

Try a life experiment: give something to somebody today, even if you don't think they deserve it — especially if you don't think they deserve it. See what effect it has on you, your mind, your body, your sense of being present and alive. If you give with an expectation of getting something in return, then see what effect that expectation has. If you give just for the sake of giving, then see what effect that has. There's an old saying: 'Give what you think you lack!' The great philosopher Shakespeare said much the same thing in *Hamlet*: 'Assume a virtue if you have it not.' As with most ancient ideas there's a modern equivalent: 'Fake it till you make it!' There's also a law of nature at work — whatever we practise we will get good at, for better or for worse.

The science of happiness

We might think that happiness is something that we either have or don't have. This might be true on one level, but a lot of very wise people gave the subject a lot of consideration for a very long time (and they probably started out in caves) before science finally came along to help out. Science tells us scientifically what wisdom traditions tell us wisely: that doing some things is likely to make us happier than is doing other things. The result of the application of science to the study of happiness can be seen in studies that give us a clear idea of what's associated with happiness, and what therefore may help lead us to it.

A large international meta-analysis of the things that make us happy was conducted in Holland in 1994. This means that somebody, in this case a Dutch psychology professor, statistically examined the results of many individual studies undertaken on happiness and found some results that were obvious to non-scientists, and also some that were surprising. This analysis combined the individual findings of 603 studies undertaken between 1911 and 1995, in 69 countries. The result was the 2027-page World Database of Happiness, which revealed some interesting findings.[2]

- Money, you may not be surprised to read, isn't all that important in making us happy or unhappy. People who have enough of the stuff are actually happier than those who have too much of it, as well as happier than those who don't have enough of it — enough to meet their basic needs. It seems that if we have a great deal of money or hardly any then we tend to worry about it, which can make us unhappy.

- Being married, especially if we happen to be male, makes us happier and healthier, except if it's a particularly unhappy marriage.

- Being healthy is good for our happiness, but people who are good at being happy usually manage to stay happy even in the face of illness.

- Having or not having children doesn't make a happiness difference.

- A really important cause of happiness is whether we feel self-actualised. This means waking up in the mornings feeling like we're living our life according to our deep values — our script — and playing the part that we feel we were born to play, rather than waking up feeling like going back to sleep. It has something to do with meaning, direction and purpose in life.

Recent scientific studies have come up with an objective measure of happiness. This measure is so objective that when these researchers plugged people's brains into an electroencephalograph — a machine that can read their brainwaves, if not their minds — their brainwave characteristics objectively confirmed their subjective reports on their state of happiness. A study in Russia showed objectively that a group of people who meditated were significantly happier than a group of people who didn't meditate.[3] More recently, Magnetic Resonance Imaging (MRI) has been used to measure the brain regions active when we are happy. As the abovementioned studies showed, the left prefrontal cortex (the frontal area of the brain important for all our executive or higher functions) is particularly important in this respect. An active left prefrontal cortex and a quiet stress centre are particularly conducive to being happy. In fact, the man labelled 'The Happiest Man in the World', much to his embarrassment, is a French Buddhist monk by the name of Matthieu Ricard. His prefrontal brain patterns were way off the scale.

Deepak Chopra has presented a happiness formula that he created on the basis of many scientific studies of happiness. This formula basically states that our happiness level is partly determined by things we can't easily change, such as our genes or our karma, but is also determined by things that we can change, such as our thinking processes. We can therefore improve our happiness by undergoing cognitive therapy or by meditating. This is similar to the conclusions drawn in positive psychology — that we have our genetic make-up, our circumstances, and we have variables we can voluntarily change, such as our thoughts and behaviours.

Meditation is a mindfulness practice in that it's about transcending thoughts rather than changing them. Being able to transcend the thinking mind — to go beyond it — helps us to think more flexibly. So, does mindfulness make us happier, and if it does, how?

Mindfulness, a happy ending

We have presented scientific evidence throughout this book that demonstrates that mindfulness can improve the quality of life of people with a range of clinical conditions, and also of people without clinical conditions. Happiness is an important, possibly the most important, part of quality of life. A study in Holland showed that mindfulness greatly improves the quality of life, even of people with cancer, and that this improvement in quality of life includes increased joy.[4] There's not much point in eking out a few more months of life if we're not going to pay attention enough to appreciate it. If mindfulness can greatly improve the joy experienced by people with cancer, perhaps it can improve this in all of us.

We do a great many things in the name of happiness, just as we do them in the name of love, but we often do these things without much success because we do them mindlessly rather than mindfully. It might seem like drinking two bottles of wine before dinner or eating two boxes of chocolates, or both, might make us happy — certainly we're unlikely to do this for any reason other than the pursuit of happiness — but such activities tend not to turn out quite as well as we hoped they would.

There's nothing wrong with pleasure, but trying to stimulate the brain's pleasure centres with the intention of creating happiness gives us only a short-term burst of enjoyment and then a down. The next time we need more stimulation to produce the same effect, then more, then more. Next we have an addiction that causes anxiety if we don't keep appeasing it. This isn't a recipe for freedom but for disaster — compulsion and depression. Although we can look at this process from the perspective of the individual, it's just the same for the whole community, with our collective addiction to the pursuit of short-term gratification. Now that we're reaching the end of this book we can enjoy a chocolate or a glass of wine as an exercise in mindfulness, which means savouring it. We can taste it fully but we're also mindful enough to note that moment when the savouring is about to turn into indulgence. That's the time to stop. This mindful measure will *sustain* happiness.

Ultimately, reality is that which is, in the present moment; this might be the sounds of a Beethoven sonata or it might be the pangs of a sore toe. Being mindful means facing up to reality as it's happening right here, right now, and not choosing to ignore it until something better comes along.

If we do a life experiment of wishing we were somewhere else when something we don't like presents itself, then note the outcome of the experiment. Does it make the situation go away? Does it help us to bear the situation with equanimity? Does it help us to respond to the situation? Is it an exercise in futility? If we find that strategy doesn't work, we could experiment with mindfully getting on with the situation and not wasting time wishing reality were other than what it is.

If we do a life experiment of wishing a situation we like would stay the way it is forever, then note the outcome of that experiment. Does clinging to the situation make the happiness stay? Does it help us to move on with life to savour whatever comes next? Does clinging cause fear, frustration and anxiety? Is it an exercise in futility? If we find that strategy doesn't work, we could experiment with savouring the things we enjoy and then mindfully letting go and not wasting time wishing reality were other than what it is.

The basic tenets of mindfulness — awareness and acceptance, no matter what of — might seem about as sexy and as useful to our happiness as filing our tax return on time or eating a plate of boiled turnips. The interesting thing here, though, is that if we pay full attention to our experience then we will realise that we already have what we are chasing. Happiness is actually our natural state, and all we have to do to realise this is to stop looking for something better — to value what we have by giving it our full attention. The problem might not be that we have to get happiness from somewhere, but rather we simply need to stop thinking our way out of it.

Our experience will teach us everything we need to know, if we provide the curiosity and attention to learn what our experience is there to teach us. The funny thing is, when we learn something from our experiences because we pay attention to them, even the challenging experiences, we learn something valuable from them. This creates a kind of alchemy that helps to change the experience from something bad (that is, I wish it never happened) to something good (that is, I am better off for having gone through it). The people we most admire throughout history for their courage and wisdom have all taught us this lesson. Possibly the most poetic statement to this effect comes from Shakespeare in his play *As You Like It*:

> *This is no flattery: these are counsellors*
> *That feelingly persuade me what I am.*
> *Sweet are the uses of adversity,*
> *Which, like the toad, ugly and venomous,*
> *Wears yet a precious jewel in his head;*
> *And this our life exempt from public haunt*
> *Finds tongues in trees, books in the running brooks,*
> *Sermons in stones and good in every thing.*
> *I would not change it.*

There was once an advertising executive in New York who thought that it might be nice to provide some simple stories of wisdom to children instead. Theodor Geisel wrote many wonderfully wise books for children and others (under the name Dr Seuss), including a mindfulness primer called *I Had Trouble Getting To Solla Sollew*. The hero of this story decided one day to leave town in search of enlightenment because he had troubles. Things that flew swooped him. Things that crawled bit his toes. Somebody advised him to go to a place called Solla Sollew, and why not? After quite a few adventures that metaphorically described all of our life adventures, including being conscripted into an army led by a heroic maniac and having to fight an arbitrary and ferocious enemy with nothing but a heroic pea-shooter, the hero finally made it to Solla Sollew. The trouble was that even though there were no troubles in

Solla Sollew (at least very few), it was closed. There was a giant key-turning worm in the keyhole of the entrance gate to the fabulous and trouble-free city, who wouldn't let anyone open the gate. The citizens of Solla Sollew were all far too high-minded to force this worm to stop turning people away, so the situation continued. This turned out to be a blessing in disguise for our hero because he used this experience to attain genuine happiness, rather than a grudge. The hero realised that his happiness was at home waiting for him, if he simply returned and gave his full attention to his life with all its ups and downs, light and dark, no matter what his mind thought of it.

This brings us back to Jiddu Krishnamurti's secret of happiness that he promised his expectant audience. The secret of happiness is: 'I don't mind what happens!'

CHAPTER 25

Mindfulness and enlightenment

To be fully mindful is to be enlightened. To be fully enlightened is to be beyond words!

In this book we have looked at mindfulness from a practical point of view. As we have seen, there are many applications for mindfulness that are of great benefit to us in our daily life, but is there even more to mindfulness than this? Mindfulness and related contemplative practices have been very much at the heart of the world's great wisdom and spiritual traditions for millennia. From a practical perspective, the spiritual applications of mindfulness seem unimportant or irrelevant. In fact, many people interested in mindfulness are only interested in it from a practical point of view, and only if it can come without all the spiritual, 'new-age' packaging that's often associated with meditation.

We have tried to present mindfulness in a way that's down to earth rather than off the planet, and that's relevant to a wide range of people, but it would be remiss of us not to explore the deeper potential of mindfulness. If this is of no interest to you then please stop reading now before it's too late!

From an enlightenment or spiritual perspective, all of the pragmatic benefits of mindfulness that we discussed in the first 24 chapters are just side effects, as useful as they may be in helping us relieve and/or transcend suffering.

The meaning of enlightenment

Just what is enlightenment and how do we get it? This leads us to other related but often overlooked questions, including: What is suffering, and how do we free ourselves from it? Gautama the Buddha (there are many other Buddhas and potential Buddhas) once said, 'The truth of suffering must be explored to its end …' So what does this actually mean? Some wisdom traditions seem to be telling us that suffering is unavoidable. But are they really? The Christian Old Testament tells us that we were in a pretty good paddock, once. We fell out of divine favour because we wanted to know more than what was good for us, and so our Paradise turned into our Paradise Lost when Adam and Eve ate the forbidden fruit. We've all had existential indigestion ever since, apparently.

Other wisdom traditions also give us stories of a fall from the grace of our Golden Age, which we lost because we wanted something more, and our craving for something other than what we have began. Whether we gained happiness or lost contentment in the process is the kind of question that could keep us chatting around the campfire for a very long time. Ancient Greek mythology gives us the story of Prometheus, who wanted to make mortals as good as gods — all knowing know-alls — so he stole their divine secret spark one dark and starry night. Prometheus wasn't only cast out of Paradise for his troubles, like Adam and Eve were, but also chained to a rock to contemplate some eternal truths at his leisure.

The main message from all these myths and allegories is that at our core we're much more than we realise and we have far greater strength and wisdom than we generally have access to. Growing in wisdom is therefore a form of coming home, a type of transcendence, a return to our innermost self, a return to the simplicity and innocence that is innate in us. To be removed from this core is, to quote Shakespeare again in *Hamlet*, 'to suffer the slings and arrows of outrageous fortune'.

Most of us have a pretty good idea of *what* suffering is, but often we're not so clear on *why* it is. We suffer when we see a gap between what we think we want (or want to avoid) and what we think we have (or can't put up with). The solution to bridging that gap might seem simple — either get more or want less. Most of us opt for trying to get or avoid more rather than wanting or avoiding less. That takes its toll over time and often brings us into conflict with the world and the other people in it.

When we're very young and we want our toy truck or our parents to be with us always and for some reason we lose sight of them, even if only for a little while, then we can get upset. When we're not quite so young and we want our sports car or our fabulous new boyfriend or girlfriend to be with us always and for some reason we lose sight of them, even if only for a little while, we can get upset. When we're even less young and we want our physical pain or emotional anguish to leave us, even if only for a little while, and they don't, we can get upset. At one level, suffering comes from non-acceptance of what is and craving for what isn't, but is there something deeper going on that explains what's really happening when we suffer?

There are some venerable religious and philosophical traditions out there that seem to be telling us that the human condition has to involve pleasure and pain, and if we get too moved by these and begin grasping and recoiling from them then that leads to suffering in one form or another. Does that mean that we're hopeless cases?

Mindfulness and enlightenment — a happy ending

The bottom line of all wisdom traditions is that they describe individual suffering and universal hope. Greek mythology gives us the story of Pandora and her box. Like Eve in Paradise and Alice in Wonderland, Pandora grew curiouser and curiouser — until she ended up so curious that she dealt with her temptation just as Oscar Wilde advised us all to deal with it much later: 'The best way to deal with temptation is to yield to it.' According to Pandora's myth, all of our troubles started when she opened her forbidden box, but so did something else. Deep and dormant beneath all of the escaping evils in the box that symbolised the human heart was something even stronger than evil — hope. Hope is at the heart of truth and evil is its opposite.

Don't despair then, no matter how much we think we're suffering, no matter how anxious or depressed or out of control we think we are and how hopeless we think our life is. According to the Christian wisdom tradition there is sin (ignorance), but there is also salvation (recognising a greater truth). According to the Buddhist wisdom tradition there is suffering (the first noble truth), but there is also salvation (the fourth noble truth), which also comes from recognising a deeper reality than the one we have just 'thunk up' for ourselves. According to philosophy in general there is the suffering of not knowing who we really are, but there is also the antidote of finding out. Our Paradise isn't lost at all, it has simply been mislaid.

We would consider it a no-brainer that if we were experiencing physical pain then we should pay attention to what's going on so we could do something about it. Perhaps our hand is on a hotplate, maybe a bone is broken or maybe we have a speck of sand in our eye. Our attention allows us to move our hand, put a splint on our broken limb or remove the speck. Well, that's mindfulness. Just numbing and ignoring the pain leaves the problem to fester and get worse. That's avoidance or inattention.

Mindfulness is also indispensable for understanding the very nature of the mental and emotional suffering we experience so that we might do something about that too. As tempting as avoidance and unmindfulness are, we will never understand what's behind the suffering in the first place if we use them as our way of dealing with it. Wisdom doesn't come without attention, but paying attention to the things we find most uncomfortable isn't for the faint-hearted, so it also requires courage. To understand what's real or true we must observe with an unbiased attitude. We have already explored these issues in coping with situations such as depression, and all the principles are the same here — it's just that the perspective is larger, even universal, when we think of wisdom.

How do we reclaim our natural Paradise then, by whatever name we call it — enlightenment, salvation, wisdom, God, sanity? Our best wisdom traditions tell us just what our best movies, books and songs tell us: all we need to do is to recognise that we already have what we want and need. This is the key to a reunion with our true self that is greater than the sum of our many parts. The *Wizard of Oz* is a story about a character who is a wizard at one level, and a fraud at a deeper level, and a true wizard at an even deeper level. He gave a great truth to a girl and a scarecrow and a lion and a tin man who had all gone to considerable trouble to find him: we all already have a home and a heart and a reasoning mind and the courage to live, because we're alive, we just didn't know it.

Being mindful means simply being alive to our infinite living potential, which is available to us all — right here, right now. Being mindful means choosing to remain conscious, of all of our experiences, no matter how bad or good our mind judges them to be, rather than choosing to trade our consciousness for a dream of finding something better than real — somewhere, someday. Being mindful teaches us the very nature of permanence and impermanence. Being mindful naturally leads us to enlightenment because enlightenment just means living in the light of who we really are, rather than in the dark of who we think we are. Being mindful — being fully aware and accepting and appreciative of our reality — will transform even our most damning and complicated life sentences into a single and simple word: freedom. Perhaps we're standing in the way of our own freedom, not because things have a hold of us, but because we have a hold of them — and we won't let go.

One of the authors once found himself up a mountain in a pine forest in northern India. He had just left a monastery called Tushita near the village of Dharakot, which he had visited and from which he had bought a book on an ancient belief system that had provided the basis for the development of some powerful mindfulness practices. He was so inspired by the mindful living practices of the monks at the monastery and their peace and happiness that he could hardly wait to go down the mountain to his hotel in Dharamsala and get stuck into the secrets of mindfulness.

Perhaps because he was mindlessly thinking about mindfulness and all the wonderful benefits that it would soon offer him, he stumbled on a rock and dropped his book. A nearby monkey seized its chance and the book and made off up the mountain with it. As the mindless author chased it through beautiful pine trees, he didn't see the beauty of the trees, nor hear the pine needles rustling under his feet as he ran, nor smell the subtle pine fragrance. Eventually he found the monkey and the book, but now the monkey wasn't alone, and he was. He was surrounded by monkeys including a very large one with very long and fierce teeth who bared them threateningly at the solitary human who was fully aware now — of his fear — and was fully unaware that one day he would help produce a mindfulness user's guide. The monkey leader glared at the human. The human glared at the monkey leader. There was an impasse.

'Let it go, Doc!' A girl's voice cried out from down the mountain. 'Just let it go!'

There is no secret to mindfulness, just as there is no secret to enlightenment or to life. Don't look for it, be it.

more from the mindfulness series

mindfulness AT WORK

How to avoid stress, achieve more and enjoy life!

DR STEPHEN MCKENZIE

Mindfulness at Work reveals how the practice of mindfulness — the ability to focus our attention on what is rather than be distracted by what isn't — can be a powerful antidote to the distractions and stresses of our modern lives, especially our working lives.

ISBN 978-1-921966-19-4

www.mindfulnessatwork.com.au

mindfulness FOR LIFE (CD)

Techniques and applications

DR CRAIG HASSED AND DR STEPHEN MCKENZIE

Mindfulness for Life — the CD — is a complete guide to mastering the art of paying attention to what is going on in our lives right now. The CD supports the book and helps you attain a state of full awareness. Stop daydreaming and start living your life in the present moment!

ISBN 978-1-921966-43-9

www.mindfulnessforlife.com.au

mindful learning

Reduce stress and improve brain performance for effective learning

DR CRAIG HASSED AND DR RICHARD CHAMBERS

Mindful Learning provides practical insights and exercises on how to apply mindfulness in any educational setting. Whatever your age, whatever your learning environment, mindfulness can make a positive difference, and *Mindful Learning* shows you how.

ISBN 978-1-921966-39-2

www.mindfullearning.com.au

EXISLE
PUBLISHING

www.exislepublishing.com

ENDNOTES

Chapter 1

1 Killingsworth, M.A., Gilbert, D.T., 'A Wandering Mind is an Unhappy Mind', *Science*, 12 November 2010, Vol. 330, no. 6006, p. 932, DOI: 10.1126/*science*.1192439

2 James, W., *Principles of Psychology*, Dover, 1890, Harvard University Press, 1983

3 Benson, H., *The Relaxation Response*, William Morrow and Co, New York, 1975

4 Tolle, E., *The Power of Now*, Namaste Publishing, Vancouver, 1997

5 www.mindandlife.org

6 Doidge, N., *The Brain that Changes Itself*, Scribe, Melbourne, 2008

Chapter 2

1 Killingsworth, M.A., Gilbert, D.T., 'A Wandering Mind is an Unhappy Mind', *Science*, 12 November 2010, Vol. 330, no. 6006, p. 932, DOI: 10.1126/*science*.1192439

Chapter 3

1 Gusnard, D.A., Akbudak, E., Shulman, G.L., Raichle, M.E., 'Medial prefrontal cortex and self-referential mental activity: relation to a default mode of brain function', *Proceedings of the National Academy of Sciences of the United States of America*, 2001;98(7):4259–64

2 Lazar, S.W., Kerr, C.E., Wasserman, R.H., et al, 'Meditation experience is associated with increased cortical thickness', *Neuroreport*, 2005;16(17):1893–1897

3 Hassed, C., *Know Thyself*, Michelle Anderson Publishing, Melbourne, 2002

4 Letter of 1950, as quoted in *The New York Times* (29 March 1972) and *The New York Post* (28 November 1972)

Chapter 4

1 Mathers, C.D., Loncar, D., 'Projections of global mortality and burden of disease from 2002 to 2030', *PLoS Medicine* 2006, Nov;3(11):e442

2 Kirsch, I., et al, *PLoS Medicine* 2008, Feb;5(2):e45 DOI:10.1371/journal.pmed.0050045

3 Fournier, J.C., DeRubeis, R.J., Hollon, S.D., et al, *JAMA*, 6 January 2010;303(1):47–53

4 Killingsworth, M.A., Gilbert, D.T., *Science*, 12 November 2010, Vol. 330, no. 6006, p. 932, DOI: 10.1126/science.1192439

5 Grossman, P.J., Niemann L., Schmidt, S., Walach, H., 'Mindfulness-based stress reduction and health benefits. A meta-analysis', *Psychosomatic Research*, 2004;57(1):35–43

6 McEwen, B.S., 'Protection and damage from acute and chronic stress: allostasis and allostatic

overload and relevance to the pathophysiology of psychiatric disorders', *Annals of the New York Academy of Sciences*, 2004;1032:1–7

7 Wilson, R.S., Evans D.A., Bienias, J.L., Mendes de Leon, C.F., Schneider, J.A., Bennett, D.A., 'Proneness to psychological distress is associated with risk of Alzheimer's disease', *Neurology*, 2003;61(11):1479–85

8 Pedersen, W.A., Wan, R., Mattson, M.P., 'Impact of aging on stress-responsive neuroendocrine systems', *Mechanisms of Ageing & Development* 2001;122(9):963–83.

9 Fahrenkopf, A.M., Sectish, T.C., Barger, L.K., et al, *BMJ*, doi:10.1136/bmj.39469.763218.BE

10 Zeidan, F., Johnson, S.K., Diamond, B.J., David, Z., Goolkasian, P., *Conscious Cogn.* 2010 Jun;19(2):597–605, E-pub 3 April 2010

11 Taylor, J., Wilson, G.S., Applying Sports Psychology, 2005

12 McEvoy, S.P., Stevenson, M.R., Woodward, M., *Accid Anal Prev.*, 2007 Nov;39(6):1170–6.

13 Hallowell, E.M., *Harvard Business Review* 2005 Jan;83(1):54–62, 116

14 Grossman, P.J., Niemann, L., Schmidt, S., Walach, H., 'Mindfulness-based stress reduction and health benefits. A meta-analysis', *Psychosomatic Research*, 2004;57(1):35–43

15 Ma, S.H., Teasdale, J.D., 'Mindfulness-based cognitive therapy for depression: replication and exploration of differential relapse prevention effects', *J Consult. Clin. Psychol.* 2004;72(1): 31–40

16 Sharplin, G.R., Jones, S.B., Hancock, B., et al, 'Mindfulness-based cognitive therapy: an efficacious community-based group intervention for depression and anxiety in a sample of cancer patients', *Med J Aust.*, 6 September 2010;193(5 Suppl):S79–82

17 Teasdale, J.D., Moore R.G., Hayhurst, H., Pope, M., Williams, S., Segal, Z.V., 'Metacognitive awareness and prevention of relapse in depression: empirical evidence', *J Consult. Clin. Psychol.*, 2002;70(2):275–87

18 Chiesa, A., Serretti, A., 'A systematic review of neurobiological and clinical features of mindfulness meditations', *Psychol. Med.* 2010;40:1239–52

19 Rubia, K., 'The neurobiology of meditation and its clinical effectiveness in psychiatric disorders', *Biol. Psychol.*, 2009;82:1–11

20 Witek-Janusek, L., Albuquerque, K., Chroniak, K.R., et al, 'Effect of mindfulness-based stress reduction on immune function, quality of life and coping in women newly diagnosed with early stage breast cancer', *Brain Behav. Immun.* 2008;22:969–81

21 Way, B.M., Creswell, J.D., Eisenberger, N.I., Lieberman, M.D., 'Dispositional mindfulness and depressive symptomatology: correlations with limbic and self-referential neural activity during rest', *Emotion*, Vol 10(1), February 2010, 12–24

22 Biegel, G.M., Brown, K.W., Shapiro, S.L., Schubert, C.M., 'Mindfulness-based stress reduction for the treatment of adolescent psychiatric outpatients: A randomized clinical trial', *Journal of Consulting and Clinical Psychology* 2009 vol. 77 (5) pp. 855–66 http://dx.doi.org/10.1037/a0016241

23 Goldin, P.R., Gross, J.J., 'Effects of mindfulness-based stress reduction (MBSR) on emotion regulation in social anxiety disorder', *Emotion*, 2010 Feb;10(1):83–91

24 Hassed, C., de Lisle, S., Sullivan, G., Pier, C., 'Enhancing the health of medical students: outcomes of an integrated mindfulness and lifestyle program', *Adv. Health Sci. Educ. Theory Pract.*, 2009;14:387–398

25 Warnecke, E., Quinn, S., Ogden, K., Towle, N., Nelson, M.R., 'A randomised controlled trial of the effects of mindfulness practice on medical student stress levels', *Med. Educ.*, 2011 April;45(4):381–8. doi: 10.1111/j.1365-2923.2010.03877.x

26 McKenzie, S., Hassed, C., Gear, L., 'Medical and Psychology students' knowledge of and attitudes towards mindfulness as a clinical intervention' (in press)

27 Krasner, M.S., Epstein, R.M., Beckman, H., et al, 'Association of an educational program in mindful communication with burnout, empathy, and attitudes among primary care physicians', *JAMA*, 23 September 2009;302(12):1338–40

28 Franco, C., Mañas, I., Cangas, A.J., Moreno, E., Gallego, J., 'Reducing teachers' psychological distress through a mindfulness training program', *Span J Psychol.*, 2010, Nov;13(2):655–66

29 www.theage.com.au/national/education/when-the-mind-matters-20090612-c5da.html

30 Joyce, A., Etty-Leal, J., Zazryn, T., Hamilton, A., Hassed, C., 'Exploring a mindfulness meditation program on mental health of upper primary children: A pilot study', *Advances in School Mental Health Promotion*, 2010;3(2):16–24

31 Davis, L.W., Strasburger, A.M., Brown, L.F., 'Mindfulness: an intervention for anxiety in schizophrenia', *J Psychosoc. Nurs. Ment. Health Serv.*, 2007 Nov;45(11):23–9

32 Chadwick, P., Hughes, S., Russell, D., Russell, I., Dagnan, D., 'Mindfulness groups for distressing voices and paranoia: a replication and randomized feasibility trial', *Behav. Cogn. Psychother.*, 2009 Jul;37(4):403–12, E-pub 23 June 2009

33 Pawlak, R., Margarinos, A.M., Melchor, J., et al, *Nature Neuroscience*, 2003;6(2):168–74

34 www.mindandlife.org

35 Hölzela, B.K., Carmody, J., Vangela, M., et al, 'Mindfulness practice leads to increases in regional brain gray matter density', *Psychiatry Research: Neuroimaging*, 2010 (in press)

36 Newberg, A.B., Wintering, N., Waldman, M.R., et al, 'Cerebral blood flow differences between long-term meditators and non-meditators', *Conscious Cogn.*, 4 June 2010 (E-pub ahead of print)

37 Lazar, S.W., Kerr, C.E., Wasserman, R.H., et al, 'Meditation experience is associated with increased cortical thickness', *Neuroreport*, 2005;16(17):1893–1897

38 Luders, E., Toga, A.W., Lepore, N., Gaser, C., 'The underlying anatomical correlates of long-term meditation: larger hippocampal and frontal volumes of grey matter', *Neuroimage*, 15 April 2009;45(3):672–8

39 Hölzel, B.K., Carmody, J., Vangel, M., et al, 'Mindfulness practice leads to increases in regional brain gray matter density', *Psychiatry Res.*, 30 January 2011;191(1):36–43

40 Friedland, R.P., Fritsch, T., Smyth, K., et al, 'Patients with Alzheimer's disease have reduced activities in midlife compared with healthy control-group members', *Proceedings of the National Academy of Science USA*, 10.1073/pnas.061002998

41 Scarmeas, N., Levy, G., Tang, M.X., et al, 'Influence of leisure activity on the incidence of

Alzheimer's disease', *Neurology* 2001;57(12):2236–42

42 Verghese, J., Lipton, R.B., Katz, M.J., Hall, C.B., Derby, C.A., Kuslansky, G., Ambrose, A.F., Sliwinski, M., Buschke, H., 'Leisure activities and the risk of dementia in the elderly', *New England Journal of Medicine*, 2003;348(25):2508–16

43 Lutz, A., Brefczynski-Lewis, J., Johnstone, T., Davidson, R.J., 'Regulation of the neural circuitry of emotion by compassion meditation: effects of meditative expertise', *PLoS One*, 26 March 2008;3(3):e1897

44 Krasner, M.S., Epstein, R.M., Beckman, H., et al, 'Association of an educational program in mindful communication with burnout, empathy, and attitudes among primary care physicians', *JAMA*, 23 September 2009;302(12):1338–40

45 Buckner, R.L., Snyder, A.Z., Shannon, B.J., LaRossa, G., Sachs, R., Fotenos, A.F., Sheline, Y.I., Klunk, W.E., Mathis, C.A., Morris, J.C., Mintun, M.A., 'Molecular, structural, and functional characterization of Alzheimer's disease: evidence for a relationship between default activity, amyloid, and memory', *J Neurosci.*, 2005;25(34):7709–17

46 Grossman, P.J., Niemann, L., Schmidt, S., Walach, H., 'Mindfulness-based stress reduction and health benefits. A meta-analysis', *Psychosomatic Research*, 2004;57(1):35–43

47 Epel, E., Daubenmier, J., Moskowitz, J.T., Folkman, S., Blackburn, E., 'Can meditation slow rate of cellular aging? Cognitive stress, mindfulness, and telomeres', *Annals of the New York Academy of Sciences*, 2009 August;1172:34–53

48 Rogojanski, J., Vettese, L.C., Antony, M.M., Mindfulness, 2011;2(1):14–26. DOI: 10.1007/s12671-010-0038-x

49 Vieten, C., Astin, J.A., Buscemi, R., Galloway, G.P., 'Development of an acceptance-based coping intervention for alcohol dependence relapse prevention', *Subst. Abus.*, 2010 April;31(2):108–16

50 Brewer, J.A., Sinha, R., Chen, J.A., et al, 'Mindfulness training and stress reactivity in substance abuse: results from a randomized, controlled stage I pilot study', *Subst. Abus.*, 2009 Oct–Dec;30(4):306–17

51 Bowen, S., Chawla, N., Collins, S.E., et al, 'Mindfulness-based relapse prevention for substance use disorders: a pilot efficacy trial', *Subst. Abus.*, 2009, Oct–Dec;30(4):295–305

52 Bowen, S., Witkiewitz, K., Dillworth, T.M., et al, 'Mindfulness meditation and substance use in an incarcerated population', *Psychol. Addict. Behav.*, 2006, Sep;20(3):343–7

53 Baer, R.A., Smith, G.T., Allen, K.B., 'Assessment of mindfulness by self-report: the Kentucky inventory of mindfulness skills', Assessment, 2004;11(3):191–206

54 Shapiro, S.L., Brown, K.W., Thoresen, C., Plante, T.G., 'The moderation of Mindfulness-based stress reduction effects by trait mindfulness: results from a randomized controlled trial', *J Clin. Psychol.*, 2011 Mar;67(3):267–77. doi: 10.1002/jclp.20761, E-pub 22 December 2010

55 Kristeller, J., Hallett, C., 'An Exploratory Study of a Meditation-based Intervention for Binge Eating Disorder', *J Health Psychol.*, 1999;4:357–63

56 Kristeller, J.L., Wolever, R.Q., 'Mindfulness-based eating awareness training for treating binge eating disorder: the conceptual foundation', *Eat Disord.*, 2011, Jan;19(1):49–61

57 Proulx, K., 'Experiences of women with bulimia nervosa in a mindfulness-based eating disorder treatment group', *Eat Disord.*, 2008 Jan–Feb;16(1):52–72

58 Speca, M., Carlson, L.E., Goodey, E., Angen, M., 'A randomized, wait-list controlled clinical trial: the effect of a mindfulness meditation-based stress reduction program on mood and symptoms of stress in cancer outpatients', *Psychosom. Med.*, 2000;62(5):613–22

59 Carlson, L.E., Speca, M., Patel, K.D., Goodey, E., 'Mindfulness-based stress reduction in relation to quality of life, mood, symptoms of stress and levels of cortisol, dehydroepiandrosterone sulfate (DHEAS) and melatonin in breast and prostate cancer outpatients', *Psychoneuroendocrinology*, 2004;29(4):448–74

60 Carlson, L.E., Speca, M., Patel, K.D., Goodey, E., 'Mindfulness-based stress reduction in relation to quality of life, mood, symptoms of stress, and immune parameters in breast and prostate cancer outpatients', *Psychosomatic Medicine*, 2003;65(4):571–81

61 Kabat-Zinn, J., Lipworth, L., Burney, R., 'The clinical use of mindfulness meditation for the self-regulation of chronic pain', *J Behav. Med.*, 1985;8(2):163–90

62 Singh, B.B., Berman, B.M., Hadhazy, V.A., Creamer, P., 'A pilot study of cognitive behavioral therapy in fibromyalgia', *Altern. Ther. Health Med.*, 1998;4(2):67–70

63 Astin, J.A., Berman, B.M., Bausell, B., Lee, W.L., Hochberg, M., Forys, K.L., 'The efficacy of mindfulness meditation plus Qigong movement therapy in the treatment of fibromyalgia: a randomized controlled trial', *J Rheumatol.*, 2003;30(10):2257–62

64 Perlman, D.M., Salomons, T.V., Davidson, R.J., Lutz, A., 'Differential effects on pain intensity and unpleasantness of two meditation practices', *Emotion*, 2010, Feb;10(1):65–71

65 Davidson, R.J. Kabat-Zinn, J., Schumacher, J., Rosenkranz, M., Muller, D., Santorelli, S.F., Urbanowski, F., Harrington, A., Bonus, K., Sheridan, J.F., 'Alterations in brain and immune function produced by mindfulness meditation', *Psychosomatic Medicine.*, 2003;65(4):564–70

66 Pace, T.W., Negi, L.T., Adame, D.D., et al, 'Effect of compassion meditation on neuroendocrine, innate immune and behavioral responses to psychosocial stress', *Psychoneuroendocrinology*, 2009 Jan;34(1):87–98

67 Cohen, L., Warneke, C., Fouladi, R.T., Rodriguez, M.A., Chaoul-Reich, A., 'Psychological adjustment and sleep quality in a randomized trial of the effects of a Tibetan yoga intervention in patients with lymphoma', *Cancer*, 2004;100(10):2253–60

68 Britton, W.B., Haynes, P.L., Fridel, K.W., Bootzin, R.R., *Psychosomatic Medicine.*, 2010 Jul;72(6):539–48

69 Tacon, A.M., McComb, J., Caldera, Y., Randolph, P., 'Mindfulness meditation, anxiety reduction, and heart disease: a pilot study', *Family & Comm. Health*, 2003;26(1):25–33

70 Astin, J.A., 'Stress reduction through mindfulness meditation. Effects on psychological symptomatology, sense of control, and spiritual experiences', *Psychotherapy Psychosomatic.*, 1997;66(2):97–106

Chapter 6

1 McEwen, B.S., 'Protection and damage from acute and chronic stress: allostasis and allostatic overload and relevance to the pathophysiology of psychiatric disorders', *Annals of the New York Academy of Sciences*, 2004;1032:1–7

2 Lin, J., Dhabhar, F.S., Wolkowitz, O., Tillie, J.M., Blackburn, E., Epel, E., 'Pessimism correlates with leukocyte telomere shortness and elevated interleukin-6 in post-menopausal women', *Brain Behav. Immun.*, 2009, May;23(4):446–9

3 Humphreys, J., Epel, E.S., Cooper, B.A., Lin, J., Blackburn, E.H., Lee, K.A., 'Telomere Shortening in Formerly Abused and Never Abused Women', *Biol. Res. Nurs.*, 8 March 2011 (E-pub ahead of print)

4 Epel, E.S., Blackburn, E.H., Lin, J., et al, 'Accelerated telomere shortening in response to life stress', *Proc. Natl. Acad. Sci. USA*, 2004;101(49):17312–5

5 O'Donovan, A., Epel, E., Lin, J., Wolkowitz, O., et al, 'Childhood Trauma Associated with Short Leukocyte Telomere Length in Posttraumatic Stress Disorder', *Biol. Psychiatry*, 12 April 2011 (E-pub ahead of print)

6 Drury, S.S., Theall, K., Gleason, M.M., et al, 'Telomere length and early severe social deprivation: linking early adversity and cellular aging', *Mol. Psychiatry*, 2011, May 17 (E-pub ahead of print)

7 Puterman, E., Lin, J., Blackburn, E., et al, 'The power of exercise: buffering the effect of chronic stress on telomere length', *PLoS One.*, 2010, May 26;5(5):e10837

8 Jacobs, T.L., Epel, E.S., Lin, J., et al, 'Intensive meditation training, immune cell telomerase activity, and psychological mediators', *Psychoneuroendocrinology*, 2011, Jun;36(5):664–81, E-pub 29 October 2010

9 Hölzela, B.K., Carmody, J., Vangela, M., et al, 'Mindfulness practice leads to increases in regional brain gray matter density', *Psychiatry Research: Neuroimaging*, 2010 (in press)

Chapter 7

1 Dusek, J.A., Otu, H.H., Wohlhueter, A.L., Bhasin, M., Zerbini, L.F., Joseph, M.G., Benson, H., Libermann, T.A., 'Genomic counter-stress changes induced by the relaxation response', *PLoS ONE.*, 2 July 2008;3(7):e2576

2 Siegel, D., *The Mindful Brain: Reflection and Attunement in the Cultivation of Well-Being*, W.W. Norton, New York, 2007

3 Chiesa, A., Serretti, A., 'Mindfulness based cognitive therapy for psychiatric disorders: a systematic review and meta-analysis', *Psychiatry Res.*, 2011, May 30;187(3):441–53, E-pub 16 September 2010

4 Kabat-Zinn, J., Massion, A.O., Kristeller, J., Peterson, L.G., Fletcher, K.E., Pbert, L., Lenderking WR, Santorelli SF, 'Effectiveness of a meditation-based stress reduction program in the treatment of anxiety disorders', *The American Journal of Psychiatry*, Vol. 149 (7), 1992, pp. 936–43

5 Miller, J.J., Fletcher, K., Kabat-Zinn, J., 'Three-year follow-up and clinical implications of a

mindfulness meditation-based stress reduction intervention in the treatment of anxiety disorders', *General Hospital Psychiatry*, Vol. 17 (3), 1995, pp. 192–200; PMID: 7649463

6 Davidson, R.J., Kabat-Zinn, J., Schumacher, J., Rosenkranz, M., Muller, D., Santorelli, S.F., Urbanowski, F., Harrington, A., Bonus, K., Sheridan, JF., 'Alterations in brain and immune function produced by mindfulness meditation', *Psychosomatic Medicine*, Vol. 65 (4), 2003, pp. 564–70

7 Way, B.M., Creswell, J.D., Eisenberger, N.I., Lieberman, M.D., 'Dispositional mindfulness and depressive symptomatology: Correlations with limbic and self-referential neural activity during rest', *Emotion*, Vol 10(1), February 2010, 12–24

8 Hofmann, S.G., Sawyer, A.T., Witt, A.A., Oh, D., 'The effect of mindfulness-based therapy on anxiety and depression: A meta-analytic review', *Journal Of Consulting And Clinical Psychology*, April; Vol. 78 (2), 2010, pp. 169–83

9 Schachter, S., Singer, J., 'Cognitive, Social, and Physiological Determinants of Emotional State', *Psychological Review*, 69, 1962, pp. 379–399

Chapter 8

1 www.beyondblue.org.au

2 Beck, A.T., *Cognitive Therapy and the Emotional Disorders*, International Universities Press, New York, 1976

3 Mathers, C.D., Loncar, D., 'Projections of global mortality and burden of disease from 2002 to 2030', *PLoS Med.*, 3 November 2006;3(11):e442

4 *The Diagnostic and Statistical Manual of Mental Disorders, Fourth Edition*, Text Revision, American Psychiatric Association, Washington, 2000

5 Beck, A.T., 'Thinking and depression', *Archives of General Psychiatry*, Vol. 9, 1963, pp. 324–333

6 Beck, A.T., 'Thinking and depression: 2', *Archives of General Psychiatry*, Vol. 10, 1963, pp. 561–71

7 Seligman, M., *Helplessness: On Depression, Development and Death*, Freeman, San Francisco, 1975

8 Seligman, M., *Learned Optimism*, A.A. Knopf, New York, 1991

9 McKenzie, S.P., *An information processing approach to psychopathology involving a computer simulation of depression*, Deakin University, Geelong, 1986

10 Fournier, J.C., DeRubeis, R.J., Hollon, S.D., et al, 'Antidepressant drug effects and depression severity: a patient-level meta-analysis', *JAMA*, 6 January 2010;303(1):47–53

11 Brewer, J., Bowen, S., Smith, J., Marlatt, A., Potenza, M., 'Mindfulness-based treatments for co-occurring depression and substance use disorders: What can we learn from the brain?' *Addiction*, 2010; Vol 105(10), pp. 1698–1706

12 Kirsch, I., 'Antidepressants and the placebo response', *Epidemiological Psychiatry Soc.*, Oct–Dec 2009;18(4):318–22

13 Tolle, E., *The Power of Now*, Namaste Publishing, Vancouver, 1997

14 Langer, E., Russell, T., Eisenkraft, N., 'Orchestral performance and the footprint of

mindfulness', *Psychology of Music*, Vol 37(2), April 2009, pp. 125–36

15 Manicavasgar, V., Parker, G., Perich, T., 'Mindfulness-based cognitive therapy vs cognitive behaviour therapy as a treatment for non-melancholic depression', *Journal Of Affective Disorders*, April 2011, 1573–2517; Vol. 130 (1–2), pp. 138–44

16 Thompson, N.J., Walker, E.R., Obolensky, N., Winning, A., Barmon, C., Diiorio, C., Compton, M.T., 'Distance delivery of mindfulness-based cognitive therapy for depression: project UPLIFT', *Epilepsy & Behavior*, November 2010; Vol. 19 (3), pp. 247–54

17 Williams, M., Teasdale, J., Segal, Z., Kabat-Zinn, J., *The Mindful Way Through Depression*, Guilford Press, New York, 2007

Chapter 9

1 *Macquarie Concise Dictionary* (4th Ed.), Macquarie Dictionary Publishers, Sydney, 2006

2 Collins D., Lapsley, H,. *The costs of tobacco, alcohol and illicit drug abuse to Australian Society in 2004/05. NCADA monograph*, Australian Government Publishing Service, Report No. 30. Canberra, 2008

3 Witkiewitz, K., Bowen, S., 'Depression, craving, and substance use following a randomized trial of mindfulness-based relapse prevention', *J Consult. Clin. Psychol.*, 2010, Jun;78(3):362–74

4 Witkiewitz, K., Marlatt, G., 'Mindfulness-based relapse prevention for alcohol and substance use disorders: the meditative tortoise wins the race', *J Cognit. Psychother.*, 2005; 19; 221–230

5 Vieten, C., Astin, J.A., Buscemi, R., Galloway, G.P., 'Development of an acceptance-based coping intervention for alcohol dependence relapse prevention', *Substance Abuse*, 2010 April;31(2):108–16

6 Brewer, J.A., Sinha, R., Chen, J.A., et al, 'Mindfulness training and stress reactivity in substance abuse: results from a randomized, controlled stage I pilot study', *Substance Abuse*, 2009, Oct–Dec;30(4):306–17

7 Bowen, S., Witkiewitz, K., Dillworth, T.M., et al, 'Mindfulness meditation and substance use in an incarcerated population', *Psychol. Addict. Behav.*, 2006 Sep;20(3):343–7

Chapter 10

1 Cussen, A., Sciberras, E., Ukoumunne, O., Efron, D., 'Relationship between symptoms of attention-deficit/hyperactivity disorder and family functioning: a community-based study', *Eur J Pediatr.*, 9 July 2011 (E-pub ahead of print)

2 Hallowell, E.M., 'Overloaded circuits: why smart people underperform', *Harvard Business Review*, 2005, Jan;83(1):54–62, 116

3 Klingberg, T., Forssberg, H., Westerberg, H., 'Training of working memory in children with ADHD', *Journal of Clinical and Experimental Neuropsychology*, 2002;24:781–91

4 Ashcraft, M.H., Kirk, E.P., 'The relationships among working memory, math anxiety, and performance', *J Exp Psychol Gen.*, 2001, Jun;130(2):224–37

5 Beilock, S.L., Carr, T.H., 'When high-powered people fail: working memory and "choking

under pressure" in math', *Psychol Sci.*, 2005;16(2):101–5

6 Christakis, D.A., Zimmerman, F.J., DiGiuseppe, D.L., McCarty, C.A., 'Early television exposure and subsequent attentional problems in children', *Pediatrics*, 2004, Apr;113(4):708–13

7 Aronson, M., 'Does excessive television viewing contribute to the development of dementia?' Medical Hypotheses, 1993;41(5):465–6

8 Lindstrom, H.A., Fritsch, T., Petot, G., et al, 'The relationships between television viewing in midlife and the development of Alzheimer's disease in a case-control study', *Brain Cogn.*, 2005, Jul;58(2):157–65

9 Friedland, R.P., Fritsch, T., Smyth, K. et al, 'Patients with Alzheimer's disease have reduced activities in midlife compared with healthy control-group members', *Proceedings of the National Academy of Science USA*, 10.1073/pnas.061002998

10 Dr Clifford Nass on his studies at Stanford University from Dretzin, R., Rushkoff, D., 'digital_nation life on the virtual frontier', pbs.org Frontline, February 2010, Web, 14 April 2011

11 www.ucsdcfm.wordpress.com/2011/07/01/our-brains-are-evolving-to-multitask-not-the-ill-usion-of-multitasking/

12 Levine, L.E., Waite, B.M., Bowman, L.L., 'Electronic Media Use, Reading, and Academic Distractibility in College Youth', *Cyber Psychology & Behavior*, Vol. 10, Issue 4, August 2007, EBSCOhost, Web, 16 April 2011

13 Poldrack, R., 'Multi-Tasking Adversely Affects the Brain's Learning Systems', psych.ucla.edu., July 2006, Web, 14 April 2011

14 McEvoy, S.P., Stevenson, M.R., Woodward, M., 'The contribution of passengers versus mobile phone use to motor vehicle crashes resulting in hospital attendance by the driver', *Accid. Anal. Prev.*, 2007, Nov;39(6):1170–6, Epub 9 April 2007

15 Rosen, C., 'The Myth of Multitasking', *The New Atlantis*, www.thenewatlantis.com. Spring 2008, Web, 14 April 2011

16 Stone, L., 'Beyond Simple Multi-Tasking: Continuous Partial Attention', www.lindastone.net, November 2009, Web, 14 April 2011

17 Ophir, E., Nass, C., Wagner, A.D., 'Cognitive control in media multitaskers', PNAS.org., *Proceedings of the National Academy of Sciences of the United States of America*, July 2009, Web, 15 April 2011

18 Black, D.S., Milam, J., Sussman, S., 'Sitting-meditation interventions among youth: a review of treatment efficacy', *Pediatrics*, 2009 Sep;124(3):e532–41

19 Krisanaprakornkit, T., Ngamjarus, C., Witoonchart, C., Piyavhatkul, N., 'Meditation therapies for attention-deficit/hyperactivity disorder (ADHD)', *Cochrane Database Syst Rev.*, 16 June 2010;(6):CD006507

Chapter 11

1 Main, C.J., Spanswick, C.C., (2001), *Pain management: an interdisciplinary approach*, Elsevier, p. 93

2 Breivik, H., Collett, B., Ventafridda, V., Cohen, R., Gallacher, D., (2006), 'Survey of chronic

pain in Europe: prevalence, impact on daily life, and treatment', *Eur. J Pain*, 10(4):287–333, E-pub 10 August 2005

3 www.thebigview.com/buddhism/fourtruths.html

4 Singer, T., Seymour, B., O'Doherty, J., Kaube, H., Dolan, R.J., Frith, C.D., 'Empathy for pain involves the affective but not sensory components of pain', *Science*, 20 February 2004;303(5661):1157–62

5 Eriksen, H.R., Ursin, H., 'Subjective health complaints, sensitization, and sustained cognitive activation (stress)', *J Psychosom. Res.*, 2004;56(4):445–8

6 Ursin, H., Eriksen, H.R., 'Sensitization, subjective health complaints, and sustained arousal', *Annals of the New York Academy of Sciences*, 2001, Mar;933:119–29

7 Elias, A.N., Wilson, A.F., 'Serum hormonal concentrations following transcendental meditation — potential role of gamma aminobutyric acid', *Med. Hypotheses*, 1995 Apr; 44(4):287–91

8 Harte, J.L., Eifert, G.H., Smith, R., 'The effects of running and meditation on beta-endorphin, corticotropin-releasing hormone and cortisol in plasma, and on mood', *Biol. Psychol.*, 1995, Jun;40(3):251–65

9 Watts, A., *The Watercourse Way*, Pantheon Books, New York, 1975

10 Kabat-Zinn, J., Lipworth, L., Burney, R., 'The clinical use of mindfulness meditation for the self-regulation of chronic pain', *Journal of Behavioral Medicine*, Vol 8(2), June 1985, pp. 163–190

11 McCracken, L., Thompson, M., 'Components of mindfulness in patients with chronic pain', *Journal of Psychopathology and Behavioral Assessment*, Vol 31(2), June 2009, pp. 75–82

12 Schütze, R., Rees, C., Preece, M., Schütze, M., 'Low mindfulness predicts pain catastrophizing in a fear-avoidance model of chronic pain', *Pain*, Vol. 148(1), January 2010, pp. 120–127

13 Zeidan, F., Gordon, N., Merchant, J, Goolkasian, P., 'The effects of brief mindfulness meditation training on experimentally induced pain', *The Journal of Pain*, Vol. 11(3), March 2010, pp. 199–209

Chapter 12

1 Kausman, R., *If Not Dieting, Then What?*, Allen & Unwin, Melbourne, 2004

2 www.ifnotdieting.com.au/cpa/htm/htm_home.asp

3 Kausman, R., 'Tips for long-term weight management', *Aus. Fam. Phys.*, 2000;29(4):310–3

4 Dalen, J., Smith, B.W., Shelley, B.M., et al, 'Pilot study: Mindful Eating and Living (MEAL): weight, eating behavior, and psychological outcomes associated with a mindfulness-based intervention for people with obesity', *Complement. Ther. Med.*, 2010 Dec;18(6):260–4, E-pub 11 November 2010

5 Thomley, B.S., Ray, S.H., Cha, S.S., Bauer, B.A., 'Effects of a brief, comprehensive, yoga-based program on quality of life and biometric measures in an employee population: a pilot study', *Explore* (NY), 2011, Jan–Feb;7(1):27–9

6 Edelman, D., Oddone, E.Z., Liebowitz, R.S., et al, 'A multidimensional integrative medicine intervention to improve cardiovascular risk', *J Gen. Intern. Med.*, 2006, Jul;21(7):728–34

7 Harrison, A., Tchanturia, K., Treasure, J., 'Attentional bias, emotion recognition, and emotion regulation in anorexia: state or trait?', *Biol. Psychiatry*, 15 October 2010;68(8):755–61

8 Kristeller, J.L., Wolever, R.Q., 'Mindfulness-based eating awareness training for treating binge eating disorder: the conceptual foundation', *Eat Disord.*, 2011, Jan;19(1):49–61

9 Proulx, K., 'Experiences of women with bulimia nervosa in a mindfulness-based eating disorder treatment group', *Eat Disord.*, 2008 Jan–Feb;16(1):52–72

Chapter 13

1 Parks, C.G., DeRoo, L.A., Miller, D.B., et al, 'Employment and work schedule are related to telomere length in women', *Occup. Environ. Med.*, 2011 Aug;68(8):582–9

2 Gatt, J.M., Nemeroff, C.B., Schofield, P.R., et al, 'Early life stress combined with serotonin 3 A receptor and brain-derived neurotrophic factor valine 66 to methionine genotypes impacts emotional brain and arousal correlates of risk for depression', *Biol. Psychiatry*, 1 November 2010;68(9):818–24

3 Nowotny, B., Cavka, M., Herder, C., et al, 'Effects of acute psychological stress on glucose metabolism and subclinical inflammation in patients with post-traumatic stress disorder', *Horm. Metab. Res.*, 2010 Sep;42(10):746–53

4 Dusek, J.A., Otu, H.H., Wohlhueter, A.L., et al, 'Genomic counter-stress changes induced by the relaxation response', *PLoS ONE*, 2 July 2008;3(7):e2576

5 Iribarren, C., Sidney, S., Bild, D.E., et al, 'Association of hostility with coronary artery calcification in young adults: the CARDIA study, Coronary Artery Risk Development in Young Adults', *JAMA*, 2000 May 17;283(19):2546–51

6 Wilbert-Lampen, U., Leistner, D., Greven, S., et al, 'Cardiovascular events during World Cup soccer', *NEJM*, 2008; 358 (5):475–483

7 Castillo-Richmond, A., Schneider, R.H., Alexander, C.N., et al, 'Effects of stress reduction on carotid atherosclerosis in hypertensive African Americans', *Stroke*, 2000 Mar;31(3):568–73

8 Linden, W., Stossel, C., Maurice, J., 'Psychosocial interventions for patients with coronary artery disease: a meta-analysis', *Arch. Int. Med.*, 1996;156(7):745–52

9 Ornish, D., Brown, S.E., Scherwitz, L.W., et al, 'Can lifestyle changes reverse coronary heart disease? The Lifestyle Heart Trial', *Lancet*, 21 July 1990;336(8708):129–33

10 Ornish, D., Scherwitz, L.W., Billings, J.H., et al, 'Intensive lifestyle changes for reversal of coronary heart disease', *JAMA*, 16 December 1998;280(23):2001–7

11 Page, S.J., Murray, C., Hermann, V., Levine, P., 'Retention of Motor Changes in Chronic Stroke Survivors Who Were Administered Mental Practice', *Arch. Phys. Med. Rehabil.*, 29 August 2011 (E-pub ahead of print)

12 Sullivan, M.J., Wood, L., Terry, J., et al, 'The Support, Education, and Research in Chronic Heart Failure Study (SEARCH): a mindfulness-based psychoeducational intervention improves depression and clinical symptoms in patients with chronic heart failure', *Am. Heart Journal.*, 2009 Jan;157(1):84–90

Chapter 14

1 www.wcrf-uk.org/research_science/recommendations.lasso

2 Ornish, D., Weidner, G., Fair, W.R., et al, 'Intensive lifestyle changes may affect the progression of prostate cancer', *Journal of Urology*, 2005;174(3):1065–9

3 Frattaroli, J., Weidner, G., Kemp, C. et al, 'Clinical events in prostate cancer lifestyle trial: results from 2 years of follow-up', *Urology* 2008 Dec;72(6):1319–23

4 Ornish, D., Magbanua, M., Weidner, G., et al, 'Changes in prostate cancer gene expression in men undergoing an intensive nutrition and lifestyle intervention', *PNAS*, 2008;105(24):8369–74

5 Ornish, D., Lin, J., Daubenmeir, J., et al, 'Increased telomerase activity and comprehensive lifestyle change: a pilot study', *Lancet Oncology*, 2008 Nov;9(11):1048–57

6 Rock, C.L., Flatt, S.W., Natarajan, L., et al, 'Plasma carotenoids and recurrence-free survival in women with a history of breast cancer', *J Clin. Oncol.*, 20 September 2005;23(27):6631–8

7 Verheus, M., van Gils, C.H., Keinan-Boker, L., et al, 'Plasma phytoestrogens and subsequent breast cancer risk', *J Clin. Oncol.*, 20 February 2007;25(6):648–55, Epub 2 January 2007

8 Xiao Ou Shu, Ying Zheng, Hui Cai, et al, 'Soy Food Intake and Breast Cancer Survival', *JAMA*, 2009;302(22):2437–2443

9 Chlebowski, R.T., Blackburn, G.L., Thomson, C.A., et al, 'Dietary fat reduction and breast cancer outcome: interim efficacy results from the Women's Intervention Nutrition Study', *J Natl. Cancer Inst.*, 20 December 2006;98(24):1767–76

10 Slattery, M., Potter, J., Caan, B. et al, 'Energy balance and colon cancer — beyond physical activity', *Cancer Research*, 1997;57:75–80

11 Colditz, G., Cannuscio, C., Grazier, A., 'Physical activity and reduced risk of colon cancer', *Cancer Causes and Control*, 1997;8:649–667

12 Thune, I., Lund, E., 'The influence of physical activity on lung cancer risk', *International Journal of Cancer*, 1997;70:57–62

13 Rockhill, B., Willett, W., Hunter, D., et al, 'A prospective study of recreational activity and breast cancer risk', *Natl. Cancer Inst.*, 1999;159:2290–6

14 Holmes, M.D., Chen, W.Y., Feskanich, D., et al, 'Physical activity and survival after breast cancer diagnosis', *JAMA*, 2005;293(20):2479–86

15 Pierce, J.P., Stefanick, M.L., Flatt, S.W., et al, 'Greater survival after breast cancer in physically active women with high vegetable-fruit intake regardless of obesity', *J Clin. Oncol.*, 2007;25(17):2345–51

16 Giovannucci, E.L., Liu, Y., Leitzmann, M.F., et al, 'A prospective study of physical activity and incident and fatal prostate cancer', *Arch. Intern. Med.*, 2005;165(9):1005–10

17 Haydon, A.M., Macinnis, R.J., English, D.R., Giles, G.G., 'Effect of physical activity and body size on survival after diagnosis with colorectal cancer', *Gut*, 2006;55:62–67

18 Santos, M.C., Horta, B.L., do Amaral, J.J., et al, 'Association between stress and breast cancer in women: a meta-analysis', *Cad. Saude. Publica.*, 2009;25 Suppl 3:S453–63

19 Penninx, B.W., Guralnik, J.M., Pahor, M., Ferrucci, L., Cerhan, J.R., Wallace, R.B., et al,

'Chronically depressed mood and cancer risk in older persons', *J Natl. Cancer. Inst.*, 1998;90:1888–93

20 Sharplin, G.R., Jones, S.B., Hancock, B., et al, 'Mindfulness-based cognitive therapy: an efficacious community-based group intervention for depression and anxiety in a sample of cancer patients', *Med. J Aust.*, 6 September 2010;193(5 Suppl):S79–82

21 Foley, E., Baillie, A., Huxter, M., et al, 'Mindfulness-based cognitive therapy for individuals whose lives have been affected by cancer: a randomized controlled trial', *J Consult. Clin. Psychol.*, 2010 Feb;78(1):72–9

22 Carlson, L.E., Speca, M., Faris, P., Patel, K.D., 'One year pre-post intervention follow-up of psychological, immune, endocrine and blood pressure outcomes of mindfulness-based stress reduction (MBSR) in breast and prostate cancer outpatients', *Brain Behav. Immun.*, 2007;21(8):1038–49

23 Fang, C.Y., Reibel, D.K., Longacre, M.L., et al, 'Enhanced psychosocial well-being following participation in a mindfulness-based stress reduction program is associated with increased natural killer cell activity', *J Altern. Complement. Med.*, 2010 May;16(5):531–8

Chapter 15

1 Online etymology dictionary, www.etymonline.com/index.php?search=dementia&searchmode=none

2 Scarmeas, N., Levy, G., Tang, M., et al, 'Influence of leisure activities on the Incidence of Alzheimer's disease', *Neurology*, 2001; 57 (12): 2236–42

3 Craik, F.I., Bialystok, E., Freedman, M., 'Delaying the onset of Alzheimer disease: bilingualism as a form of cognitive reserve', *Neurology*, 9 November 2010;75(19):1726–9

4 Buckner, R.L., et al, 'Molecular, structural, and functional characterization of Alzheimer's disease: evidence for a relationship between default activity, amyloid, and memory', *J Neurosci.*, 2005;25(34):7709–17

5 Gusnard, D.A., Akbudak, E., Shulman, G.L., Raichle, M.E., PNAS USA 2001;98(7):4259–64

6 Yaffe, K., Vittinghoff, E., Lindquist, K., et al, 'Post-traumatic stress disorder and risk of dementia among U.S. veterans', *Presentation O2-02-02, ICAD, Vienna*, 13 July 2009

7 Le Carret, N., Auriacombe, S., Letenneur, L., Bergua, V., Dartigues, J.F., Fabrigoule, C., 'Influence of education on the pattern of cognitive deterioration in AD patients: the cognitive reserve hypothesis', *Brain Cogn.*, 2005 Mar;57(2):120–6

8 Hughes, T.F., Chang, C.C., Vander Bilt, J., Ganguli, M., 'Engagement in reading and hobbies and risk of incident dementia: the MoVIES project', *Am. J Alzheimers Dis. Other Demen.*, 2010 Aug;25(5):432–8

9 Peters, R., 'Ageing and the brain', *Postgraduate Medical Journal*, 2006; 82(964):84–8

10 Langer, E., Beck, P., Janoff-Bulman, R., Timko, C., 'An exploration of relationships among mindfulness, longevity, and senility', *Academic Psychology Bulletin*, 1984, Vol. 6(2): 211–226

Chapter 16

1 Ayas, N., et al, 'A prospective study of sleep deprivation and coronary heart disease in women', *Archives of Internal Medicine*, 2003, 163, 205–209

2 National Sleep Foundation, 2006

3 Markel, H., 'Lack of sleep takes its toll on student psyches', *New York Times*, 2 September 2003, p. D6

4 Eoh, H., Chung, M., Kim, S., 'Electroencephalographic study of drowsiness in simulated driving with sleep deprivation', *International Journal of Industrial Ergonomics*, Vol 35(4), April 2005, pp. 307–320

5 Herbert, T. Cohen, S., 'Stress and immunity in humans: A meta-analytic review', *Psychosomatic Medicine*, 1993, 55, 364–379

6 Roth, T., 'Narcolepsy: Treatment issues', *Journal of Clinical Psychiatry*, 2007, 68 (16–19)

7 Gross, C.R., Kreitzer, M.J., Reilly-Spong, M., Wall, M., Winbush, N.Y., Patterson, R., Mahowald, M., Cramer-Bornemann, M., 'Mindfulness-based stress reduction versus pharmacotherapy for chronic primary insomnia: a randomized controlled clinical trial', *Explore*, Mar–Apr 2011;Vol. 7 (2), pp. 76–87

8 Ong, J., Sholtes, D., 'A mindfulness-based approach to the treatment of insomnia', *Journal of Clinical Psychology*, November 2010;Vol. 66 (11), pp. 1175–84

9 Ong, J.C., Shapiro, S.L., Manber, R., 'Mindfulness meditation and cognitive behavioral therapy for insomnia: a naturalistic 12-month follow-up', *Explore*, 2009 Jan–Feb;Vol. 5 (1), pp. 30–6

Chapter 17

1 Ornish, D., Brown, S.E., Scherwitz, L.W., et al, 'Can lifestyle changes reverse coronary heart disease? The Lifestyle Heart Trial', *Lancet*, 21 July 1990;336(8708):129–33

2 Ornish, D., Weidner, G., Fair, W.R., et al, 'Intensive lifestyle changes may affect the progression of prostate cancer', *Journal of Urology*, 2005;174(3):1065–9

3 Hassed, C, *The Essence of Health: the seven pillars of wellbeing*, Random House, Sydney, 2008

4 Hassed, C., de Lisle, S., Sullivan, G., Pier, C., 'Enhancing the health of medical students: outcomes of an integrated mindfulness and lifestyle program', *Adv. Health Sci. Educ. Theory Pract.*, 2009;14:387–398

5 Fawzy, F., et al, 'Malignant melanoma; Effects of an early structured psychiatric intervention, coping and affective state on recurrence and survival six years later', *Arch. Gen. Psychiatry*, 1993;50:681–89

6 Fawzy, F.I., Canada, A.L., Fawzy, N.W., 'Malignant melanoma: effects of a brief, structured psychiatric intervention on survival and recurrence at 10-year follow-up', *Arch. Gen. Psychiatry*, 2003;60(1):100–3

7 Rogojanski, J., Vettese, L.C., Antony, M.M., 'Role of sensitivity to anxiety symptoms in responsiveness to mindfulness versus suppression strategies for coping with smoking cravings', *J Clin Psychol.*, April 2011;67(4):439–45. doi: 10.1002/jclp.20774, E-pub 8 February 2011

Chapter 18

1 www.meditationcapsules.com

2 www.umassmed.edu/uploadedFiles/cfm2/special/craig-hassed-final.pdf

3 McCann, D., Barrett, A., Cooper, A., et al, 'Food additives and hyperactive behaviour in 3-year-old and 8/9-year-old children in the community: a randomised, double-blinded, placebo-controlled trial', *Lancet*, 3 November 2007;370(9598):1560–7; erratum in: *Lancet*, 3 November 2007;370(9598):1542

4 Swing, E.L., Gentile, D.A., Anderson, C.A., Walsh, D.A., 'Television and video game exposure and the development of attention problems', *Pediatrics*, 2010 Aug;126(2):214–21

5 Landhuis, C.E., Poulton, R., Welch, D., Hancox, R.J., 'Does childhood television viewing lead to attention problems in adolescence? Results from a prospective longitudinal study', *Pediatrics*, September 2007;120(3):532–7

6 Zimmerman, F.J., Christakis, D.A., 'Associations between content types of early media exposure and subsequent attentional problems', *Pediatrics*, November 2007;120(5):986–92

7 Lillard, A.S., Peterson, J., 'The Immediate Impact of Different Types of Television on Young Children's Executive Function', *Pediatrics*, Published online 12 September 2011 (DOI: 10.1542/peds.2010-1919)

8 Klingberg, T., Forssberg, H., Westerberg, H., 'Training of working memory in children with ADHD', *Journal of Clinical and Experimental Neuropsychology*, 2002;24:781–91

9 Ashcraft, M.H., Kirk, E.P., 'The relationships among working memory, math anxiety, and performance', *J Exp. Psychol. Gen.*, 2001 Jun;130(2):224–37

10 Beilock, S.L., Carr, T.H., 'When high-powered people fail: working memory and "choking under pressure" in math', *Psychol. Sci.*, 2005;16(2):101–5

11 www.ucsdcfm.wordpress.com/2011/07/01/our-brains-are-evolving-to-multitask-not-the-ill-usion-of-multitasking/

12 Dr Clifford Nass on his studies at Stanford University from Dretzin, R., Rushkoff, D., 'digital_nation life on the virtual frontier', pbs.org Frontline, February 2010, Web, 14 April 2011

13 Levine, L.E., Waite, B.M., Bowman, L.L., 'Electronic Media Use, Reading, and Academic Distractibility in College Youth', *Cyber Psychology & Behavior*, Vol. 10, Issue 4 August 2007, EBSCOhost, Web, 16 April 2011

14 Ophir, E., Nass, C., Wagner, A.D., 'Cognitive control in media multitaskers', *PNAS.org. Proceedings of the National Academy of Sciences of the United States of America*, July 2009, Web, 15 April 2011

15 Slagter, H.A., Lutz, A., Greischar, L. et al, 'Mental training affects distribution of limited brain resources', *PLOS Biology*, June 2007;5(6):e138. DOI:10. 1371/journal.pbio.0050138

16 Zeidan, F., Johnson, S.K., Diamond, B.J., David, Z., Goolkasian, P., 'Mindfulness meditation improves cognition: evidence of brief mental training', *Conscious Cogn.*, June 2010;19(2):597–605, E-pub 3 April 2010

17 Poldrack, R., 'Multi-Tasking Adversely Affects the Brain's Learning Systems', psych.ucla.edu.,

July 2006, Web, 14 April 2011

18 Joyce, A., Etty-Leal, J., Zazryn, T., Hamilton, A., Hassed, C., 'Exploring a mindfulness meditation program on mental health of upper primary children: A pilot study', *Advances in School Mental Health Promotion*, 2010;3(2):16–24

19 www.ggs.vic.edu.au/Positive-Education/Overview.aspx

20 www.otl.curtin.edu.au/tlf/tlf1999/miller.html

21 www.mindsetonline.com/

22 Biggs, J., *Student Approaches to Learning and Studying*, Australian Council for Educational Research, Melbourne, 1987

23 Bullimore, D., *Study Skills and Tomorrow's Doctors*, W.B. Saunders, Edinburgh, 1998

24 Dubecki, L., 'Students happy to cheat the system', *The Age*, 1 August 2002, News 3

Chapter 19

1 Willich, S.N., Lowel, H., Lewis, M., et al, 'Weekly variation of acute myocardial infarction. Increased Monday risk in the working population', *Circulation*, 1994;90(1):87–93

2 Manfredini, R., Casetta, I., Paolino, E., et al, 'Monday preference in onset of ischemic stroke', *American Journal of Medicine*, 2001;111(5):401–3

3 Peters, R.W., Brooks, M.M., Zoble, R.G., et al, 'Chronobiology of acute myocardial infarction: cardiac arrhythmia suppression trial (CAST) experience', *American Journal of Cardiology*, 1996;78(11):1198–201

4 Peters, R.W., McQuillan, S., Resnick, S.K., Gold, M.R., 'Increased Monday incidence of life-threatening ventricular arrhythmias. Experience with a third-generation implantable defibrillator', *Circulation*, 1996;94(6):1346–9

5 Rozanski, A., Blumenthal, J.A., Kaplan, J., 'Impact of psychological factors on the pathogenesis of cardiovascular disease and implications for therapy', *Circulation*, 1999;99:2192–2217

6 Sokejiana, S., Kagamimori, S., 'Working hours as a risk factor for acute myocardial infarction in Japan: a case control study', *BMJ*, 1998;317(7161):775–780

7 Willcock, S.M., et al, 'Burnout and psychiatric morbidity in new medical graduates', *Med. J Aust.*, 2004;181(7):357–60

8 Hassed, C., de Lisle, S., Sullivan, G., Pier, C., 'Enhancing the health of medical students: outcomes of an integrated mindfulness and lifestyle program', *Adv. Health Sci. Educ. Theory Pract.*, 2009;14:387–398

9 Fahrenkopf, A.M., Sectish, T.C., Barger, L.K., et al, 'Rates of medication errors among depressed and burnt out residents: prospective cohort study', *BMJ*, DOI:10.1136/bmj.39469.763218.BE (published 7 February 2008)

10 Hallowell, E.M., 'Overloaded circuits: why smart people underperform', *Harvard Business Review*, January 2005;83(1):54–62, 116

11 www.ucsdcfm.wordpress.com/2011/07/01/our-brains-are-evolving-to-multitask-not-the-ill-usion-of-multitasking

12 Rosen, C., 'The Myth of Multitasking', *The New Atlantis*, www.thenewatlantis.com, Spring

2008, Web, 14 April 2011

13 Ophir, E., Nass, C., Wagner, A.D., 'Cognitive control in media multitaskers', PNAS.org., *Proceedings of the National Academy of Sciences of the United States of America*, July 2009, Web, 15 April 2011

14 Haynes, A.B., Weiser, T.G., Berry, W.R., et al, 'A surgical safety checklist to reduce morbidity and mortality in a global population', *N. Engl. J Med.*, 29 January 2009;360(5):491–9

15 Slagter, H.A., Lutz, A., Greischar, L., et al, 'Mental training affects distribution of limited brain resources', *PLOS Biology*, June 2007;5(6):e138. DOI:10. 1371/journal.pbio.0050138

16 Zhaoping, L., Guyader, N., 'Interference with bottom-up feature detection by higher-level object recognition', *Curr. Biol.*, 9 January 2007;17(1):26–31

17 Epstein, R., Siegel, D., Silberman, J., 'Self-monitoring in clinical practice: a challenge for medical educators', *J Cont. Educ. Health*, Prof 2008;28(1):5–13

18 Epstein, R.M., 'Mindful practice in action (II): Cultivating habits of mind', *Fam. Syst. Health.*, 2003;21: 11–17

19 Sibinga, E.M., Wu, A.W., 'Clinical Mindfulness and Patient Safety', *JAMA*, 2010;304(22): 2532–3

20 Krasner, M.S., Epstein, R.M., Beckman, H., et al, 'Association of an educational program in mindful communication with burnout, empathy, and attitudes among primary care physicians', *JAMA*, 23 September 2009;302(12):1338–40

21 Theorell, T., Karasek, R.A., 'Current issues relating to psychosocial job strain and cardiovascular disease research', *J Occup Health Psychol.*, 1996;1(1):9–26; erratum in: *J Occup. Health Psychol.*, 1998;3(4):369

22 Covey, S., *Seven Habits of Highly Effective People*, Simon and Shuster, New York, 1989

Chapter 20

1 Young, J.A., Pain, M.D., 'The Zone: evidence of a universal phenomenon for athletes across sports', *Athletic Insight*, 1999;1(3):21–30

2 Csíkzentmihályi, M., *Flow: The psychology of optimal experience*, Harper & Rowe, New York, 1990

3 Cited in Harung, H., Travis, F., Blank, W., Heaton, D., 'Higher development, brain integration, and excellence in leadership', *Management Decision*, 2009, 47(6):872–894

4 Taylor, J., Wilson, G., (eds.), 'Applying sport psychology: From researcher and consultant to coach and athlete', Champaign, IL: Human Kinetics, 2005

5 www.news.bbc.co.uk/2/hi/6243787.stm

6 Zhaoping, L., Guyader, N., 'Interference with bottom-up feature detection by higher-level object recognition', *Curr. Biol.*, 9 January 2007;17(1):26–31

Chapter 21

1 www.psychology.about.com/od/personalitydevelopment/a/emotionalintell.htm

2 Goleman, D., *Emotional Intelligence*, Bantam Books, New York, 1995

3 Baer, R.A., Smith, G.T., Allen, K.B., 'Assessment of mindfulness by self-report: the Kentucky

inventory of mindfulness skills', *Assessment*, 2004;11(3):191–206

4 Hunt, N., Evans, D., 'Predicting traumatic stress using emotional intelligence', *Behav. Res. Ther.*, 2004;42(7):791–8

5 Kemp, A.H., et al, 'Toward an integrated profile of depression: evidence from the brain resource international database', *J Integr. Neurosci.*, 2005;4(1):95–106

6 Brown, R.F., Schutte, N.S., 'Direct and indirect relationships between emotional intelligence and subjective fatigue in university students', *Psychosom. Res.*, 2006;60(6):585–93

7 Pau, A.K., et al, 'Emotional intelligence and stress coping in dental undergraduates — a qualitative study', *Br. Dent. J.*, 2004;197(4):205–9

8 Lutz, A., Brefczynski-Lewis, J., Johnstone, T., Davidson, R.J., 'Regulation of the neural circuitry of emotion by compassion meditation: effects of meditative expertise', *PLoS ONE*, 26 March 2008;3(3):e1897

9 Shapiro, S.L., Brown, K.W., Thoresen, C., Plante, T.G., 'The moderation of Mindfulness-based stress reduction effects by trait mindfulness: results from a randomized controlled trial', *J Clin. Psychol.*, March 2011;67(3):267–77. doi: 10.1002/jclp.20761, Epub 22 December 2010

10 Krasner, M.S., Epstein, R.M., Beckman, H., et al, 'Association of an educational program in mindful communication with burnout, empathy, and attitudes among primary care physicians', *JAMA*, 23 September 2009;302(12):1284–93

11 Benson, S., Truskett, P.G., Findlay, B., 'The relationship between burnout and emotional intelligence in Australian surgeons and surgical trainees', *ANZ J Surg.*, 2007;77 Suppl 1:A79

Chapter 24

1 Killingsworth, M.A., Gilbert, D.T., 'A Wandering Mind is an Unhappy Mind', *Science*, 12 November 2010, Vol. 330, no. 6006, p. 932 DOI: 10.1126/science.1192439

2 Veenhoven, R., *World database of happiness: Correlates of happiness: 7837 findings from 603 studies in 69 nations 1911–1994, Vols. 1–3*, Erasmus University Rotterdam, Rotterdam, 1994

3 Aftanas, L., Golosheikin, S., 'Changes in Cortical Activity in Altered States of Consciousness: The Study of Meditation by High-Resolution EEG', *Human Physiology*, Vol. 29(2), Mar–Apr 2003, pp. 143–151

4 Kieviet-Stijnen, A., Visser, A., Garssen, B., Hudig, W., 'Mindfulness-based stress reduction training for oncology patients: patients' appraisal and changes in well-being', *Patient Education And Counseling*, 2008;72(3):436–42

INDEX